LIGHT IN THE DARK ROOM

Light in the Dark Room
Photography and Loss

Jay Prosser

University of Minnesota Press – Minneapolis – London

An earlier form of chapter 5 appeared as "A Palinode on Photography and the Transsexual Real," *a/b: Autobiography Studies* 14 (1999): 71–92.

Poetry by Gordon Parks, from *Moments without Proper Names,* is reprinted with permission.

Excerpts of unpublished writings and letters by Elizabeth Bishop are reproduced with permission of Special Collections at Vassar College Libraries and the Houghton Library at Harvard University.

Published by the University of Minnesota Press
111 Third Avenue South, Suite 290
Minneapolis, MN 55401-2520
http://www.upress.umn.edu

Library of Congress Cataloging-in-Publication Data

Prosser, Jay.
    Light in the dark room : photography and loss / Jay Prosser.
        p.   cm.
    Includes bibliographical references and index.
    ISBN 0-8166-4483-7 (hc : alk. paper) — ISBN 0-8166-4484-5 (pb : alk. paper)
    1. Photography—Philosophy.   2. Loss (Psychology).   I. Title.
    TR183.P76 2004
    770'.1—dc22

                                                                        2004015600

Printed in the United States of America on acid-free paper

The University of Minnesota is an equal-opportunity educator and employer.

12 11 10 09 08 07 06 05   10 9 8 7 6 5 4 3 2 1

For my teachers, Nancy and Ken. Guiding lights.

It is as if someone were to point out the way
to one who had got lost,
or to bring an oil-lamp into a dark place,
so that those with eyes could see what was there.

—*The Long Discourses of the Buddha*

CONTENTS

ACKNOWLEDGMENTS

I THANK THE UNIVERSITIES IN THE UNITED KINGDOM that have allowed me a forum for this work. My own has been considerate in allocating leave and support. Mick Gidley here has been caring and encouraging throughout. Vassar College Special Collections, especially Dean Rogers, smoothed my research on Elizabeth Bishop. And I thank the authors, artists, and collections for granting permission to reproduce their work here.

I'm particularly indebted to my contacts in Brazil: To SENAPULLI, the Brazilian National Seminar of Professors in English, for inviting me there in the first place and for taking me back. To the Universidade Federal de Santa Catarina for my deep week with colleagues and students. And to my friends Maria Lúcia Milléo Martins, Gláucia Renate Gonçalves, and Dilvo Ristoff for the generosity of their work, their friendship, and for helping me round Brazil.

The British Academy funded me in my initial research trip on Brazil, and the Arts and Humanities Research Board helped me complete. To Laura Marcus and Jane Gallop, the readers for that grant, and to the readers for this manuscript, I am grateful for their open, moving response and their wisdom. The enthusiasm, commitment, and kind like-mindedness of Andrea Kleinhuber, my editor at the University of Minnesota Press, have been a buoy. Margaretta Jolly read much of this writing with patience and untrammeled generosity. My family, especially my mother, held me in their love and belief.

But the dedication of this book is for Nancy K. Miller and Ken Bails, because their conversation really does have the power to turn me about.

LIGHT IN THE DARK ROOM

W E TREAT PHOTOGRAPHS as if they had a kind of presence. Photography is the commonest way for us to record our own and our loved ones' lives. And we arrange photographs in our rooms of our beloved, often because they cannot be with us there—often (and eventually) because they are dead. Photography is the medium in which we unconsciously encounter the dead. Yet herein lies photography's hidden truth. Photographs are not signs of presence but evidence of absence. Or rather the presence of a photograph indicates its subject's absence. Photographs contain a realization of loss. This book on photography enters into that loss.

Photographs contain a realization of loss in the fundamental sense that every photograph represents a past real moment that actually happened but is no longer. It is a myth that photographs bring back memories. Photographs show not the presence of the past but the pastness of the present. They show the irreversible passing of time. Our most lyrical writers on photography have understood the tense of photography. Walter Benjamin: in "the cult of remembrance of loved ones, absent or dead," "the aura emanates from early photography in the fleeting expression of a human face."[1] Susan Sontag: "Photography is a message from time past," "a trace, something directly stenciled off the real, like a footprint or a death mask."[2] Roland Barthes: "what I see . . . has been here, and yet immediately separated; it has been absolutely, irrefutably present, and yet already deferred."[3] For all, photography is a melancholic object. Not an aide-mémoire, a form

1

for preserving memory, it is a memento mori. Photography is not only a reminder of our loved ones' death, it tells our impending own. It is evidence of the fact of death itself. Photography's commentators have been less concerned to convey the significance of the realization of loss in photography. There are two senses to photography's realization. Photography makes real the loss. But then it makes possible the apprehension of this loss. This is my recovery. As offering insight into the inexorable loss that *is* life, photography captures a reality that we would otherwise not see, that we would choose *not* to see. It holds out the promise of a kind of enlightenment. It is this that makes me enter the dark room of photography.

The earliest responses to photography understood this mystical quality. Some of the first photographs were shown in magic shows; its innovation was thought to make visible the invisible.[4] To some eyes so apparently miraculous was the new medium, so unprecedented its realism, that something of the divine seemed to inhabit photography. Only God had previously had, only God *should* have, that kind of reproductive power. Photography's emergence was coincident with a decline in religious belief. Along with the development of other forms of technological reproduction, the invention of photography was both enabled by, and contributed to, the death of God. But perhaps something of the faith in the divine as ultimate reality and elucidating force transferred from God to photography. Certainly the first names for photography suggest the marveling in a form of creation almost beyond human capacity, that required limited human intervention: *heliographs,* or "sun-drawings." It was as if light alone produced the image. The name eventually chosen, *photography,* means "light-writing."[5]

As a modern technological form photography emerged in the middle of the nineteenth century when the discovery of a certain combination of chemicals made possible the fixing of images first on metal, then on glass, and finally in the form in which it has been predominantly practiced, on celluloid film printable on paper. But photography has a much longer history prior to its chemical invention. The Han Dynasty Chinese (from 200 BCE), who were possibly the first to use spectacles and lenses, were among the most advanced in optical technology in the world.[6] The Chinese Lantern contains in embryo the Magic Lantern. The thin paper shade of the Chinese lamp serves to catch in a play of light and shadow the movements and objects around it, what would later be more firmly outlined and the shades distinguished by the slide projector, or Magic Lantern. The effects of light in a dark room become evident in any country that is hot enough one needs to shut out the light to keep out the sun. Plato might have dismissed the shadows on the wall of his cave. But his most famous student,

Aristotle, succumbed to the magic that happens when you sit inside a darkened room and allow a bright light to bring in a piece of the world outside. Aristotle, in effect, knew all about the camera obscura. The camera obscura, literally a "dark room," was the earliest form of a camera. It consisted of a darkened space in which a hole or window cut into one wall projected onto the opposite inside wall the scene outside the room. Initially because light reflects objects, the scene appeared in the image in inverted form. Later a mirror was added to the "lens" of the window and the dark room; and this combination, lens, mirror, and dark room, remains the basis of every photographic mechanism today. The "room" of the camera may have shrunk, the camera become progressively more box-like and eventually handheld. But the camera retains, in its name, a reference to that magical space one originally occupied: the dark room where one went to receive an illuminated version of reality.

Photography's powers of realization have been more determining of the history of representation than we think. For centuries artists used the camera obscura as an aid to achieving greater realism in their drawings and paintings. In the nineteenth century the camera obscura was propagated into the camera lucida, which introduced a prism into the design, thereby refracting the reflected light onto a drawing surface and allowing for even greater realism. The artist David Hockney has presented evidence that suggests camera obscuras were in use at least since the Renaissance and that the camera may even have spurred the massive advances toward the attainment of realism and accurate perspective that *was* the Renaissance.[7] So dominant became the kind of naturalism that could only have been achieved by the lens-mirror combination that soon all painting aspired to photographic reproductive realism. Reproductive realism remained the aspiration of most painting until the second half of the nineteenth century. At this point painting, in the form of modern art, turned back to an impressionistic rendering of the world, now deliberately naïve and mediated. Photography could again have been pivotal. For if painting had so long aspired to *be* photography, how was it going to survive the advent of a mere machine that far exceeded the artist's capacity for realism? Amid prophecies of its obsolescence, painting would have to distinguish itself radically from photography. And it did. We are still dealing with the repercussions of the antirealistic turn in representation. One is that modernist and postmodernist photography is most typified by photographs that turn against, or complicate, photographic realism. Modernist and postmodernist photography is photography that aspires now to the condition of painting. Like digital photography and the manufacture of photographic images on computers that looks set to supersede film/paper as the means of photographic development, artistic modernist and postmodernist photography has changed forever the notion of photographic realism.

The changes in photography have tallied with changes in our models of realism in representation generally. We have traveled from a notion of reality as reproducible (the naïve or credulous realism ushered in by the Renaissance); to a notion of reality as hidden or subjective (the first half of the antirealistic turn in modernism); to a notion of reality as impossible or invented, or more radically as an effect of representation (the second half of antirealism in postmodernism). We are confronted now with a notion of reality as lost, with an apprehension of reality as consisting in that which can only be lost. The history of representation in modernity can be told through the story of how reality became lost. The model of representation we now face is one that began to be sketched at the turn of the twentieth century, when in part the shock of modernity and its technologies demanded a new description of relations between word and thing, world and image. The terms for the model emerged from structuralist linguistics, but they soon spread to describe every operation of representation in the human sciences, including those in the visual arts. The model now rendered the relation between representation and reality as between *sign* and *referent*. The *sign* was further split into two parts, *signifier* and *signified,* the marks on the page and the meaning they connote respectively. And in poststructuralism and postmodernism there was a growing sense of a gap between signifier and signified, resulting in questions about whether representation can ever close on meaning, about how exactly representation touches reality. An increasing concern with the terms of signification meant a demotion in status of the referent. The referent was sidelined, deferred. The referent, which carried the weight of vestigial reality, went almost out of the picture.

This "almost" is important though. It is within modernity's creeping sense of reality as lost, leading to late postmodernity's yearning for a lost reality, that I read photography in this book. Photography has poignancy now as a realization of reality as lost. The photographic instant that actually happened but is now over coincides in elegiac timing with our apprehension of reality. In his history of the representation of reality in modernity, the art historian and theorist Hal Foster has introduced a term for describing our contemporary relation to reality, "traumatic realism." With the crisis in representation that was modernity, the "symbolic order in crisis," reality in the form of the referent split off from the sign and can now only return—as the repressed can only return in trauma—as the real.[8] Traumatic realism can also be rendered Lacanian realism. I want to go back to Foster's source to emphasize the key role photography plays in the emergence of an apprehension of reality as lost. Lacan's *real* is particularly useful for understanding how this model of reality is historically apposite. Lacan took up *real* as a noun and made it a fundamental psychoanalytic category in 1953[9]—precisely the moment when structuralism and the terms of signification began to infuse academic disciplines and therefore theories of representation. The real emerged in Lacan when we began to lose the referent in theory. This was also the moment that crystallized, in different ways, the work of the authors whose photographs I examine in this book. They come from different sides of the representational divide. A semiotician and structuralist critic who spent his career debunking reality and analyzing signs writes in his relation to photographs about the worst loss from his life. Following him a structuralist anthropologist who uncovered in his subjects the signs of culture looks back at his old photographs and finds in them a reality he couldn't represent in his anthropological writing. A documentary photographer, who worked to photograph his culture as thoroughly as an anthropologist, recovers in his photographs a loss from his own life he couldn't document. And a poet who prized above all the factuality of her poetry encounters, in the process of collecting photographs, the inevitable detractions of realism. From different points along the continuum of representation the four meet in a realization that photography can reveal a real that previously escaped them and that remains, in echo of the mystical conception of photography, elusive of their lived reality.

In Lacan the real is not reality. It is that which escapes reality. The real only becomes apparent to us in "the return, the coming-back" of trauma.[10] Yet in the return of the real we realize we missed reality in the first place and are doomed to remain remiss of it. We meet the real in "an essential encounter—an appointment to which we are always called with a real that eludes us" (53). The real returns as if by chance or accident, what Lacan calls, using the Aristotelian term, *tyche;* but because it returns as a result of trauma there is something inexorable in the return of the real. "What is repeated in fact is always something that occurs—the expression tells us quite a lot about its relation to the *tuché—as if by chance*" (54). Lacan's realism is illustrated through vision, or more accurately the gaze, since he makes a distinction between gaze and vision where gaze returns the real overlooked by the more credulous and conscious vision of reality ("I see" as equivalent to "I know"). The gaze founders this post-Renaissance model with the real. Modernist poet Paul Valéry's statement for self-consciousness, "*I saw myself seeing myself*" (80), captures the traumatic doubling of the gaze, when our vision seems to turn back on ourselves, reflected and refracted, and we catch ourselves unawares. "What isolates this apprehension of thought by itself is a sort of doubt, which has been called methodological doubt" (80), and in this moment self-realization is uncovered as "illusion" (83). Lacan's anecdotal sardine can has the same effect of derealization. The sardine can, which floats on the sea, refracts back his sight of it as a gaze at him. Glinting in the lens of the sun and the mirror of the water, it seems to be looking right at him, giving him the feeling of being, in the old sense, unreal, out of the picture.

Photography with its reflective and refractive dynamics belongs in the realm of the gaze. To encounter the real in Lacan is "tirer" (67), which means "to draw" as in to draw lots (chance) and to draw curtains (revelation), but also "to shoot" as in to shoot a photograph. "I am *photo-graphed*" (106), Lacan writes, of this moment when the gaze of the sardine can hits him. When we are photographed, especially when we see ourselves in a

Hans Holbein the Younger, *Jean de Dinteville and Georges de Selve ("The Ambassadors")* (1533). Copyright National Gallery, London. Reproduced with permission.

photograph, we are at our most real. We are most ourselves and yet simultaneously we see our annihilation as subjects. The conundrum is one of time inextricable from representation. If that is me in the photograph, what is the status of my existence *here and now*? In its re-presentation of a moment that is over, the photograph foretells our own future nonexistence. This is why Lacan writes "photo-graphed" in its "fragmented form" as he often says he does (106), in order to indicate the splitting between reality and representation, between the light and the writing. Lacan's visualist explanations of the real come best in the death's-head in Holbein's *The Ambassadors*. The Renaissance work is not only as precise as a photograph, in its acute realism and in the fall of light and shadow on the optical instruments (sundials, astronomical equipment, celestial and terrestrial globes showing the new Americas—possibly a telescope) which give us the exact time and place of the scene. The painting, whose science is its mystery, is also thought one of the most likely to have used a camera obscura to have done so, or that the artist worked inside the room/camera, with a sheet of glass, a single candle, and the necessary darkness.[11] The clue may be the distorted skull at the bottom of the painting. The skull can be seen in perspective only with the help of a lens to correct the distortion and a mirror to project the image anew. With the naked eye the skull can be recognized only if we approach the picture from such an angle that we can no longer see Holbein's human subjects or the technology for mastering reality behind them. Lacan writes that the most real thing in the picture is the distorted skull, which is "an anamorphic ghost," since "Holbein makes visible for us something that is simply the subject as annihilated—annihilated that is, strictly speaking, the imaged embodiment of the *minus-phi (gk) of castration*" (89). He "reflects our own nothingness, in the figure of the death's head" (92). Holbein's skull is the most famous example of anamorphosis in art, the technique in which a distorted image can be changed back to reveal its correct (realistic) projection. Photography too, with its mirrors and lenses, works according to anamorphic optics, to reveal the excessively real, the reality that escapes straight-on representation. Such anamorphic optics, Lacan writes, "allow vision to escape. They are within the grasp of the blind" (92); "How we try to apprehend that which seems to elude us" (93).

Photography's realizations in an age that has repressed the referent can only be unconscious. "The camera introduces us to unconscious optics as does psychoanalysis to unconscious impulses," wrote Benjamin, himself fleeing modernity and with concern at its technological reproductions.[12] Jacqueline Rose remarks that references to the camera and optics in psychoanalysis outnumber those to psychoanalysis in visual theory.[13] Freud himself compared the unconscious to a camera, at the beginnings of psychoanalysis and not far along in the history of photography. In *The Interpretation of Dreams* Freud writes: "we should picture the instrument which carries our mental functioning as resembling a compound micro-scope or photographic apparatus," that is as enlarging and imprinting.[14] And Freud later described trauma as a photograph. The child receives im-pressions like "a photographic exposure which can be developed after any interval of time and transformed into a picture."[15] In both uses the loss of the real, its inscriptive force and yet its unrealizability, is the basis for the analogy between unconscious realization and photography. What cannot be realized in reality can only be unconsciously realized later in trauma: photo-graphed. It is to Freud's concept of realization in trauma that Lacan makes reference when he elaborates his return of the real, to an episode in *The Interpretation of Dreams*. A man falls asleep next to a room in which his dead child's body is surrounded by candles and is being kept watch over by an old man—inadequately, for he has fallen asleep. The bereaved father dreams his child comes to his bedside and *"whispered to him reproachfully: Father, don't you see I'm burning?"*[16] He awakens to find one of the candles has overturned, started a fire, and already burned part of his dead child's body. For Lacan what returns in the dream is "the missed reality that causes the death of the child," a real which, since the child is dead, is "too late now" (58). The gap between dream and reality "constitutes awaken-ing" (57), but since one cannot recover the dead (or can one? Photography raises this question about raising the dead) it is an awakening to loss. Photography is "a firebrand" (59) in a dark room, a dream of light that is always "too early or too late" (69). In their photographs in this book my authors chase referential ghosts: dead loved mothers; lovers who resurrect dead mothers; the subjects who've made their careers; the subjects left out of their careers; and ultimately a self they hadn't realized.

For photographs may be the closest we get to another's autobiography. The photographic collections we leave when we die are approximations of the life story that remains typically unwritten. And because in our life we view them through our eye and our I, photographs that have significance for us are often autobiographical, although often they are those in which this is not conscious to us. Photography's approximation of autobiography remains true even with the appearance of home movies and video cameras. The predominance of photography as a form for recording our lives may be due not simply to its lesser expense and greater ease of use. With their frozen disjointed moments, photographs are closer to the life as it is lived. Unlike the moving image of film, snapshots don't require the joining up of instants into a narrative, and especially not the explanatory voice-over making sense of the life. In those autobiographies that are written and published, photographs are increasingly used as shutes into something missing, pointers to a loss that can't be recovered in the text. In Hélène Cixous's autobiographical reflections, indicatively titled in the French *Photos de Racine* ("Rootprints"), photographs of two sets of Jewish grandparents, in pre-Weimar Germany and pre-independence Algeria, initiate the autobiography as an "album of abandonment," its author's "genealogy of graves."[17] Writing an account of his parents' marriage, Michael Ondaatje can find only one photograph of them together. Recognizing it as "the photograph I have been waiting for all my life," he publishes it as, contrary to the sense of his memoir and his memory, "the evidence I wanted that they were absolutely perfect for each other."[18] And in Gabriel Josipovici's memoir of his mother written after her death, photographs carry a referent that has been forgotten or was never actually known. "I find many of them baffling, try as I will, [to] recall," he writes as he pores over images of his mother in Egypt.[19] Even photographs that do not actually appear in autobiographies or appear only marginally as traces in the text, as in Tim Lott's attempt to make sense of his mother's suicide, only on the inside cover, exemplify photography in autobiography as loss. Lott senses in photographs of his family's life something essential out of reach of his understanding. "It is as if a sudden flashlight had been held up to illuminate my past and then switched off, leaving only an engram, a faint memory trace."[20] The engram or *graphe:* like the dream of fire that comes after the burning, the photograph seared inside autobiography elucidates not memory's presence but memory's loss, the inevitable fading of lives in our lives.

The flickering of presence and absence in the convergence of photography and autobiography, their both wavering between memory and loss, has attracted recent critics. Timothy Dow Adams pithily emphasizes the *graphe* in both photography and autobiography in order to read photographs in writing even when they are not referred to (as ghosts for example in Maxine Hong Kingston's *Woman Warrior: Memoirs of a Girlhood among Ghosts*).[21] Linda Haverty Rugg's work is more focused on the literal incidence of photography in autobiography. She finds in photography and autobiography a "referential paradox" that speaks to our confusions about reality: "A simultaneous belief in linguistic and photographic referentiality and suspicion of linguistic and photographic referentiality offer the only solution to the conundrum of the age."[22] Both critics have in common the claim that photography and autobiography are similarly representational and reality, are at once referential and signifying. But incarnating a moment that was actually there and that in all but the photograph has gone, does not photography exceed autobiography's ties to the real? Hence Lacan's choice of it as a conductor for the traumatic return of the real. Photography preserves autobiography's lost referent. Even Paul de Man, poststructuralist critic of autobiography's claims to referentiality, finds in photography an ineluctable reference that remains unconscious to him. "But are we so certain," he asks in the very sentence in which he defers the referent in autobiography, "that autobiography depends on reference, as a photograph depends on its subject?"[23] Photography embodies the vestigial reference displaced from autobiography.

Thus other recent critics who move between photography and autobiography more allusively—and who write autobiographically and with more of the snapshot moments of enlightenment of photography—are more my guiding lights in this book. Of parents and a reflecting, unreconciled child in Nancy K. Miller's *Bequest and Betrayal: Memoirs of a Parent's Death*; of incomplete and recurrent mourning in Marianne Hirsch's *Family Frames: Photography, Narrative and Postmemory*; and of families that don't reveal the silences that found them in Annette Kuhn's *Family Secrets: Acts of Memory and Imagination*—photographs are interesting in their books for embodying the intimate affects of what might otherwise escape even these perspicacious autobiography critics' conscious representation.[24] The photographs often interrupt the flow of narrative, which in all cases is a work of mourning, with traumatic realization. Such critical works are about trauma of various kinds for, true to contemporary Lacanian realism, this is how realism is now most encountered in memoirs: in real people's (and real critics') traumatic experiences.

I call this way in which photography can interrupt the narrative and return the extreme moments of autobiography *ph/autography*, which is a new description of what proves to be a not-so-new combination: all of the texts I look at here are between autobiography and photography. From an essay on photography that becomes its author's most autobiographical work, to a photographic memoir, to an autobiographical account of a photographical assignment, to an autobiographically framed album of photographs and recollections, *Light in the Dark Room* catches the lens of photography and the mirror of autobiography in interplay. My term *ph/autography*, intended to suggest how photography when we really engage it inevitably becomes autobiographical, draws on the coinage of one writer for the photographical self-portrait, the "phauto"—although as his unslashed neologism indicates, for Philippe Lejeune the currents between autobiography and photography are more free-flowing. Lejeune is in fact an autobiography critic, but he realizes something he had overlooked about autobiography, realizes loss, when he is writing about another writer writing about photography, who ultimately made his relationship to photography autobiographical—and whose ultimate relationship was an insurpassably autobiographical one with photography. Lejeune finds that he and Roland Barthes meet in discovering the referent of the actual past in the manifest presence of the visual image: "The self-portrait is the only pictorial genre that has given me the poignant feeling, which Barthes describes so well with regard to photography in *La Chambre claire (Camera Lucida)*, of having before my eyes not an image of the past, but an impression directly inscribed by it."[25]

But it is Barthes's autobiography written before *Camera Lucida*, which contained photographs and compelled the need to return and do something more autobiographical than in the autobiography in *Camera Lucida*, that prompts Lejeune to realize what he may have overlooked in writing about autobiography. In particular Barthes's autobiography prompts him to realize the loss of reference, especially in the arena of self-representation, Lejeune's home ground. Lejeune had argued that autobiography holds together as a genre because of a "referential pact" (22) between author and reader: the reader agrees to read the author, narrator, and protagonist as identical and all of these as referencing an actual person. Acknowledging that Barthes's autobiography *Roland Barthes by Roland Barthes* exerts a kind of fascination over him, Lejeune finds it "anti-*Pact* par excellence," for it "proposes a dizzying game of lucidity around all the presuppositions of autobiographical discourse—so dizzying that it ends up giving the reader the illusion that it is not doing what it is nevertheless doing. 'In the field of the subject, there is no referent'" (131–32). Barthes's autobiography is at once referential (it is his manifest autobiography) and yet declares the impossibility of reference. It propels Lejeune to realize that his referential pact had been based on a fetishized presence. But he goes on nevertheless, as Barthes does with photography, believing he finds in autobiography a direct impression of the past. He responds to Barthes: "We indeed *know* all this; we are not so dumb, but, once the precaution has been taken, we go on as if we did not know it" (132). In fact what Lejeune had cited from Barthes's autobiography turns into a statement about the nonexistence of the referent what had been Barthes's self-directed question indicating the costs of the loss of the referent. What Barthes had actually written in full was, "Do I not know that, *in the field of the subject, there is no referent?*"[26]

A statement about no reference at all would mean no autobiography—and no photography; and Barthes in *Roland Barthes by Roland Barthes,* and even more in *Camera Lucida,* clearly doesn't buy this. As J. Gratton recognizes in discussion of the misquotation that generally takes place of this of Barthes's thought, "Barthes's assertion turns out to be set in a question whose status is rhetorical: not only self-directed, but requiring no answer as such. Doubly rhetorical, in fact, in that it seems to amount to an effort of self-persuasion, as if Barthes had to remind himself of what he knew; as if somewhere along the line there were a *vouloir* at odds with this *savoir,* a resistance to the authoritative thrust of such an assertion (of assertion in general?)."[27] Barthes's desire for the referent ("vouloir") in the face of his knowledge of the loss of the referent ("savoir") is conveyed best in *Roland Barthes by Roland Barthes* in the photographs that appear in the margins of this autobiography. The photographs pick up and embody the referent of the subject Roland Barthes that is lost in the more mediated, signifying writing of *Roland Barthes by Roland Barthes.* The photographs, as Paul John Eakin has written, are "like the return of the repressed"—and thus he uses Barthes's trajectory to "reopen the file on reference in autobiography."[28] In Lejeune's reading of Barthes, and in the unfurling of Barthes's biography as a writer, photography propels realization into loss.

Lejeune's realization of the loss of the referent—his encounter with the real, then—comes in the form of what is termed a *palinode.* My access to the significance of photography is in all authors provided by a text that constitutes a palinode. In each case the turn to photography as a form for realizing loss is in truth a *re*turn to photography, and a retraction or recantation (homonym for the palinode as a "singing back or again") of a prior position on photography. These palinodes are remarkable texts in the lives of their writers. In the palinode, in which one reads oneself, one's ode or the first statement that had made one's life, writers are at their most autobiographical. Part of the work of focusing on photography in its representation in the palinode is to propose the palinode as a newly described autobiographical mode for how we might reflect on the losses and oversights inevitable in the progression of our work, as photography is a form for realizing the losses inevitable in our life. The palinodes in this book trace a retreat from models of realism that turn on either signification or reference—reality as produced versus reality as reproduced—to meet in a Lacanian model of the real as lost. They do so progressively, for my chapters work, in order, through two structuralist critics who built their professions in skepticism about reality, finding reality in the code or sign; to the documentary photographer and then realistic poet who on the contrary held as their goal (and had faith in) realism. The palinodes of all are texts that cast shadows on their previous visions. They also comprise their authors' most underread, misread—or in the case of one author unpublished and what proved to be unpublishable—texts. But bringing the blindnesses in the palinode to light can be elucidating for us. The palinode is literally the ode in reverse (*palin* means "back" or "again") and it like photography works by reversal and refraction. It brings to view what one could not see before, throws light where one was previously in the dark. Lejeune's realization about what he had overlooked in autobiography is hooked graphically in his writing as he looks back on a diagram that he had designed to demonstrate the referential pact in autobiography. In his diagram there were two blacked-out squares, and in these Lejeune realizes that he had attributed to autobiography a blinkered vision he now sees belongs to himself: the blind spots were his own. "There are two 'blind' squares, corresponding to the cases 'excluded by definition.' It is undoubtedly I who was blind" (134). If he previously saw the "image of the real," now what returns, as in the Lacanian gaze reflected by those dark spaces, is "the effect of the real" (22).

As uncovering oversight—and realizing that only the oversight or first losses made possible a true insight—the palinode in its emergence and history is caught up with the dynamics of seeing and blindness, light and darkness. The origins of the form lie in the *palinoidia* that Stesichorus of Himera sings to Helen in reparation for his insults to her, which had caused him to be struck blind. After his palinode his sight is restored.[29] Stesichorus's palinode is known to us for its citation in Plato's *Phaedrus,* where it is used to preface Socrates' renunciation of a denunciation of love he had just made. Socrates enacts the revelation achieved by his reversal in a visual scene. Covered by a cloak in his ode, he removes it in his palinode. He literally recovers the light as he figuratively discovers his insight.[30] In the genealogy of the palinode the enlightenment its author attains often comes at the end of the life and contains what the life, and the works written in it, left out. In his *Retractions* Saint Augustine looks back in his old age at his massive religious oeuvre to find it lacking the spiritual light he had always sought but that he believed he had only recently approximated.[31] Augustine's palinode may in turn have influenced Chaucer, who wrote, apocryphally on his deathbed, the "retracciouns" in which he regrets the "unkonnynge" concern with "worldly vanitees" that make up the romance and satire of his *Canterbury Tales.*[32] Nietzsche wrote "Attempt at a Self-Criticism" in recoiling reconsideration of his first book, *The Birth of Tragedy,* two years before his fatal collapse into madness.[33] In palinodes the enlightenment is often coincident with trauma, our greatest insight ensuing from our greatest loss. As heir to Socratic irony and perhaps master of the palinode in modern philosophy, Kierkegaard, puts the paradox, the sympathetic reader of the palinode "can understand that the understanding is a revocation—the understanding with him as the sole reader is indeed the revocation of the book. He can understand that to write a book that does not demand to be as important for anyone is still not the same as letting it be unwritten."[34] The key to revision—and there's something godly and realistic in it—is repetition: "If God himself had not willed repetition, the world would never have come into existence. . . . Repetition is reality, and it is the seriousness of life."[35] As we might gloss Kierkegaard's life of retractions, better to have realized loss than never to have realized at all. The light only looks bright in darkness.

I begin in chapter 1 with the seminal essay on photography as loss, Roland Barthes's *Camera Lucida*. Barthes gets real on photography when he declares he is writing a palinode. "Camera lucida" is literally the light room, but Barthes's thoughts on photography actually take shape in the dark room of his incomplete mourning for his mother. The loss of his mother propels him to see the real of photography and to retreat on his previous, structuralist skepticism toward photographic realism. Looking with Barthes at the autobiographical loss of his dead mother, I also revisit the extraordinary circumstances of Barthes's death which followed so soon after hers. The double loss frozen by *Camera Lucida* proves ultimately unrepresentable, except in photography—an original loss before speech that we are born into.

Chapter 2 reads the photographic memoir of the structuralist anthropologist who provided Barthes's initial terms for thinking about photography. Like Barthes, Claude Lévi-Strauss in his career rejected a documentary approach to cultural reality, and with it photography. Photography had a foundational role in anthropology. Lévi-Strauss worked hard against this to find the signs and symbols of complex cultures in what had been denigrated as given and simple referents. But what loss is incurred in the focus on the sign? In his last published book, his autobiographical collection of his old photographs, Lévi-Strauss returns to the outset of his career in Brazil in order to realize what is changing at its end. His wonderful, overlooked photographs tie loss to advances in global technology and want us to see something now. His need, finally, to fall back on photography in order to warn of impending and massive planetary perdition is both enabled by the latest technology and returns to a more magical, and in his inverting, appreciative terms, primitive, relationship to photography.

Chapter 3 takes up the legacy of the realistic tradition of documentary photography. It was this that generated the field of visual anthropology, to which photography in anthropology now belongs. The documentary photographer Gordon Parks has worked most successfully as a participant observer to produce what amounts to a visual anthropology of African American lives. But what is exacted in return, what are the costs of a life of documentation? Who gets to represent reality, and how? Parks worked for *Life* magazine, where we see the (U.S.) nationalization of documentary realism. I tell the story of how, at *Life*, Parks's photographs redeemed a life; but I also look at the worst instance resulting from the encounter of the *tirer:* the horrible realness involved in the "taking" of life in the act of photographing. Parks in his photographs of a Brazilian boy initially thought he was bringing light, in his words, to a dark underworld. But his return a decade later to reconsider his assignment, and his second journey to the slums of the Rio de Janeiro shantytown called "Catacumba" ("tomb"), recall more than one ghost that he had sought to use his photography to dispel.

The poet Elizabeth Bishop saw Parks's assignment in *Life* magazine while she was living in Brazil. In her poetry concerned to convey the reality of places, she was persuaded to edit a book collection of photographs for *Life's* World Library series about this country she loved and in which she had made her home. But the realism of this largely overlooked photographic edition turns out to be thwarted by political causes that entailed the suicide of Bishop's lover, the partner for whom she had settled in (and fallen in love with) Brazil. The political circumstances resulted in Bishop's deepest regret for this book. Chapter 4 recovers Bishop's original drafts and correspondence for her collection and discovers how her profound sense that she had failed to capture reality catalyzed her plans for another book about Brazil, one that would contain her own photographs and would be more autobiographical. I focus—and this marks their first encounter with criticism—on Bishop's lyrical photographs, which are as precise in their detail as her poetry and equal to if not surpassing the observant eye of her recently published paintings. I try to recover as much as possible this book Bishop said would have been about loss, all the while aware that Bishop found her losses so insuperable she did not publish the work. This may be the palinode taken to its most extreme, elusive mode.

Chapter 5 provides an instance of a palinode in the making—my own. I return to an earlier use I made of photography as referential. Contrary to the claim of my preceding book that photographs show the sex change of transsexuals, I now realize what I had left out of this manifesto about transsexual autobiography: precisely the fact that transsexual narratives can't be realized, can't be closed. My misapprehension of photography turned on a misreading of *Camera Lucida*, or more precisely a failure to take in what Barthes leaves out—a photograph of his mother that Barthes couldn't show. I, too, now touch on inevitably lost parts: photographs cut from my own and another transsexual's book, a cut footnote about photographs, and ultimately for me a sense of lost body parts. Circling back to Barthes and chapter 1, I show how reading others' losses (Bishop cites Lévi-Strauss as well as Parks) can spur our own realizations. *Light in the Dark Room* stemmed from looking, in photography, at my own autobiographical losses. This chapter was first presented in Brazil.

Why Brazil? Lévi-Strauss's photographic memoir is called *Saudades do Brasil,* and the term *saudades* appears in two other works here and runs as the spirit of them all. *Saudades* is as intrinsic to Brazil as it is to the conception of photography in this book. It is a word that Brazilians are proud of as having significance to their country. I avoid direct translation; Bishop writes there's always loss incurred in translation. But at the outset, *saudades* is best glossed as a realization of loss. My choice of these writers is considered: in reverse order, a Canadian-born (and ultimately U.S.-settled) American; an African American; a European American*ist*, all of whom moved between Brazil and the United States; and, key start, a Frenchman who, in his book on photography, sees at the end of his life the United States as the worst example for the way in which reality is subsumed into signs, in which photography is made yet another readable text. My writing about realizing loss in photography in these particular authors moves toward a larger question about where exactly we are locating reality in an age dominated by global technologies: what's left of the real in our lives when our ultimate realities seem taken by technology, with its attendant progress, acquisition, development, gain—corporate, national, and individual? The United States and Brazil are not the confines for my concerns about the losses incurred in modernity's technologization; but as the United States is the greatest source and purveyor of global technologies, and as Brazil shows some of their more obvious effects, the relations between these two countries form an apt and animated backdrop for reading loss in photography. In brief and to foreshadow: I suggest in the focus on Brazil that Brazil may (yet) contain an instance of the real lost from the dominance of the U.S. symbolic. I end, then, in my epilogue with a few autobiographical snapshots going back to my own recent trips to Brazil and my own *saudades* or realizations of losses there. Like my authors here I go with the I and the eye—in a form that, like photography, doesn't master reality but lets it go. As well as chasing some of the referents of their photographs—mostly, of course, lost—I tell how, in the Amazon on the Rio Negro, there's a particular quality of light that made me want to take, and then give, up photographs . . . and to live with the realism and illumination (attention to presence, acceptance of absence) given us by photographs.

Chapter 1

Roland Barthes's Loss

Has there been a critic whose loss has been less worked through than that of Roland Barthes? It is not that we haven't mourned Barthes. Since his death in 1980 there have been some ten book-length studies, a biography and a wealth of critical essays, and much of this material is character-ized by an incredible sense of loss. To take the most recent collection as an example, Colin MacCabe describes Jean-Michel Rabaté's *Writing the Image after Roland Barthes* as "a kind of memorial" for Barthes—and this is seventeen years after Barthes's death. Another contributor, Daniel Ferrer, states therein that "Barthes cannot be safely distanced, he is still relevant to us; the mourning period is not over, and I do not see any sign that it is coming to an end."[1] The notion that our "mourning" for Barthes might be "interminable" and "collective" is first suggested—and these words first linked—in an essay that Derrida wrote six months after Barthes's death.[2] This essay functions as a kind of anti-eulogy for Barthes, since Derrida refrains from the gesture of the obituary or funereal ode that would sum up and therefore summarily dismiss Barthes. He refuses to "pay homage . . . [to] the author who has passed away (whose tastes, curiosities, and project should, it seems, no longer surprise us)" (51). Instead Derrida incorporates Barthes as a ghost. He sketches the ghost as the return of the dead, the return of the dead in and as the living—"Neither life nor death, it is the haunting of the one by the other. . . . Ghosts: the concept of the other in the same . . . the dead other alive in me . . . a relationship of haunting which is perhaps constitutive of all logics" (41–42). The incorporation is extraordinary for it results in a kind of palinode for Derrida, as Derrida speaks subjectively and fragmentedly (dare one say sentimentally?) of what Barthes meant "for me" (35). He praises Barthes for pointing to the possibility of a "something else" beyond all language (46) and describes this almost wistfully as a "love" that "shatters" "all discourses . . . all theoretical systems" (48). *After* Roland Barthes here means Derrida speaking *in the style of* Barthes. After Barthes we are anything but *over* him. Indeed, that Barthes may be more influential now in his death than he was in his life is suggested by the sheer numerousness of these posthumous citings and by their emphasis on his loss. The criticism has become a kind of palinodic tomb for Barthes: a space not for burying him or for keeping him alive but for returning him interminably as dead—the dead in our life.

Of Barthes's texts it is especially *Camera Lucida* that holds our melancholia. It has become the epitaph on Barthes's tomb, or rather the stone we repeatedly roll back to keep Barthes's tomb open. *Camera Lucida*'s threnodic status can be explained in part by the fact that this was Barthes's last text and hence represents his most complete last word. Moreover its subject matter is death and loss, since Barthes finds in photography "that rather terrible thing which is there in every photograph: the return of the dead," as he turns to write on photography while he was in interminable mourning following the death of his mother.[3] And in the precise timing of its publication *Camera Lucida* seemed to coincide these losses—to coincide Barthes's loss of his mother with our loss of him. *Camera Lucida* was published as *La chambre claire: Note sur la phtographie* in France on January 28, 1980. Barthes was knocked down by a laundry van on February 25, 1980 and died on March 26, 1980. The English translation was published posthumously then, in 1982. As Tzvetan Todorov notes in *his* elegy for Barthes, *Camera Lucida* marks a "disturbing coincidence between the accidental (surely the right word here) and the essential."[4] Barthes's essay on photography was sparked by the *tuché*—the accident that returns the real—of Barthes's mother's death; and it collided with or elided into the *tuché* of his own death. Derrida has noted the incarnate place this book has in our interminable mourning for Barthes, and in doing so he uses a figure that suggests the elision of these double losses into a single, redoubled loss: *Camera Lucida* is a book "whose time and tempo accompanied his death as no other book, I believe, has ever kept vigil over its author" (36). The figure puts the book in our mourning for Barthes in the same place that Barthes occupied as he kept watch over his dying mother. It is as if whatever Barthes were mourning—or failing to mourn—in *her* has come to be embodied in our mourning (failing to mourn) *him*.

The more interminable our mourning for Barthes, the more *Camera Lucida* and its conception of photography as autobiographical and inextricable from loss have come into our present tense. Early critics did not know what to make of the autobiographical rawness and the notion of photography as real that characterize *Camera Lucida*. These features seemed to turn their back on the suspicion toward subjecthood and the referent for which we had canonized Barthes. Writing in 1982 for an introductory study of Barthes as a theorist, a critic of cultural mythologies from literary historian to semiologist to structuralist and poststructuralist, Jonathan Culler is obviously exasperated at *Camera Lucida*'s upset of his neat trajectory for Barthes. "How did Roland Barthes, the critic of bourgeois myth, reach this point?" For Culler, Barthes had already lost it in *Camera Lucida,* and he begins his work of mourning before Barthes's death. "Defying all the most convincing work on meaning, he affirms the powerful myth, he taught us to resist." Culler rues "this strangest moment, when what has been denigrated returns."[5] Later critics in contrast saw *Camera Lucida* as presaging new times. Elaine Hoft-March, writing in the nineties and taking specific issue with Culler's reading of Barthes as recidivist (falling back), suggests that *Camera Lucida* heralds a new feminine discourse, an imaginary relation to the mother that "upends certain gender-codified meanings, a subversion enabling him to indicate a new theoretical direction rather than to exhibit critical resignation."[6] And in 1981 even before the English translation of *La chambre claire* had been made, J. Gerald Kennedy predicted that the text would one day be recognized as heraldic. What is interesting about Kennedy's observation is the notion that *Camera Lucida* would be seen as precursory only retrospectively—that it would have to wait its time not only in order to come into but in order to be noted as ahead of its time: "As we begin to assess the impact of Barthes's work on modern critical thought, it seems unlikely that *La chambre claire* will figure as a major work. Insofar as his career has provided an accurate barometer of French intellectual trends, the book may some day mark a general turn away from structuralist and post-structuralist abstraction toward a more pragmatic and humane discourse."[7]

That that time has now come is suggested by the books enmeshing photography and autobiography cited in my introduction. So many of them see *Camera Lucida* as initiating but recognize that what it is initiating of is loss, the irrevocable moment. We have come into sympathy with *Camera Lucida* and with its notion of photography as autobiographical loss. Two of the most recent contributions to Barthes studies are focused on photography. Rabaté's collection treats the photograph as an open memorial for Barthes. Nancy Shawcross's book, the first monograph devoted to Barthes on photography—while the body of her work sees Barthes in *Camera Lucida* as disconsolate with postmodernism and reverting to modernism—in her last few sentences rightly suggests that *Camera Lucida* needs to be read in two directions at once, backwards and forwards. "Barthes's essay can be viewed as the voice of either the past or the future. Or he may be read with the duality of impulse that has marked his writings from the beginning."[8] Critics have always agreed that *Camera Lucida* marks a turn in Barthes's writings, might have disagreed about what this turn represents; but what is indisputable is that the turn was not fully exercised. Is *Camera Lucida* the beginning of Barthes's career as a novelist? The fact that Barthes was planning a novel is well known. Is it in fact this novel? Or is it rather the book Barthes says within *Camera Lucida* he was planning to write about his mother? Crucially, there is something unfulfilled, something unrealized in *Camera Lucida;* yet Barthes's swan song is all the more powerfully real because of that. Barthes's death froze realization. If we have a conception of photography as loss in autobiography and in the palinode, if this form is seminal then, it is because *Camera Lucida*, this ph/autographic palinode, photographed loss: made it real and insuperable. And this loss of Barthes—that is, our loss of him and his loss in photography—is absolutely intricated with the marvelous temporal dynamics of the palinode.

PALINODIC LIFE

Barthes is clearly not interested in writing a history of photography. But his title, *La chambre claire,* French for a camera lucida, and his cover illustration of a man using a camera lucida to portray a woman, make the anamorphic, palinodic dynamics of this earliest form of the camera immediately relevant to his text. The palinode within his text is explicit and structuring. The book is divided into two equal parts of a total of forty-eight chapters—or "notes," to use the French term from *La chambre claire*'s subtitle for Barthes's numbered fragments that, with its musical meaning also, is more appropriate than the English translation of the visual and deliberate-sounding "reflections"; for we are here in the realm of the gaze, not of vision.[9] The palinode appears exactly halfway through the book. It is promised at the end of chapter 24, entitled "Palinode" and the shortest chapter: "I would have to descend deeper into myself to find the evidence of Photography, that thing which is seen by anyone looking at a photograph and which distinguished it in his eyes from any other image. I would have to make my recantation, my palinode" (*Camera* 60). The photographs, chapter 24 acknowledges, have been "public ones, up to now" (60). Barthes's quest through photography has been accordingly "ontological" (3), an attempt to "learn at all costs what Photography was 'in itself'" (3)—a largely theoretical endeavor in mastery and knowledge of this form in keeping with the phenomenological approach suggested by the book's dedication to Sartre. But, following startlingly the discussion of the "'light' (good) desire of eroticism" in a Mapplethorpe photograph (59), the chapter promising the palinode confesses that Barthes has not yet found the essence of photography: "I had perhaps learned how my desire worked, but I had not discovered the nature (the *eidos*) of Photography" (60). Now, as Barthes descends deeper into himself to make his recantation, he immerses photography in autobiography—to produce ph/autography. As part 2 begins we know immediately we're in a different realm, a private underworld of profound sadness: "Now, one November evening shortly after my mother's death, I was going through some photographs. I had no hope of 'finding' her" (63).

This second half of *Camera Lucida,* the palinode, is a work of failed personal mourning for Barthes's mother. It is important to be precise here. *Camera Lucida* is not a work of mourning, or even of something in between melancholia and mourning, as it has been albeit intuitively read.[10] Rather it is a classical case of melancholia, corresponding to Freud's conception of melancholia as inarticulable and frozen in his famous distinction of melancholia from mourning. Even from the first part, which takes "Emotion as Departure" (viii), *Camera Lucida* is freighted with sadness and loss. The shock of grief, violence and bodily pain characterizing several of the photographs here punches through the attempt to circumscribe photographic form. Perhaps the most telling image of the autobiographical generational loss that is to follow shows a mother in Nicaragua carrying sheets around a covered corpse (her child?) (24). In the second part death acquires its referent, or rather the reason for its unnameability, its veiling or covering in the first place (that is, in the ode). The first photograph, appearing in the French edition only, of the curtains drawn almost closed performs this function of hiding and suggesting future revelation. Barthes does finally find his mother's essence, in the famous "Winter Garden Photograph," which, he writes, "achieved for me, utopically, *the impossible science of unique being*" (71). But in front of this photograph he cannot move forward in his mourning: "I suffer, motionless. Cruel, sterile deficiency: I cannot *transform* my grief, I cannot let my gaze drift; no culture will help me utter this suffering which I experience entirely on the level of the image's finitude (this is why, despite its codes, I cannot *read* a photograph): the Photograph—my Photograph—is without culture: when it is painful, nothing in it can transform grief into mourning" (90). The Winter Garden Photograph stops language, like melancholia: "The horror is this: nothing to say about the death of one whom I love most, nothing to say about her photograph. . . . I have no other recourse than this *irony:* to speak of the 'nothing to say'" (93).

This is why the Winter Garden Photograph is not reproduced within *Camera Lucida.* Instead we have Barthes's explanation of the reason that he cannot include the photograph, itself in parenthesis as if it hardly bears speaking in the primary voice of this *Note sur la photographie,* this essay on photography. Of parenthesis elsewhere in Barthes Derrida says that it "does not enclose an incidental or secondary thought but "lowers the voice—as an *aside*—out of a sense of modesty" (40). "(I cannot reproduce the Winter Garden Photograph. It exists only for me. For you, it would be nothing but an indifferent picture, one of the thousand manifestations of the 'ordinary'; it cannot in any way constitute the visible object of a science; it cannot establish an objectivity, in the positive sense of the term; at most it would interest your *studium*: period, clothes, photogeny but in it, for you, no wound)" (73). Melancholy, Freud writes, "behaves like an open wound.[11] The Winter Garden Photograph is Barthes's wound; its absence is evidence of his melancholia. It is the "petit trou" (*La chambre* 49), the little hole in the text in which Barthes's trauma lies *un*buried: sunken, profound, but uncovered. As Eakin notes, the Winter Garden Photograph is "truly . . . the most memorable photograph in the book"—and it is surely memorable because of its absence—and that it is "in order to illustrate what he has shown and what he cannot show [that] Barthes deliberately omits the 'Winter Garden Photograph.'"[12] If Barthes's absent photograph evidences that he cannot speak, show, or work through his loss, his ph/autographical palinode is compelled by this melancholia; he must move back *because* he cannot move forward in his mourning for his mother. The whole book takes its organization from this palinodic retreat/descent. As Ralph Sarkonak has noticed, *Camera Lucida* with its 48 chapters, its 24 photographs (at least those in the text, excepting the prefacing, curtaining one in the French edition then), and 12 bibliographic items has a rigid numerical—we might almost say numerological—structure. Each number is half of the previous number. The total of all numbers is 84, which Sarkonak guesses to be the age at which Barthes's mother died. He turns out to be right. Barthes's biographer, Louis-Jean Calvet, has since independently cited this figure as the age at which Henriette Binger Barthes died.[13]

The palinodic structure contains, or barely contains, *what* Barthes is failing to mourn in his mother.

The palinodic turn in the essay produces a notion of photography as itself a kind of melancholy. Like Sontag and Benjamin, Barthes speaks of the melancholy of photography yet adds to this his loss of his mother—the autobiographical to the photographical. *Camera Lucida* knows early on that "Death is the *eidos* of Photography" (15)—"the Photograph always carries its referent with itself . . . like the dead man and the corpse" (5–6); but the beginning of the palinode acknowledges that he had not made this desire or death—or this desire *for* death—his own. In the Winter Garden Photograph Barthes discovers not only the essence of his mother but the essence of photography. It is this photograph that impels him into writing the book about photography in the first place, that draws him in that Lacanian sense—"me tirait vers la Photographie" (*La chambre* 114). The Winter Garden Photograph is not part of the *studium,* to bring forward the structuring Latinate terms of *Camera Lucida. Studium* is that which can be studied or articulated about photography. *Studium* is always coded. It moves forward—it moves the subject forward—into language. The Winter Garden Photograph in which Barthes realizes the essence of photography is, to use the term *Camera Lucida* counterpoints to *studium,* the *punctum.* Initially the *punctum* is the poignant partial detail that ruptures or punctures the *studium.* Appearing "by chance" (42), not the intended material that the photographer would have us see but the involuntary, the nondeliberate, the *punctum* is described as a "lightning-like" flash (45), a "fulguration" (49) that comes to revelation deferred: "[D]espite its clarity, the *punctum* should be revealed only after the fact" (53). Identified through its essence of the *punctum* that it is Barthes's purpose to pursue, photography, like Barthes, doesn't move forward but remains frozen. Unlike cinema, it presents a moment of intense immobility, and it is this temporal immobilization that renders photography melancholic: "It is *without future* (this is its pathos, its melancholy)" (90). The *punctum* is also unspeakable. "What I can name cannot really prick me. The incapacity to name is a good symptom of disturbance" (51). Not surprisingly then, Barthes introduces the *punctum* through and as a shard of Lacan's real: "it is the absolute Particular, the sovereign Contingency, matte and somehow stupid, the *This* (this photograph and not Photography), in short, what Lacan calls the *Tuché,* the occasion, the Encounter, the Real, in its indefatigable expression" (4). *Punctum* in photography carries the gaze that ruptures our vision, an undrifting gaze (before the Winter Garden Photograph, the photographic *punctum* of the book, Barthes "cannot let [his] gaze drift"). It is what we do not consciously notice about the photograph. It is the "blind field" (57) that we can only "see" when we "shut [our] eyes" having looked at the photograph (55). *Punctum* is derived from the Latin "to prick" ("this wound, this prick" [26]), in echo of *trauma* from the Greek for "wound." In sum, the *punctum* is the photographic incarnation of Barthes's melancholia. It is loss that won't be healed.

Barthes's terms for photography, *punctum* and *studium,* guide us how to read the palinode in relation to the ode. The palinodic organization has challenged critics. The ode/palinode structure is less than a "scission en deux parties dissymétriques et inajustables" a splitting into two parts asymmetrical and irreconcilable, as Chantal Thomas has suggested.[14] And it is more than a "signal that Barthes wants the reader to *glisser* [slide] between the two parts . . . while simultaneously approaching part two as a clean slate on which to begin his inquiry into photography," as Shawcross has conversely proposed (75). The palinode is between these two models. It chiastically reverses the ode so that we do transition across the two parts but to note how the second part retreats on (descends from) the first. The second part is best understood as the *punctum* to the first part's *studium* that has stayed largely in the realm of that which can be studied or spoken about the photograph. The palinode punctures through the study of the ode with the poignant autobiographical detail—the unspeakable that moves us about Barthes's essay *Camera Lucida.* And as *Camera Lucida* descends deeper into Barthes's subjectivity and his grief, it punctures and reverses conventional discourse on photography as a whole. It is the *punctum* in writing on photography. Barthes departs from the *savoir* of photography, a mastery or knowledge of the form, into his *vouloir,* a desire to point toward that which moves him subjectively about photography and whose eventual *eidos* is death. Barthes is not interested in writing *about* photography. This he calls "scientia" (7). He dismisses most other writing about photography about and like the *studium* as an education into "savoir" (*La chambre* 51). "What did I care about the rules of composition of the photographic landscape, or, at the other end, about the Photograph as a family rite?" (7). "The photograph touches me if I withdraw it from its usual blah-blah" (55). "I wanted to explore [photography] not as question (a theme) but as a wound" (21).

In pursuing this *punctum* or wound *Camera Lucida* not only contains a palinode, it becomes a startling palinode of Barthes's previous work, particularly his work on photography. As Shawcross has neatly documented, Barthes's work on photography underwent shifts. She notes four, and I suggest the following as turning points. In the fifties at the beginning of his career Barthes was the mythologist analyzing the mythology or ideology of the photograph in contexts such as, in his *Mythologies*, Edward Steichen's anthropological exhibition, "The Family of Man." In the sixties as a semiologist and structuralist he read the "rhetoric of the image"—the title he gave to an essay that is exemplary in treating photography as a linguistic-like structure that can be broken down into "signifieds" and "signifiers." As a poststructuralist in the seventies Barthes placed photographs at the beginning of his autobiography, *Roland Barthes by Roland Barthes,* now crucially in excess of the writing, in the margins of the unraveling linguistic structures. Much of this work is *studium*.[15] In his mythologist and structuralist phases for example, Barthes was writing about photography precisely as a cultural "family rite" (on Steichen) or about its "rules of composition" ("Rhetoric of the Image"). Shawcross suggests that what Barthes produces in *Camera Lucida* is a difficult "third form" that resists classification, a text between fiction, autobiography, and essay—although one that reverts to modernist and even nineteenth-century mythologies of photography (68 and passim). Yet while Barthes's thinking on photography underwent shifts and these seem to correspond to the phases recognized as marking Barthes's career—typically from mythologist to structuralist (to semiotician) to poststructuralist; or structuralist to poststructuralist to something in excess (Kennedy), or in reversion (Shawcross, Culler)—photography serves not simply to indicate those shifts but more interestingly, ab initio, to resist them. Photography is the form that has something in it already and evident in Barthes all along to enable and propel the palinode: the return to something in excess of the writing.

In "The Photographic Message," an essay published in 1961 from the same structuralist era as "The Rhetoric of the Image," Barthes identifies most clearly what is distinct about photography. The essay is a self-declared "structuralist analysis," but it is important for showing how photography resists structuralist analysis—for suggesting, as odes do when read retroactively through the palinode, an existent tension.[16] Photography for Barthes is a "structural paradox" (19). On the one hand like any other text analyzed by structuralists, photography works according to various "connotation procedures" (20), the text/captions, photographic composition, and layout in publication that seek to "connote" the photographic message: the "blah-blah" that here Barthes *is* interested in reading. On the other hand photography "transmit[s] . . . literal reality," is a "perfect *analogon*" of the thing represented and hence *"it is a message without a code"*

(20). Connotation is countered by denotation, and it is denotation that exclusively constitutes photography, for connotation, Barthes acknowledges, is "not strictly part of the photographic structure" (20). A paradox, photography already contravenes the notion of reality as produced by codes that was the structuralist *doxa* or opinion. This structuralist orthodoxy Barthes had represented in, say, an essay from the same decade as "The Photographic Message" entitled "The Reality Effect," in which "the *referential illusion*" is said to characterize verisimilitude in the literature of modernity—interestingly from around the beginnings of photography: Flaubert's *Madame Bovary* is Barthes's example.[17] Or again the approach to reality as produced is evident even in the later structuralist-transitioning-to-poststructuralist *S/Z*, where the "referential code" similarly shows how reality is coded in Balzac's *Sarrasine*.[18] These ideas are in line with Lejeune's "image of the real," not his "effect of the real."[19] And it is surely to "The Photographic Message" that Barthes refers back when he writes in *Camera Lucida* that he did not try to escape from the "photographic paradox" (20), that he was already a realist when he asserted that the photograph was an image without a code.

And yet—and here's the real structural paradox of photography, the paradox *for* structuralism in the real that *is* photography—Barthes in "The Photographic Message" recognizes that we cannot isolate the pure denotative state that is the *eidos* of photography. Denotation moves necessarily into connotation, the message into the code; reality can only be accessed through representation, and for Barthes as a structuralist critic representation is understood through language. "From this point of view, the image—grasped immediately by an inner language itself—in actual fact has no denoted state, is immersed for its very social existence in at least an initial layer of connotation, that of the categories of language" (*Image* 28–29). *Connotation* in "The Photographic Message" corresponds to *studium* in *Camera Lucida*: "connotation is present in *studium*" (*Camera* 26), and both are derived from "culture" (*Image* 22; *Camera* 28). *Denotation,* which points to the thing itself, will become the much more traumatic, wounding, but similarly "deictic" (pointing) *punctum* (*Camera* 5). In other words "The Photographic Message" shows that Barthes already knows the *eidos* of photography but can't—a paradox for him as a structuralist as well as in photography—stay with or articulate it. Toward the end of the essay, however, he foretells in an eerie prophecy what might happen to enable him to grasp and write the real that is distinct about photography:

These few remarks sketch a kind of differential table of photographic con-
notations, showing, if nothing else, that connotation extends a long way.
Is this to say that a pure denotation, a *this-side-of language,* is impossible?
If such a denotation exists, it is perhaps not at the level of what ordinary
language calls the insignificant, the neutral, the objective, but on the contrary at the level of absolutely traumatic images. The trauma is a suspension of language, a blocking of meaning. (*Image* 30)

This is what happens in *Camera Lucida* then. It is the trauma of losing his
mother that suspends the connotation procedures of photography, levers up
the structural codes, and sparks his return forty years later to seize photography through one particular photograph as the *this-side-of language* that
it is. And *photography* in the process becomes *Photography*: capitalized and
iconized, a talismanic gate or *trou* ("hole") through which Barthes falls to
the underworld of Lacan's similarly capitalized Real; "je tombai," "I fell," is
the first verb for Barthes in *La chambre claire* and it describes his first relation to photography (13). The earlier essay, which comes close to the distinctness of photography, shows that the paradox of photography already
laid bare a tension between representation and reality; for photography is
a reality that does not signify. This *paradox of* photography becomes in
Camera Lucida a *palinode in* photography—in fulfillment of this prophecy
of how to return to a moment before.

In fulfillment of this prophecy Barthes's last work on photography
becomes a palinode of his entire career, or at least the critical part that
had made up the bulk of it: the criticism. Barthes, our cultural critic par
excellence, decoder of languages, and then playful unthreader of systems,
in the wake of his mother's loss writing about photography in *Camera
Lucida,* a text doubly in extremis, looks back and questions the discourses
that had made up his career. His draw to photography *(tirer)* opens up the
confusion—indeed he is drawn to photography surely *because* it opens up
confusion, is a paradoxical mode as he inferred before. This is a point made
early on in *Camera Lucida*:

> Then I decided that this disorder and this dilemma, revealed by my de-
> sire to write on Photography, corresponded to a discomfort I had always
> suffered from: the uneasiness of being a subject torn between two lan-
> guages, one expressive, the other critical; and at the heart of this critical
> language, between several discourses, those of sociology, of semiology,
> and of psychoanalysis—but that, by ultimate dissatisfaction with all of
> them, I was bearing witness to the only sure thing that was in me (how-
> ever naïve it might be): a desperate resistance to any reductive system. (8)

As we descend into the palinode of *Camera Lucida* we move inexorably away from the languages of criticism, sociology, semiology, and even psychoanalysis, into the expressive, the autobiographical—from a critique of the highly linguistic, to the pointing at the ineffable. This doubt in the languages that had made up Barthes's career had already been hinted at, but in the characteristic Barthesian distancing third person in the antecedent (by two books) autobiography, *Roland Barthes by Roland Barthes*: "what if all his life *he had chosen the wrong language?*" (*Roland Barthes* 115). In this ambivalence, in this doubt, the autobiography hews the pathway for the ph/autographical palinode. As I said in my introduction Eakin notes that the photographs in *Roland Barthes by Roland Barthes* are the return of the repressed in the autobiography, are the most autobiographical thing about that autobiography. The photographs cohere the body into identity—Roland Barthes—even in the playful, split, evacuating subject of that poststructuralist autobiographical writing. It is notable that in *Camera Lucida* Barthes has resolved the split subject and writes wholly and integratingly in the first person—as if the ph/autographical palinode were the more autobiographical book, which, in its revelation of a profound self, it is. But in the prevenient autobiography we realize that Barthes had always made turns in on himself, had constantly suffered doubts about the loss of the expressive from the critical, the real from its code. Critics have recognized that, if he had not always had a strictly palinodic way of working, Barthes's work operates through shifts, whether these are seen as two "ecstasies," three "subjects," or three "paradoxes."[20] These shifts may be correlated to those in theory, but they move off its edge to something ethical or moral as Kennedy suggests—a Kierkegaardian trajectory from aesthetics to ethics eventually to the spiritual, in its increasing concern with pursuing an elusive, transcendent real over analysis of form or structure and in its apprehension of where this real lies. Barthes more than any other is a theorist whose trajectory has kept pace with, indeed set but also repeatedly revoked the times. In a chart entitled "Phases" in *Roland Barthes by Roland Barthes,* Barthes describes how "each phase" in his writing life, here given as "social mythology," "semiology," "textuality," and "morality," is "reactive" (145). And what he reacts to is the *"doxa,"* which he defines as "popular opinion" (71). In other words he makes these turns out of his theoretical phases, these *para-doxa*—which he had been crucial in helping render dominant—just as the rest of us were getting into them. And consummately at the moment when the referent was being deferred in theory, when Derrida and de Man were being read (and Jane Gallop's date of "around 1981" for the point at which feminism encountered theory in the academy might serve as a useful watershed for the general arrival of theory in the U.S./U.K. academy),[21] Barthes went out of theory, not only in these books with autobiography and then ph/autography but crucially, coincidentally, with his death. No wonder our sense of *interruptus,* of some unspeakable loss frozen and photographed in *Camera Lucida.* Our entry into theory coincides with Barthes's final exit.

Barthes's oeuvre thus represents a project of "perpetual self-correction," as Sontag writes in her introduction to the *Barthes Reader,* which has the advantage of being able to look back and select from all of his writings.[22] In the autobiography Barthes writes that his "foible" is to produce serial "introductions," "postponing the 'real' book til later" (*Roland Barthes* 173). This foible, the nonrealization of the "perfect Book" (173)—which we will see carried to fulfillment in our poet in a later chapter when she doesn't produce the book and this is what is so perfect about it—Barthes calls "prolepsis" (173). But prolepsis only results in *analepsis,* which is the need to go back and restore that constitutes the palinode. Analepsis is less the opposite of the predictive prolepsis than its retrodictive inevitability. The putting-off-till-later requires the return of what was left unfinished; and the deferral, which always, Barthes suggests, has reality in its sights—is always a deferral *of* reality (which then returns as the real)—sets up the conditions for a return: "But the dilatory, denial of reality (of the realizable), is no less alive for all that: these projects live, they are never abandoned; suspended, they can return to life at any moment" (173). Yet the return to life is never a nostalgic recovery of what was there, the return, say, of the dead into life. It is instead the discovery of a new place or text that includes recognition of the loss, of the oversight—of the dead as interminably lost, living *as dead.* Barthes's language suggests that such recognition involves a kind of spiritual pilgrimage and is perhaps the enlightenment that comes at the end of an initiate's journey: "Yet for him, it is not a question of recovering a pre-meaning, an origin of the world, of life, of facts, anterior to meaning, but rather to imagine a post-meaning: one must traverse, as though the length of an initiatic way, the whole meaning in order to be able to extenuate it, to exempt it" (87). Barthes's image of history—and his favored image (via Vico)—of the spiral encapsulates this palinodic reversal that yet creates something new in return: "history proceeds in a spiral, and things of the past return, but obviously not in the same place; thus there are states, values, behavior, 'writings' of the past that may return, but in a very modern place."[23] And what he seeks in the return is always the real—the exemption from meaning. In the autobiography Barthes writes that his project has always been one of return and that from his first book, *Writing Degree*

Zero, he has been seeking the same thing, a place or a moment—moment frozen as place—that does not signify, a utopia before or outside cultural connotation. Of his first book he writes, looking back on himself in the third person in the autobiography, "Evidently he dreams of a world which would be *exempt from meaning*. . . . This began with *Writing Degree Zero*, in which is imagined 'the absence of every sign'" (*Roland Barthes* 87).

But why this palinodic way of working, this *tirer* into anamorphic inversions culminating in *Camera Lucida*—this desire for the "zero degree" that pulls him back? There must have been a sense of irrevocable loss motivating such returns, such compelled attempts to recover the real. Critics have posed this almost as a psychological question, and this seems right, to wonder about—to *worry* about—the psychic implications of such a self-retracting (undermining?) mode. Antoine Compagnon asks "what he was running after, why he had to give up any position he had just conquered, as though the best, or only defense were to run away, radicalize and overturn his views on the spot."[24] Or back to Culler's bewilderment: "he tries to uproot his seedlings as they sprout."[25] And Stephen Ungar, in relation specifically to the palinode in *Camera Lucida* and in response to the question of why not simply *begin* with part 2, why does Barthes invoke terms and tones he later rejects, identifies that the palinode allows for a kind of self-analysis, a critical focus on the self.[26] Barthes had a term in his autobiography for this pulling the rug from under his own feet, "self-criticism"—like Nietzsche and as in Lejeune's palinode and possibly where Lejeune (in his fascination for Barthes's self-ambivalence) got it from. Self-criticism, turning to criticize and correct the self, is the palinode in generic form: not in relation to a specific text but a way of working, a methodology. But as for Lejeune "self-criticism . . . is an impossible undertaking,"[27] Barthes also writes in his definition that "nothing is more a matter of the image-system, of the imaginary than (self-) criticism" (*Roland Barthes* 120). Although *Roland Barthes by Roland Barthes* would seem to be a classic piece of self-criticism as Barthes writes of himself in the third person and "it is a *recessive* book (which falls back, but which may also gain perspective thereby)" (119), Barthes writes here under the heading "Le livre du Moi—The book of the Self"—that what disappears in self-criticism is the self so that one is left in self-analysis with an ungraspable real. Thus Lejeune's description, in his discussion of self-criticism, of *Roland Barthes by Roland Barthes* as Barthes's most *un*autobiographical book is absolutely correct. The zero degree, a world exempt from meaning, proves unoccupiable. In a fragment in *Roland Barthes by Roland Barthes* entitled "La coincidence," which is where he asks himself that famous, often-truncated question of the autobiography, "Do I not know that *in the field of the subject, there is no referent?*" (56), Barthes wonders about how one represents, how one joins with a past self. He makes an analogy between self-criticism in writing—"When I pretend to write on what I have written in the past" (56)—and listening to himself playing music. In the moment of analysis of the self, the mediation—of self, of the gap between past and present—disappears. Self-realization, grasping of the past self, elides or rather *coincides* (the title of the fragment) the self into the thing itself. The self becomes referent—and then real. Self-criticism in Barthes's analogy disappears or voids the self. When he listens to a recording of himself playing Bach or Schumann, "very soon I no longer hear myself; what I hear is, however pretentious it may seem to say so, the *Dasein* of Bach and of Schumann, the pure materiality of their music; because it is my utterance, the predicate loses all pertinence" (55–56). What is said about Bach or Schumann (the predicate, the playing) loosens its hold (its pertinence), and as in writing on the self "there occurs . . . a movement of abolition," an abolition that is "a simple idea: simple as the idea of suicide" (56).

Barthes's first book had begun his career with this quest for how to free representation, in this case literature, from the weight of forms: how to recover from the clichéd language, the technical reflexes, automatic reflections, and literary self-consciousness that Barthes noted had burdened literature over the course of history into Literature. And he uses the very same term there, repeated in his musical analogy years later in his autobiography, for the abolition of mediation. Such abolition can be achieved but only at the risk of suicide, silence. He seeks "this precarious moment of History in which literary language persists only the better to sing the necessity of its death. . . . This art has the very structure of suicide."[28] If in retrospect we can see that Barthes's work had always quested this suicidal, self-abolishing art, it is in his return to photography that he finally finds it—the abolition of language, of code, of mediation: a message without a code in the representation of death. But in an uncanny, preternatural sense, is it not also possible that with his last work, *Camera Lucida*—in writing about photography after his mother's death—Barthes's *life* took the structure of a suicide? Did his life not turn in on itself after the writing? After his mother's death, in his melancholia—which is after all *depression*—Barthes writes in *Camera Lucida* that he has nothing to live for except his writing. "Once she was dead I no longer had any reason to attune myself to the progress of the superior Life Force . . . (unless, utopically, by writing, whose project henceforth would become the unique goal of my life)" (72). This near evacuation of a desire to live and write is quite different from the last lines of the prevenient autobiography, where a persistent and tenacious desire is expressed as motivating and making possible writing: "And afterward? What to write now? Can you still write anything? One writes with one's desire, and I am not through desiring" (*Roland Barthes* 188). But if you've discovered in photography a form that abolishes (finally) mediation and language—an art that realizes the structure of suicide, accessed through death, with desire left behind—what is left of life? Barthes goes on in *Camera Lucida,* eerily, presciently to speak of his own death: "From now on I could do no more than await my total, undialectical death" (72). Barthes's biographer, Calvet, who has said that, after Barthes's childhood illness, depression "was to be his most typical mood" (39), asks of Barthes's death: "The question still remains: was this a form of suicide?"(252). For not only did Barthes not actually die from the road injuries of his accident. The forensic surgeon's report concluded that the actual cause of death was pulmonary complications from the TB that Barthes had endured since a child; Calvet writes: "It was as if, thirty-five years later, Saint-Hilaire-du-Touvet and Leysin [the sanatoria where Barthes had spent his youth] had finally taken their revenge on the body that had escaped them" (253)—what was put off "til later" returns. Calvet also suggests that Barthes had some unconscious pull toward death: a death wish. He notes that at first Barthes's condition gave doctors and friends no cause for concern. Barthes could speak after his accident and was sufficiently well to be unhappy in his environment, complaining about being stuck in hospital and interrupted by unwanted visits that intruded on this introspective self. Yet while he seemed well enough, something in Barthes would not recover: "his body was not responding to treatment: it was as if his body could not get going again" (251). Calvet interviewed friends who wonder whether Barthes had lost the desire to live, particularly after his mother's death, and who suggest that there was a sense of something willed—something willful—in Barthes's death: "Some visitors felt that the doctors were annoyed by his resistance or refusal to get better" (252).

And of the accident itself it was in some respects peculiarly nonaccidental, more in line with the "coincidence" not only of which Todorov speaks, but of which Barthes writes in *Roland Barthes by Roland Barthes* in which the mediating watchfulness of the self is abolished into the real. Apparently Barthes was looking *right in the direction of the van* that ran him over. "Were his thoughts elsewhere?" Calvet asks (249). A gaze without seeing. This was a child's death, Todorov notes, not unkindly. Or a depressive's, a melancholic's. James Beighton, in MA work, has simply but persuasively correlated Barthes's inattention at his accident and what he calls "Le texte symptomal" from Barthes's later writings—their undeniable tonal fatigue—to the *Diagnostic and Statistical Manual of Mental Disorders*'s diagnostic criteria for depression and to recent studies of depression that have stressed its inarticulability, its unrepresentability.[29] Beighton suggests that there were many signs that Barthes was suffering from depression at the end of his life after his mother's death. And Julia Kristeva, who after speaking with him around this time found Barthes depressed, writes that, whatever difference she may find as a post-Freudian between depression and melancholia, "Freudian theory detects everywhere the same *impossible mourning for the maternal object*." The depressive/melancholic suffers from the loss of signification or meaning—"symbolic abdication," which leaves the sufferer in the realm of the real. After speechlessness, there is only death: "Melancholia then ends up in asymbolia, in loss of meaning: if I am no longer capable of translating or metaphorizing, I become silent and die."[30] Along with *Camera Lucida* Barthes's journals written after his mother's death, "Deliberation" and "Soirées de Paris," the latter published posthumously (and it's so painful one wonders about the rightness of this), are overwhelming in their sense of desolation—and all of it hinged onto Barthes's mother's death. "Soirées de Paris," beginning with an epigraph from Schopenhauer's suicide note, feels like *Barthes*'s suicide note: "I have a melancholy life, that finally, I'm bored to death by it."[31] Literally. It is as if art really did achieve the structure of a suicide: as if *that* Photograph really did take Barthes's soul.

As Barthes approximates more closely the palinode throughout his career and finally produces it after his mother's death in *Camera Lucida,* what constitutes the "zero degree" and the recognition of it, its realization, becomes enmeshed in the Orpheus myth. Following Maurice Blanchot and the modernist movement, for whom the Orpheus myth is installing of modernism, a symbol for looking back beyond custom in the attempt to revive an art that had died, Barthes had long been fascinated by the Orpheus myth—by his look back. Blanchot had written that in looking back "Orpheus had done no more than obey the profound necessity of art"; Orpheus chooses inspiration, carelessness, and desire over laws and the familiar and thus, to draw out the title of Blanchot's essay, "Writing begins with Orpheus' gaze"; "everything depends on the decision to look back."[32] In *Writing Degree Zero* Barthes uses the Orpheus myth to capture—both murderous and suicidal—the task of the modern writer who must ignore all the conventions and laws of literature in order to recover a pure language or form from Literature. The writer must recover writing without discourse, the *vouloir* without *savoir*. The modern writer confronts the

"Orphean problematics of modern Form" (67). If "This art has the very structure of suicide," it is because "This language [of the writer: which "is not so much a fund to be drawn as an extreme limit" (16)] is like Orpheus who can save what he loves only by renouncing it, and who, just the same, cannot resist glancing round a little; it is a Literature brought to the gates of the Promised Land: a world without Literature, but one to which writers would nevertheless have to bear witness" (81–82). In order to retrieve, to *reprieve* what they love, writers must cede Literature—but nevertheless use literature to do so. The Orpheus myth appears again in *Roland Barthes by Roland Barthes*, in a fragment titled "Recession," to show that "blind spot" in representing the self—"only in the fashion of Orpheus: without ever turning around, without ever looking" (152–53). The myth reappears in the essay "Literature and Signification," to express the irrevocability of, now, reality: "One could say that literature is Orpheus returning from the underworld; as long as literature walks ahead, aware that it is leading someone, the reality behind it which it is gradually leading out of the untamed—that reality breathes, walks, lives, heads toward the light of a meaning; but once literature turns round to look at what it loves, all that is left is a named meaning, which is a dead meaning."[33] And the Orpheus myth is cited in *A Lover's Discourse,* with Barthes showing some self-consciousness about how much *he* is turning to look back at the Orpheus myth: "I cannot *write myself.*" To use the word "'suffering' expresses no suffering," and hence "Someone would have to teach me that one cannot write without burying 'sincerity' (always the Orpheus myth: not to turn back")[34] But it is above all in *Camera Lucida* that Barthes not only cites the Orpheus myth, in relation to the photographer whose insight ("la voyance" [*La chambre* 80], which Richard Howard, Barthes's translator, renders as "second sight" [*Camera* 47]), consists not in "seeing" but in giving the sense to the photograph of pure accidental presence, the detail (the *punctum*) that will gaze back at Barthes: "above all, imitating Orpheus, he must not turn back to look at what he is leading—what he is giving to me!" (47). Beryl Schlossman glosses this as "the moment when the referent slips away forever. The myth of Orpheus captures this moment in the fateful turn, the moment when Orpheus turns to look at Eurydice."[35] In *Camera Lucida* Barthes *enacts* the Orpheus myth, because he *does* look back, finally, fatally, fails the injunction to look forward, to progress. Orpheus is, of course, a myth about melancholia—about unsuccessful, refused mourning. Orpheus, whose love is "too much" to "endure [his] grief" in Ovid's version of this myth, loses his recently married wife to death. Contravening all the rules of nature and culture, transforming his life into as near death as possible in order to recover her from the dead, he descends to the underworld to plead for her return ("I would have to descend deeper into myself"). His song is so moving that the gods agree—but then Orpheus transgresses their condition not to look back at Eurydice and the outcome is her second, eternal death followed soon by his own: "Eurydice slipped into the depths. Orpheus stretched out his arms, straining to clasp her and be clasped; but the hapless man touched nothing but yielding air, Eurydice dying now a second time."[36] After her death Orpheus himself meets a violent death, ripped apart by women who desire him but whom he cannot love (for Ovid and for some other renderers Orpheus was the first homosexual as well as consummate poet).[37] The price of their reunion is death. But why look back—a question that surely is what fascinates about the myth—if not in order to look upon death itself, or because the love is so extreme it overrides the injunction, can't abide the gods' law? That previous Barthes critics have noted Barthes's use of the Orpheus myth without collating either Barthes's citations of it or each others' suggests, strangely and at odds with Barthes, the injunction not to look back has been heeded.[38] But the palinode says one must look back. In this the Orpheus myth is the *mythos,* the mythic motif we might say, of the palinode.

Who or what is the Eurydice that vanishes in the moment of Barthes's looking, of really looking? In the Orpheus myth she is death. But she is also the object of an extreme love that is a refusal of mourning. Blanchot writes that Orpheus looks round at Eurydice not because he wishes to see her live but because he wishes to see her dead—to love her in the fullness of death, we might say then. For Barthes, Eurydice is equivalent to the zero degree that his art has always quested. Hence he looks back to, invokes and constantly revokes, both myth (Orpheus) and what is in fact a term of temperature measure (the zero degree comes from the Celsius scale) together. Initially, what Barthes means by the *zero degree* is no meaning, or exemption from meaning. But the zero degree comes to acquire its meaning or its object. First, what is zero degree but death, and if art quests zero degree no wonder it has the structure of a suicide. Emptiness, the void. But in *Camera Lucida,* via an expressed extreme love, the zero degree/Eurydice becomes finally incarnated in Barthes's mother after her death. Deferred from the first book to the last ("à l'origine de l'oeuvre, la nostalgie du réel"),[39] the zero degree comes to rest in an extreme love for a dead mother. In *Camera Lucida* Barthes finds that, although it comes closest of all forms of representation, in photography his "body never finds its zero degree, no one can give it to me (perhaps only my mother? For it is not indifference which erases the weight of the image . . . but love, extreme love)" (12). Behind the palinodic retraction of *Camera Lucida,* then, the ultimate referent of the look back that is this book is an extreme—extreme to a degree that has not been seen before (for indeed how can one see "zero"? how to circumscribe the extreme?)—love for Barthes's mother. What is the most extreme love but a love almost outside of love, in the excess, in the "almost"—that begins what we think of as love? Barthes's interest in the Orpheus myth culminates in transgressing the interdiction of what one loves—not to look back in love—and this takes him into the verges of another myth, of generational transgressions: the Oedipus myth.

PALINODIC LOVE

Like Orpheus with Eurydice, Barthes loses his mother twice over. That there are two palinodes in *Camera Lucida* has been suggested by criticism (Sarkonak), but not that their ultimate referent is love for the mother, a love that is itself palinodic, a desire to go back (transgressing narrative rules) in all kinds of ways. The first palinode, in the ode part of *Camera Lucida,* moves Barthes from the *studium* to the *punctum* as the accidental detail that makes its way into the photograph. This is how the *punctum* is originally defined. The photograph "is never distinguished from its referent (from what it represents)" (5); "the referent adheres" (6); "every photograph is somehow co-natural with its referent" (76); "I call the 'photographic referent' not the *optionally* real thing to which an image or a sign refers but the *necessarily* real thing" (76); "it is Reference, which is the founding order of photography" (77). This is one of the most reiterated tenets of *Camera Lucida,* and it puts into retraction ("reacts to") Barthes's previous work on the sign and his emphasis on attending to the codes of photography. Yet while it may be reference that is the *founding* order of photography, the final order of photography becomes the real. The second, far more powerful palinode is the *loss* of this referent, as the *punctum* is recast from detail or object to time. Reflected in the titles of the two chapters from part 1 and part 2 respectively, "*Punctum*: Partial Feature" (chapter 7) and "Time as *Punctum*" (chapter 8), this recasting entails a recognition of the pastness of the referent in the photograph, as Barthes looks back, looks back in an Orphean move, to realize that what the photograph represents is a lost referent. Photography's reference is in the past tense: "I can never deny that *the thing has been there.* There is a superimposition here: of reality and the past" (76). "Ça-a-été," "interfuit" (*La chambre* 120, 121): photography's past is aorist, an ontology that certainly occurred but that is irrevocably over, "the Intractable" (77). Photography itself then becomes not only melancholic but palinodic, for it gives us the thing only to retract or lose it, only to present it as already lost. Photography is marked by "a strictly revulsive movement which reverses the course of the thing" and which Barthes calls "the photographic ecstasy" (119)—madness or love; madness *in* love. It is this pastness of the referent, the repeal of presence, that makes photography so fatal, so inextricably tied to death.

Barthes says that photography's desire is "fantasmatic, driving from a kind of second sight [here is *"voyance"*] which seems to bear me forward to a utopian time, or to carry me back to somewhere in myself: a double movement which Baudelaire celebrates in *Invitation au voyage* and *La Vie intérieure*. . . . it is as if *I were certain* of having been there or of going there" (40). Where is this place one is certain of having been and of going there if not a place from before birth and after death? Barthes immediately connects this certain retrospective and prospective space to the Freudian maternal body, which Freud says is the only place we can be sure we have already been there and to which we retain the desire to return.[40] Barthes writes that there is "nothing Proustian in a photograph" (82), by which he means that photography does not recall the past, cannot return memory: it is not "an aid to memory" but a "counter-memory" then;[41] or even stronger, not an aide-mémoire but a memento mori. Photography "does not take a nostalgic path out of memory" (85). Even for Proust there is nothing really "Proustian" in a photograph. The narrator of *Remembrance of Things Past* does not console himself with a photograph of his grandmother after her death. And at Albertine's death the photograph forms an analogy for, at first, the horrible livedness of her death, its refusal to move from living death to a memory he can mourn. "Things past" are instead sparked famously in Proust's opus by the smell, the scent, the taste of a madeleine with a cup of tea; photography is almost too real for the psychological world of Proustian memory. For Barthes photography is a horrific haunting, the incarnation of the dead, not a carrying across *(metaphor)* to life. "In Photography, the presence of the thing (at a certain past moment) is never metaphoric. . . . if the photograph then becomes horrible, it is because it certifies, so to speak, that the corpse is alive, as *corpse*: it is the living image of the dead" (78–79). This is why photography can become invested with Barthes's melancholy ("the melancholy of Photography itself" [79]). The form itself makes irrevocable loss. Photography instead "has something to do with resurrection"; it is not memory but "reality in a past state"—the presence of death—and hence our astonishment at photography is "religious" (82).

Barthes's palinodic retraction of the *punctum* as pure presence is impelled by his palinodic approach to the Winter Garden Photograph, by finding then losing his mother's presence, and by the palinodic reference that *is* this photograph. Going through photographs of her that November evening, with a light in a dark room, "alone in the apartment where she had died, looking at these pictures of my mother, one by one, under the lamp, gradually moving back in time with her, looking for the truth of the face I had loved" (67), Barthes, in the evocative French, "remonte." Variously translated by Howard into the English as "moving back," "worked back," and "traversing" (71), the verb *remonter,* used in *La chambre claire* in two closely spaced chapters four times (106, 111), is a double movement. It is "to go back" (in time), to "date back," "to descend," "to have again"; but also simultaneously but inversely "to go towards," "to get on one's feet again," "to wind up" (a clock)—or "to set upright" (an oil lamp for instance). *Remontant* is the dynamic of the palinode, of Barthes's approach to the photograph, and of the subject of the photograph. Looking for the image that will return her to him, Barthes moves back in time with his mother, starting with the most recent images taken in the summer before her death. The Winter Garden Photograph shows her as a child of five in a conservatory, a "winter garden." The photograph is not of his mother but his "mother-as-child" (71), or again in the more evocative French, "mère enfant" (*La chambre* 128 and passim). The French elides or coincides the generational differences, slips over the *relative* (metaphoric) conjunction *as*—and puts the mother in the place of the child. The child (Barthes) finding his mother in the child is of course a palin*dromic* dynamic (a reversal in the second set of terms of the order in the first: child; mother; child). But this is not a word game. *Palin-* represents the truth of their final relationship for Barthes, the ultimate reality. "This movement of the Photograph (of the order of photographs) I have experienced in reality" (71). At the end of her life, *their* life, during her illness Barthes nursed her: "she had become my little girl, uniting for me with that essential child she was in her first photograph. . . . I who had not procreated, I had, in her very illness, engendered my mother" (72).

The scene of the photograph is itself caught up in the recursiveness of time and relationship. It is in its representation of closeness a foretelling of a separation that has yet to happen—but that of course has happened by the time Barthes comes upon the photograph. Again these inversions are best in the original. The photograph shows Barthes's mother alongside her slightly older brother: "Le frère et la soeur, unis entre eux, je le savais, par la désunion des parents, qui devaient divorcer peu de temps après, avaient posé côte à côte, seuls" (106). The palindromic juxtapositions, the balancing of this sentence, are startling in Barthes's language. The children are "unis entre eux . . . par la désunion des parents": "*united* by the *disunion* of

their parents"—with Barthes's knowledge ("je le savais") separating, yet
the copula of, the inverting phrases. The children "avaient posé côte à côte,
seuls": "had posed *side by side alone,*" again impelled togetherness making
them alone, or rather surely their aloneness forcing them together. And
finally the double movement of time: the parents "qui devaient divorcer,"
"who were to"—imperfect indicative but with the sense of something futural about the verb *devoir*—"to be fated," "to be about to," "divorce." The
description of the scene of the photograph, packed into this one sentence,
is a tight weave of the chiastic inversions (the back and forth and up and
down, the proximity and separation) that also describe the relationship
of Barthes to his mother in the body of *Camera Lucida.* One final point
before we leave the scene of the Winter Garden Photograph, on the idea
of the winter garden: what could be more an inversion of time and more
unnatural, more against the laws of nature and generation, than a garden
(with palms) in winter? It was the house, Barthes writes settling on it to
represent his mother's death, where his mother was born.

How we get from *this* photograph to Barthes's relationship with his
mother is through *other* photographs that *remontent.* Other readers have
recently noted (with the attention to Barthes on photography) the remarkable generational slips that are made in relation to other photographs in
Camera Lucida. In these they find the absent Winter Garden Photograph,
metaphorized or indicated if not deictically revealed. Most notably there is
a photograph by Nadar that appears in the midst of note 28 as Barthes describes and discusses the Winter Garden Photograph and makes his move
back in time with his mother. This photograph, under which Barthes cites
Nadar as "the world's greatest photographer" (68), shows an old woman,
grey, probably sick, with dark rings under her eyes, but still striking. It is
the photograph that could most be "allegorically in Nadar's beautiful and
sensual portrait of a woman with dark eyes and luminous white hair," as
Schlossman puts it, Barthes's aging and sick mother absent in the absent
Winter Garden Photograph.[42] In the edition of Nadar's works from which
Barthes takes the image this photograph is listed as Nadar's *mother,* but it
is catalogued in the Bibliothèque Nationale in Paris as Nadar's *wife.* In his
caption Barthes keeps open the ambiguity of the photograph, and in so
doing, Daniel Grojnowski writes in his research on the provenance of the
photograph, expresses the desire of a child, "un désir d'enfant."[43] Barthes's
caption reads: "Nadar: The Artist's Mother (or Wife)" (68). If the slip
consciously adheres to the confusion surrounding the referent of Nadar's
photograph, nevertheless it is crucially significant to the generational slips
in the unconscious logic of the narrative of *Camera Lucida.* Like *mère*

« Quel est, à votre avis,
le plus grand photographe du monde?
— Nadar. »

"Who do you think is the world's greatest photographer?—Nadar." "Nadar: The Artist's Mother (or Wife)," from Roland Barthes, *Camera Lucida.*

enfant, the parenthesis in Barthes's caption (and Derrida's remarks that Barthes's parentheses do "not enclose an incidental or secondary thought" but rather "[lower] the voice" "out of a sense of modesty" could not be more pertinent—as if the parenthesis marks off the crucial but unspeakable thought), runs the relationship backward to skip a generation—but here not to skip two generations so that his mother becomes his child, the reflection of his reality, but a single generation so that the artist's mother *could be* his wife (the projection of his fantasy?). Family palindromes. Diana Knight believes, compellingly but ultimately falling short of the mood of *Camera Lucida* (for it makes the book seem too contrived, too conscious), that "the Winter Garden photo is simply an invention" and is instead a "transposition of the 'real' photo ('The Stock')."[44] "The Stock," which is the only photograph appearing in *Camera Lucida* to come from the author's private collection, shows an old man with a girl and boy who although slightly younger than the five and eight of Barthes's winter garden subjects nevertheless seem to share their same age differential, and the little girl has the same "brightness of . . . eyes," the same "physical luminosity" (66) Barthes attributes to his mother elsewhere in *Camera Lucida.* "The Stock" appears in a note entitled "Lineage" (103) where *another* generational mistake/uncertainty occurs: "Sometimes I am mistaken, or at least I hesitate: a medallion represents a young woman and her child: surely that is my mother and myself? But no, it is *her* mother and her son (my uncle)" (103). Knight notes "another confusion of generations" (140) in Barthes's comments on a photograph by Van der Zee, again parenthetical: "the sister (or daughter)" (*Camera* 43).

Knight takes these generational slips back to Barthes's homosexuality and her sense that what he sees in the Winter Garden Photograph, and hence in his mother, is acceptance of his homosexuality, "the example of this mother's goodness" (141). I'd insist we take them further back, back to the "love, extreme love," the zero degree of meaning that Barthes suggests only his mother can offer him—did give him. It is love for the mother that is extreme. Obviously this love is extreme in the face of her death. Barthes speaks of resurrection of his mother twice, and clearly his investment is to *remonter* (to raise again but also himself to go towards) his dead mother. His is an insufferable grief: "why is that I am alive *here and now?*" (84). In other words, after the death of my mother how can I still be alive? But *remonter* expresses a desire that was even shaping of their life. He dreams about her (he only dreams about her), but it is never quite her. Instead, "love's dreadful regime" is the "almost" (66): "Le presque" (*La chambre*

104). The almost, a proximity that is too much but not quite enough, a desire for equivalence or conjunction or identity that is held apart by just a gap (the curtains)—a just: might this not also describe an impossible, overwhelming love between generations that, in its most representable but literal form, is named incest? One wants the parenthesis here to express a love that slips through language. Homosexuality is conventionally the unspeakable love, but what's more primordial and unspeakable? Barthes writes that he and his mother had no need for language: "in a sense I never 'spoke' to her, never 'discoursed' in her presence, for her; we supposed, without saying anything of the kind to each other, that the frivolous insignificance of language, the suspension of images, must be the very space of love, its music" (72); and, "she never made a single 'observation'" (69). The suspension of images as the space of love has a double meaning. The images are suspended in their freezing of time and history, but suspended also in the sense of their absence—as in the absence of the Winter Garden Photograph. The last complete piece of writing that Barthes produced, a talk on Stendhal that he was due to give in Milan and that was found lying on his desk after his death (he never gave it), was entitled "On échoue toujours de parler ce qu'on aime": "one always fails in speaking of what one loves."[45] In *A Lover's Discourse,* the book that Barthes wrote just before moving to *Camera Lucida,* in spite of the book's title and its articulacy and the embrace of its articulacy (*A Lover's Discourse* is Barthes's most popular work, the one through which he entered popular discourse), love is also above all inexpressible. In a fragment entitled "Inexpressible Love," which is where the Orphic injunction in *A Lover's Discourse* not to turn back appears, Barthes confronts the impossibility of putting love into language: "On the one hand, this is saying nothing; on the other it is saying too much: impossible to *adjust.* . . . Love has of course a complicity with my language (which maintains it), but it cannot be *lodged* in my writing" (98). And yet at the end of this fragment, to know this loss, to see that the real cannot be lodged, is suspended as absence, is to make writing possible: "to know that writing compensates for nothing, sublimates nothing, that it is precisely *there where you are not*—this is the beginning of writing" (100). Barthes makes the same point a theoretical one in his "Inaugural Lecture" to the Collège de France. In a talk that infamously calls language "quite simply fascist," Barthes writes of the impossible double bind between representation and the real: "literature is categorically realist, in that it never has anything but the real as the object of desire," not because it can realize desire but because it can't: "From our ancient times to the efforts of our avant-garde, literature has been concerned to represent something. What?

I will put it crudely: the real. The real is not representable, and it is because men ceaselessly try to represent it by words that there is a history of literature."[46] As Blanchot writes, it was because Orpheus lost Eurydice that he sang; return, representation issues from loss.

What is the love that is inexpressible, that is not simply representable as unspeakable—for this would be the homosexuality that Barthes "spoke" in coded form elsewhere (in *Roland Barthes by Roland Barthes*, the goddess H.)—but that has no need for language, that ultimately may be this absence of or antecedence to language? Is it not a love that a child has for its mother, not so much a "pre-Oedipal love" (I don't want to psychoanalyze: Barthes insists he has lost not "the mother" but *his* mother [75]; hence the shortfall—or overstep—of Elaine Hoft-March's neatly packaged Oedipal reading), as an exclusive, perfect original love, a love that, if we are fortunate, we are born into and that no other love can replace? Here is where *Camera Lucida is* Proustian. For Proust's narrator, the consuming love for his mother with which *Remembrance of Things Past* begins, so that he must kiss her goodnight at the risk of banishment from her, means that from then on "reality will take shape in the memory alone." No love can give him "that untroubled peace" and that past original love must be the paragon—of his love for Albertine, and even for his grandmother, since Proust transposes his own real dead mother to his fictional dead grandmother.[47] All Proust's remembrance comes from this. Barthes acknowledges mother-love as his connection to Proust since in another late essay, which suggests Proust as his guide for whatever Barthes was going to go on to write—Proust, he says, was "seeking a form which will accommodate suffering (he has just experienced it in an absolute form through his mother's death)"—Barthes writes that "it is at the painful price of this inversion [of the irreplaceable mother's kiss] that Proust's *Search . . .* , night after night, will be written."[48] As Kennedy writes of Barthes's "nothing to say" at his mother's death, "There was nothing to say because there was so much that wanted saying."[49] This is the referent of the palinode.

Barthes lived with his mother, chose to live with his mother all her life, a situation that our culture would conventionally see as requiring "discourse." Gabriel Josipovici, an English academic who lived with *his* mother all *her* life, wrote *his* memoir of his mother and his life with her. The title, *A Life*, refers to the inextricability of their lives, to their singular life. His mother, Sacha Rabinovitch, in one of those odd "coincidences" so pervasive of Barthes's story, made the English translation of the Blanchot essay on Orpheus that got Barthes rolling on the Orpheus myth. We know from *Camera Lucida* (the opening of the palinode) that Barthes was planning "to write a little compilation about her" (63), his mother; and with its use of photographs in the attempt to recover the dead, its recognition of the reversal of roles ("how inevitable") of mother and child at the end of the life as the child feeds his sick, dying mother, and in its writing in a period of evident ongoing grief after his mother's death, it is tempting to see Josipovici's book as a lot like *Camera Lucida* or the kind of book Barthes would have written had he been able to say more, had the book been more explicitly about his mother and less (ostensibly) about photographs.[50] *A Life* is above all an attempt to come to terms with the separation *and* the intrication of a mother's and son's lives. Josipovici is heterosexual. It is for this reason and more besides that I believe that this mother-love, pace Freud, has nothing to do with the gender of the projected sexual object-choice; for all that follows is *inconsequential*. Josipovici considers the Oedipal discourse that might surround their love, even quotes a poem by Sacha (who was a published poet as well as a translator) on the riddle of the Sphinx. He ultimately refutes such discourse:

> Was it my weakness that kept me by her? Had she, in her desire to protect me after what she felt had been the traumatic years of my earliest childhood, made me dangerously dependent on her? Or was the whole Freudian vocabulary and mind-set of devouring mothers and submissive sons a cliché by which the west had been enthralled? [Josipovici's mother is from the East, a Sephardic Jew.] I was certainly the best friend she had ever had, and she, to her surprise, had turned out to be the best friend I could have hoped for. Perhaps our relationship was a miracle which needed to be nurtured rather than denied. (186)

Or as he puts the explanation for their closeness more simply: "we found each other better company than anyone else" (159). Or, in response to the question of whether it was Josipovici's "weakness or my strength that had led to my making my life with her" (214), he quotes the closing lines of Sacha's poem on Oedipus: "Riddles are for asking. / They are better left unsolved" (224). Barthes was also aware of the psychoanalytic "discourse" that surrounded such love. In *Roland Barthes by Roland Barthes* the first autobiographical (author) photograph in the pages of photographs that begin the autobiography shows Barthes as a child in his mother's arms—captioned "The Demand for Love" (8)—already two-thirds the size of his mother (between seven and ten?), conventionally too "grown up" to be making a demand for such proximity, such holding: such *presque*. Yet in *Camera Lucida* Barthes somewhat defensively—rightly defensively—in terms very close to Josipovici refuses any discursive explanation of their proximity that has been dictated to by anthropology and psychoanalysis. "As if our experts cannot conceive there are families 'whose members love one another'" (74). The Winter Garden Photograph requires him to forget two social institutions—"the Family, the Mother" (74). He loves his mother looking back before anthropological and psychoanalytic conventions. He inverts the diagnostic syllogism he has been subjected to in his grief that imputes some blame for his melancholia with his staying too long with her. "It is always maintained that I should suffer more because I have spent my whole life with her; but my suffering proceeds from *who she was;* and it is because she was who she was that I lived with her" (75). Her being is the missed-out origin of his grief and his love, if one needs one.

It's a platitude to read in *Camera Lucida* a love letter or elegy to the dead mother, but what is it as both? What does it mean to proclaim one's love for one's mother—and such a limitless love as this—after she is dead, to a dead living in Barthes's melancholia? The pull of *Camera Lucida* is always from death to love, or love to death, as if Barthes were in love with death—or dead to love. (But what's the difference? Closing his journal "Soirées de Paris" and writing soon after his mother's death, Barthes despairs of finding love with another single other: "knowing it was over, and that more than O. was over: the love of *one* boy" [*Incidents* 73].) Love is soldered to death in *Camera Lucida,* and again one wants the French to convey this. The photograph is affixed to its referent with "la même immoblité amoureuse ou funèbre" (17): the same stillness of love or death. Classical phenomenology before *Camera Lucida* had never spoken of "désir ou deuil" (41), desire or grief; or Barthes kept with him like a treasure "mon désir ou mon chagrin" (42)—my desire or my sorrow. And from speaking of the desire in Mapplethorpe photographs at the end of the ode section of *Camera Lucida,* Barthes moves to immerse himself in his mother's death that begins the palinode section. Love and death, Proust, the great novel that Barthes never wrote—here in *Camera Lucida* are what Barthes writes he sees in photography: "l'amour et la mort" (115). In French (think the trio of the reading of the tarot cards toward the end of Bizet's *Carmen,* in which Carmen's friends are foretold love at the very same time she is prophesied death), the pronounced consonants ("l," "m") and the echoed assonances ("am," "ou"/"or") bring Barthes's repeated two words much closer—inseparable—than our contrasting Anglo-Saxon/ Anglo-Norse sounds. As in most palinodes, it is sound, the echoes of the palin*drome*, that comes to put in motion what is most real, that which escapes the sense of language ("discourse") in this form that elides past and present, referent and self—music or sound that expresses the "coincidence"

(Roland Barthes by Roland Barthes) that is perhaps ultimately the best way to describe Barthes's relationship with his mother.

Is there a way to say—but in music or in photography—they simply coincided? In "One Always Fails in Speaking of What One Loves" Barthes writes that music as a space *"outside of language"* (*Rustle* 302) expresses love, generating a "kind of aphasia" (303). In *Camera Lucida* he compares the Winter Garden Photograph to "the last music that Schumann wrote before collapsing, that first *Gesang der Frühe* which accords with both my mother's being and my grief at her death; I could not express this accord except by an infinite series of adjectives, which I omit, convinced however that this photograph collected all the possible predicates from which my mother's being was constituted" (70). The "Song of Dawn" that Schumann wrote right before his death, a work of light as the composer was entering *his* darkness, constitutes another palindrome, another temporal contradiction that apparently is what moved Barthes about this piece. In an essay entitled "Loving Schumann" that he wrote the same year as *Camera Lucida,* Barthes, considering what the composer means to him, suggests that to love Schumann is to be out of time, not only in the sense of to contravene the preferences of his moment but also to be archaic, mythic in a way that takes the child back to an indissoluble connection with his mother. Schumann "is truly the musician of solitary intimacy, of the amorous and imprisoned soul that *speaks to itself*. . . in short of the child who has no other link than to the other." "This is a music at once dispersed and unary, continually taking refuge in the luminous shadow of the Mother (the *lied,* copious in Schumann's work, is, I believe, the expression of this maternal unity)." To love Schumann is "to assume a philosophy of Nostalgia, or to adopt a Nietszchean word, of Untimeliness, or again, to risk this time the most Schumannian word there is: of Night. Loving Schumann, doing so in a certain fashion *against* the age . . . can only be a responsible way of loving: it inevitably leads the subject who does so and says so to posit himself in his time according to the injunctions of his desire and not according to those of his sociality. But," Barthes continues and concludes the essay, "that is another story, whose narrative would exceed the limits of music."[51]

Indeed it does. And the desire that exceeds music is taken up in the essay on photography. In photographical palinodes as suggested by Barthes's analogy between *his* photograph and Schumann's last work to express what he at a crucial point cannot, music continues to be evoked as the *contrapunctum,* the counterpoint that puts in motion what exceeds, comes before or after language. But if music picks up what cannot be said in language—is as outside the space of the sign or code expressive of the inexpressible that is love—photography, when it can suspend even the limits of music, when it can freeze into the real the love that lies outside or before sociality, can point to this extreme "narrative." In the Winter Garden Photograph Barthes finds Benjamin's "flash" in history (30), the traumatic, the way to interrupt history that Benjamin suggests *is* history.[52] "I had discovered this photograph by moving back through Time. The Greeks entered into Death backward: what they had before them was their past" (*Camera* 71). The photograph "is a prophecy in reverse: like Cassandra, but eyes fixed on the past" (87). There is a madness in this history: Orpheus trying to retrieve Eurydice— Barthes "taking into my arms what is dead, what is going to die" (117). If history is the barrier that separates him from his mother—death, a generation, the mother as child, the mother as *wife*—what about conjuring a different narrative of history, one that moves not forward but backward, regressively, *palinodically*? "Is History not simply that time when we were not born?" Barthes asks (64). What does it mean to love one's mother so much one sees her, coincidentally, as one's wife? Such a prehistorical, impossible love, history has no name for, and myth names as incest, which is the very foundation of history, of time forward, of progress. Mythically there are different conceptions of history (this different conception of history is what myth is), nonlinear, cyclical, with a reversible quality to its time. Barthes, recognized as our deconstructionist of myth, ends up back in the greatest myth—living out Orpheus and the one that is before history. The recognition is something like Culler's, except I see that what Barthes has at stake in believing in the real of the myth of photography is absolutely exquisite and absolutely true. Only masks (veils, language) enable him to read photography, to talk about "photography" at all. And when the mask dissolves as it does in the Winter Garden Photograph the soul is left. Mary Bittner Wiseman suggests that photography is emblematic of postmodernism and yet returns to the primitive; for to be primitive and postmodern, as in photography, is to be out of time. Photographs for Barthes are like masks for primitives. Magical, photographs manifest the souls of ancestors. Seeking out the primitive in photography Barthes ends *Camera Lucida* by saying we have repressed the profound madness of photography, which is its mythic heritage.

In thinking about the significance of the palinodic organization of *Camera Lucida*, critics have suggested alternative influences on Barthes. Réda Bensmaïa finds in *Roland Barthes by Roland Barthes* a reference to the Kierkegaardian palinode. While she doesn't consider *Camera Lucida*, the insistence on becoming subjective and becoming mystical in the retraction of Kierkegaard's *Concluding Unscientific Postscript* surely continues as an

influence in Barthes's final work.[53] Gary Shapiro thinks that Barthes's palinode rewrites that of *Phaedrus,* and indeed Barthes ends in a similar place
to Socrates in his retraction, in love and (as) madness ("mon désir fou" [*La
chambre* 166]).[54] But most significant for our contextualization of Barthes's
palinode is a point that Lejeune makes in his elegy for Barthes—an elegy
that like Derrida's is written in Barthes's voice ("ton sur ton"; "pastiche").
Lejeune writes that to name Barthes's form simply as "Palinodie" is to reduce *Camera Lucida* to a Western logic: "la Doxa occidentale.[55] Why should
photography be powerful to hold these extreme things after all? Because,
Camera Lucida ends by telling us, the real for Westerners is now hidden.
Death is not *in* modern society—is nowhere except in photography. Since
the second half of the nineteenth century, with a crisis in religious belief
that coincided with the invention of photography, death (the contact with
death) has moved from religion to photography. Today, Barthes writes, we
have renounced the mythic in photography, tamed it, dominating the world
instead by the sign—especially in the United States, he insists, "where
everything is transformed into images" and the sublimation in photography of the real into masks or signs "completely *de-realizes* the human world
of conflicts and desires" (118). In his last chapter Barthes offers a critique of
advanced societies and longs for a more naïve, a more primitive relationship
to images. Incredibly he calls for an abolition of images and a contact with
the real without mediation. The choice in conceiving photography he presents as that between photography as madness (the real), or photography as
tamed (the sign): photography's frozen stillness or its mediation; its silence
or its narrative movement into language. Barthes chooses madness, silence,
stillness. "I passed beyond the unreality of the thing represented, I entered
crazily into the spectacle, into the image, taking into my arms what is dead,
what is going to die, as Nietzsche did when [as he fell into madness], as
Podach tells us, on January 3, 1889, he threw himself in tears on the neck
of a beaten horse: gone mad for Pity's sake" (117). Yet in this embrace of
death lies compassion: "la Pitié" (*La chambre* 179), a welling up of pathos
in recognition of the void (and a very Kierkegaardian term as the object of
a spiritual trajectory). Gone mad *for the sake of* pity. And this madness, this
revelation of what's behind the curtains, forces Barthes to ask what he calls
"the ethical question" of *Camera Lucida* (118), which this essay extraordi-
narily poses in relation to photography: What is the status of the real in
Western society when we choose to mask death?

By far the most outstanding (notable and incongruent) influence underlying Barthes's palinode and enlightening of his mystical turn in closing
are some works on Buddhism. Cited in the bibliography that appears only

in the French version, *La chambre claire,* these constitute the text's intertextual *punctum.* Buddhism pervades Barthes's final works, is also in *Roland Barthes by Roland Barthes* and *A Lover's Discourse.* Barthes's most ostensible Buddhist text is *Empire of Signs,* from 1970. But his recognition of the emptiness of forms that *is* Buddhist reality is intellectual prior to *Camera Lucida* and stops short of the satori, of Zen. Death is strangely absent from *Empire.* This is notable because the Buddhist satori has impermanence, the nonexistence of the self—this is all going to change—at its essence. Photography is used briefly in *Empire* to evoke the emptiness Barthes idealizes in the haiku, that is the "trace," the "faint gash inscribed upon time," the "flash, a slash of light"—and, quoting Shakespeare— *"When the light of sense goes out, but with a flash that has revealed the invisible world."* The haiku is like the photograph one takes very carefully, "but having neglected to load the camera with film."[56] In *Camera Lucida* Barthes loads the film into the camera and works the analogy between photography and the haiku the other way round. Photography is now like the haiku because of its *"intense immobility"* (49). Looking back at photography, Barthes stays with the flash long enough to see that its slash of light reveals the zero degree as death. The lightness and playfulness of *Empire of Signs* contrast with the realization—and it is no longer intellectual but experienced, practiced—of *Camera Lucida.* One of the Buddhist texts that Barthes had been reading in writing *Camera Lucida, The Way of Zen* by Alan Watts, the conduit of Buddhism in the West in the sixties and seventies, emphasizes the centrality to Buddhism of the insight into loss thus: "It is precisely this realization of the *total* elusiveness of the world which lies at the root of Buddhism." Watts argues that forms—or signs—(Barthes's previous "empire") are conjured from the void to mask death. "The life of things is only conventionally separable from their death; in reality the dying is the living." And Buddhism sees that this truth is beyond form and language; Zen has "nothing to say."[57]

Barthes's realization of these central tenets of Buddhism in photography is a brilliant elucidation. In *Camera Lucida* the Lacanian real, the *This,* the *Tuché,* is also a Buddhist one—*tathata.* So that in the sentence following that in which Barthes defines the Lacanian real he performs this equation: "In order to designate reality, Buddhism says *sunya,* the void; but better still: *tathata,* as Alan Watts has it, the fact of being this, of being thus, of being so; *tat* means *that* in Sanskrit and suggests the gesture of the blind pointing" (5). The *punctum* is a satori for Barthes: "This *something* has triggered me, has provoked a tiny shock, a *satori,* the passage of a void" (49), and the definition of satori he gives is the *punctum* all over, "at once the past and the real" (82). The final word of *La chambre claire* (again absent from the English translation, lost taper) goes on the rear cover to that of another Buddhist writer, Chögyam Trungpa. The Tibetan Trungpa, who had just a few years before translated *The Tibetan Book of the Dead,* writes in his introduction there that *"Tathagata* literally means 'thus-gone,' which can be paraphrased as 'he who has become one with the sense of what is.' It is synonymous with *buddha* ('awakened')." With its journey to the underworld in its pilgrimage for the truth of the dead mother in her photograph, and with Barthes's becoming one with the sense of what has thus-gone, *Camera Lucida* is not unlike the Tibetan Book of the Dead, the Bardo Thötröl. *Camera Lucida,* too, like that prayer, is for the living as much as for the dead; singing to the dead "can show us how to live," Trungpa writes.[58] But what Barthes quotes on his rear cover is from another text by Trungpa, in which the lama discusses his lineage teacher Marpa's insight into the loss of his son. "Marpa was very upset when his son was killed, and one of his disciples said, 'You used to tell us that everything is illusion. How about the death of your son? Isn't it illusion?' And Marpa replied, 'True, but my son's death is a super-illusion.'"[59] Death is an illusion perhaps because we cannot grasp its real, because we can only view it like everything through the lens of our sense-perceptions. But the death of the one whom one loves the most is nonetheless real, and it becomes a super-illusion when our irremediable grief embodies their loss: as in a ghost, or even a photograph. As I think Barthes might take up Marpa's insight in relation to photography in the very last lines of *Camera Lucida*: "such are the two ways of the photograph. The choice is mine: to subject its spectacle to the civilized code of perfect illusions, or to confront in it the wakening of intractable reality" (119). Barthes's awakening is that he chooses to see super-illusion. It is a loss that coincides with our gain.

CHAPTER 2

CLAUDE LÉVI-STRAUSS'S
TRISTES PHOTOGRAPHIQUES

THE VIEW FROM AFAR

At the beginning of *Tristes Tropiques,* received to date as his most autobiographical work, Claude Lévi-Strauss states his antipathy toward photographic texts by anthropologists or travelers. This book or lecture accompanied with slide show, which "enjoys a kind of vogue" at the time of
Lévi-Strauss's writing in 1955, often takes the form of the "anthropologist's
return" to his career's work "to reveal his precious store of memories."[1]
Lévi-Strauss condemns not just the ways in which "actual experience is
replaced by stereotypes" and "memories have to be sorted and sifted"
(30). He condemns the hypocrisy of the enterprise: "photographs, books,
travellers' tales" have taken the place of relics of the exotic that colonizers,
those earliest explorers, brought back from their conquest, such as masks
or *pau-brasil* ("Brazil-wood") from Brazil and from which Brazil was given
its name (30). Both are part of a "quest for power" (32). But whereas the
earliest artifacts at least acknowledged their conquest, their contemporary
photographic equivalent mourns the cultures that its "monoculture" or
"mass civilization" destroys (30). The modern narrative "pretends to itself
that it is investing [primitive peoples] with nobility at the very time when
it is completing their destruction" (33). When the anthropologist-traveler
"brandishes before an eager public albums of coloured photographs, instead
of the now vanished native masks," "Perhaps the public imagines that the
charms of the savages can be appropriated through the medium of these

photographs. Not content with having eliminated savage life, and unaware even of having done so, it feels the need feverishly to appease the nostalgic cannibalism of history with the shadows of those that history has already destroyed" (34). At the end of *Tristes Tropiques* Lévi-Strauss will propose Buddhism as an alternative to this model of knowledge as destruction of the other. As offering an enlightenment into the false divisions between self and other and an idealization of childlike unguardedness, Buddhism is "a return to the maternal breast" (498).

In 1994 some forty years later, Lévi-Strauss produces a book that would seem the embodiment of that repudiated photographic traveler's tale. Written, if not in extremis, then certainly since the anthropologist was already eighty-six in the twilight of his life, *Saudades do Brasil: A Photographic Memoir* collects 180 photographs in which Lévi-Strauss looks back on his travels in Brazil, the place that had begun and remained central to his career. From the 1930s, the photographs capture a way of life in Brazil that was then rapidly passing. This was before the substantial U.S. investment that began during the Second World War, the country still had a physical frontier, and its Indians in the interior were still primitive. Lévi-Strauss would discover "bravos" or savages in 1938 in the form of the Tupi-Kawahib, a group previously thought extinct, and record them on the cusp of abandoning their way of life in the Amazon and adapting (*Tristes* 316). Expensive and beautifully produced, translated from the French and then into English and Portuguese, *Saudades do Brasil* presents as a coffee-table guide for the armchair traveler. Moreover, since *saudades do brasil* in Portuguese means most closely "nostalgia for Brazil," Lévi-Strauss's last published book appears to literalize to the letter that act of nostalgic cannibalism. The turn is recognizably palinodic, and it comes in the form of a photographic memoir.[2]

In fact Lévi-Strauss's previous work had used photography—for the first time and most substantially before *Saudades* in *Tristes Tropiques,* where his criticism of photography in anthropology is made. But what's marked and constant in his oeuvre until the photographic memoir is that he doesn't recognize the distinctness of photography as a form: that is he doesn't see or articulate its ties to the real or even to the referent, and there are certainly no autobiographical photographs, or any revealed autobiographical invest-ment in photography in line with the *punctum* that Barthes identifies in the essence of photography. Instead the photographs are used as code, or *studium,* in a way similar to Barthes's first engagements with photography. Indeed Barthes's distinction between message and code in his essay on photography "The Photographic Message" drew these terms from Lévi-Strauss's *The Raw and the Cooked*.[3] Lévi-Strauss is the key intellectual figure behind Barthes's structuralism, as Barthes's first structuralist analysis, *Mythologies,* derived its impetus from the structural study of myth proposed by Lévi-Strauss in *Structural Anthropology 1*.[4] The crisis of representation in the human sciences in the form of structuralist linguistics, the splitting of the signifier from the referent in which Barthes and Lévi-Strauss played foundational roles in their respective fields, allowed first Barthes via Lévi-Strauss and then Lévi-Strauss to see photography as code. Photographs are treated in Lévi-Strauss's structuralist work in a way consonant with his "ode," the system of structural anthropology that he founded. The crisis of representation allowed Lévi-Strauss to emphasize code and sign at the expense of the referent in his anthropology as much as in photography.

The kind of photographic anthropological narrative that Lévi-Strauss criticizes had been in existence since the middle of the nineteenth century, since anthropology and photography were invented simultaneously and immediately interwoven; for photography had an establishing function in anthropology.[5] Both forms were initially conceived as modes of observing and documenting reality. Anthropologists embraced photography for its apparent capacity for showing its referent unmediated: "for an anthropology deeply rooted in positivism, photography offered a tempting proposition: an objective vision and collection of 'facts,' facilitating systematic organization and analysis, in the service of scientific enquiry."[6] It was the documentary, superficial use of photography in previous anthropology that Lévi-Strauss rejected. His resistance to anthropological photography is consistent with structuralist tenets. He shows a distrust of the powers of the documentary, of the idea of reaching truth from the visible. Technology may one day record all native thought, yet even were it possible, he argues, documenting what is visible would not reveal significance: "The greater our knowledge, the more obscure the overall scheme. . . . it becomes impossible to visualize a system when its representation requires a continuum of more than three or four dimensions."[7] Structural anthropology exchanged the documentation of visible surfaces of cultures for a linguistic analysis of their deep structures, producing something like a cross-section of what is beneath the visible. The adaptation of Saussurean linguistics to conceive of culture as a language resulted in Lévi-Strauss locating meaning not in visible entities but in relations that because unconscious, remain hidden. Structuralism shifts from "*conscious . . .* phenomena to . . . their *unconscious* infrastructure; . . . [from] *terms* as independent entities . . . [to] the *relations* between terms; it introduces the concept of *system*" (*Structural Anthropology* 1:33). In the analysis of the myths of Brazilian Indians, in the first volume of the *Introduction to a Science of Mythology* tetralogy where we see this system best at work (for myths are key signifiers in this language), myths are said to reveal the "underlying structure" of culture (*Raw* 111). It was not enough to document; one must question the status of the referent, uncover the sign in the apparently referential, the connotative in the denotative—and culture therefore in the apparently natural. For Lévi-Strauss, because culture *is* language there is no presignifying, prediscursive, or natural stage. The paintings on the faces of the Brazilian Caduveo Indians, for example, are not mere ornamentation but signs that, like European heraldry, may be read to decode a system of class and rank and the elementary structures of kinship. The primitive or "savage mind" was a "science of the concrete" (*Savage* passim) as complex as the Western technique of structuralism that was therefore needed to decode it. Structural anthropology did not so much jettison the referent as transform it into code. Lévi-Strauss makes this the grounds on which to differentiate structuralism from its dematerializing cousin, formalism. Formalism in focusing on form—in the example of Vladimir Propp's approach to fairy tales—"destroys its object." Structuralism analyzes structure, which "is content itself, apprehended in a logical organization conceived as property of the real."[8]

How "real" can be used to refer to "structure" rather than referent or any other conception of real becomes clear in Lévi-Strauss's comments on photography in his art criticism, which reveal a distaste for the medium, for what Barthes calls its definitive "co-natural[ism] with its referent."[9] Even though he was using *the real* as a noun after Lacan had raised it to a psychoanalytic category, Lévi-Strauss's *real* is emphatically not Lacanian, disruptive of the symbolic, but absolutely consonant with code. Mirroring his own practice in structural anthropology, Lévi-Strauss was drawn to those pictorial artists who he believed encoded realism—such as even a surrealist, Anita Albus. His definition of realism as the artist's interpretation or encoding of the phenomenological object allows him to value the realism of painting over that of photography: "the physical constraints of the camera, the chemical constraints of the sensitive film, the subjects possible, the angle of view, and the lighting, allow the photographer only a very restricted freedom compared with the artist's practically unlimited freedom of eye and hand, as well as the mind."[10] When compared even to painting that is so realistic that it seeks to trick us into believing that the representation is real, trompe l'oeil, the mechanistic, reproductive inadequacy of photography is brought into greater relief:

Photographic realism does not distinguish accidents from the nature of things. . . . It remains servile to a "thoughtless" vision of the world. With trompe l'oeil, one does not represent, one reconstructs. . . . Trompe l'oeil is selective; it does not seek to render everything about the model, nor just anything. . . . With all its technical sophistication, the photographic camera remains a coarse device compared to the human hand and brain. . . . As the term *snapshot* suggests, photography seizes the moment and exhibits it.[11]

Lévi-Strauss thus dismisses the fear that photography will render realistic or naturalistic painting obsolete, for the media are antitheses. Painting's creativity is associated with life; photography, in its lifeless reproductions, with death. The only kind of painting Lévi-Strauss disparages in comparison to photography is that modeled on photographs, the "miserable productions of neofigurative artists who painted portraits or still lifes, not from life but from color photographs they slavishly try to copy. Although they are said to give new life to trompe l'oeil, the opposite is the case" (30).

As Lévi-Strauss's emphasis on the camera as "device" or machine suggests, it is particularly technology that gives photography the flaws he identifies of lack of discrimination and artistic conceptualization. His criticism of photography has a cultural association that can be drawn out through reference to Walter Benjamin's correlation, in his "Short History of Photography," of the development of photography with the increased mechanization of the marketplace. Both photography and capitalism, Benjamin writes, result in "the fragmentation of the aura": the unique property of things.[12] The reproductive realism of photography is the representational equivalent, because product, of the monoculturalization against which Lévi-Strauss directs his entire anthropology and which he predicts will result in cultural entropy. If photography is in this cultural conception "the final culmination of a western quest for visibility,"[13] the West's privileging of vision as a means to mastery of knowledge, Lévi-Strauss implicitly aligns reconstructive realism with primitive societies, and representational realism with postindustrial societies. The more technologically advanced a society, the more likely it is to reproduce an object exactly as it appears because it can do so, yet in proportion does it risk aesthetic regression: "It has often been the case in the history of art that, as the technical knowledge and skill increase, the aesthetic quality declines" (*Look* 163). If his ideal in art as in structuralism is "the promotion of an object to the rank of the sign," primitive art most embodies this ideal.[14] Lévi-Strauss writes that "preliterate peoples express themselves literally" (*Look* 178), by which paradox he means not that primitive peoples reproduce realistically but that they create the literal before the technological means of reproduction. He exemplifies this literalism—supernaturalism really, for there is in the creation of the literal in the absence of the apparent capacity to do so something magical—with accounts of rituals that reenact myths and that must conceal their reenactive status, or statues carved in the likeness of dead love-objects. (The lost beloved wife of a chief who is reincarnated in the form of a cedar tree and who accounts for the origins of the beautiful cedars along Canada's Pacific coast resonates with the refusal to accept loss of the Orpheus myth.) The more lifelike the art—the more it can become or iconize the referent in the referent's absence—the more magical, "the more part of a supernatural order" (*Look* 181). "To have their art seen as lifelike was both their privilege and their obligation. . . . the purpose of the illusion created by a work of art was to attest to the ties binding the social to the natural order" (*Look* 184). Modern Western art that rejected realism altogether fell short on the other side of photography for breaking social or worldly ties, for failing the "collective function of the work of art" (Charbonnier 73). While it might seem contradictory given his objection to photographic realism, Lévi-Strauss also criticizes modernist aesthetics for their *"academicism of the signifier"* (Charbonnier 75). This kind of art abandoned the referent. Cubism "missed the object" (*View* 250), and Picasso is singled out as "much more an admirable discourse on pictorial discourse than a discourse about the world" (*Structural Anthropology* 2:277). Self-referential, missing the object, cubism appears in Lévi-Strauss's configuration the artistic correlative of formalism.

Photographs are treated in Lévi-Strauss's oeuvre not as reproductively realistic (referential) but as close as possible to reconstructively realistic; except, unlike primitive art, photographs *do* evidence that the referent has always been there. Photographs retain, indeed are defined by, the quality of technological reproduction of an object now in the past tense. Lévi-Strauss seeks to transubstantiate the referent of the photograph into code as he does with other visible surfaces in his structuralism—to free photography from its mechanical, thoughtless, and accidental limitations: to aesthecize it. When he publishes photographs before *Saudades,* they are interspersed with the drawings and diagrams that proliferate in his anthropology and that are a favored demonstration of his structuralist method. Tellingly, John Berger describes diagrams as the "metaphorical model of Cubism," since both treat "appearances as . . . signs."[15] In his diagrams Lévi-Strauss ends up repeating the "academicism of the signifier" of which he accused cubism; and indeed his photographs are no more referential than his diagrams. In *Tristes Tropiques* where Lévi-Strauss includes both photographs and drawings of the face paintings of the Caduveo, given that the drawings were produced by native informants and by one of the first anthropologists to record the Indians, the drawings may in this case have more authenticating power. Why Lévi-Strauss chooses to include both photographs and drawings especially when they are of the same referent is perplexing, until one realizes that most of what he represents in photographs is already in code. If photographs are evidence, his photographs evidence the referent as code. This criterion for selection informs Lévi-Strauss's use of photographs from first to last, *Tristes Tropiques* to *Saudades*. In *Structural Anthropology* 1, *The Savage Mind, The Naked Man, The Way of Masks*,[16] *The Story of Lynx*,[17] photographs of Indian art, artifacts, places, and people wearing native dress; and in *Look, Listen, Read,* photographs of Western pictorial art—all show the object was already sign—as, for example, in the design of a North American Indian mask.[18] And in all instances the writing coheres the photographs into a discursive, interpretative project. The photographs are subordinated to the text, in service as illustrative of the anthropology, or, in the case of *Look, Listen, Read,* of art criticism; they do not have any revelatory power beyond the text. Lévi-Strauss does not appear interested in the form of photography. If, as historians argue, photography in anthropology is now most useful as an analogue of anthropological history, and particularly and most recently its "raw histories . . . the unprocessed and the painful,"[19] photographs in Lévi-Strauss, his uses of them pre-*Saudades*, are symptomatic of structural anthropology. Photographs as those criticized "snapshots" "seize and exhibit" the oversights of structural anthropology. Lévi-Strauss writes that the "view from afar" is apposite for "expressing what I consider the essence and originality of the anthropological approach" (*View* xi). His photographs show how structural anthropology was able to emerge as a system of knowledge only in the "view from afar."

"Le regard éloigné" (the title of one of Lévi-Strauss's books reflecting on his methodology translated as *The View from Afar*) threatened to elide the referent. In order to see structure as a "property of the real," Lévi-Strauss needed to be far enough away from the referent, and his flattening out of the referentiality of photography into code, diagram, illustration is indicative. When we juxtapose the most famous structuralist diagram of a Bororo village appearing in *Tristes Tropiques* and *Structural Anthropology* 1 with a photograph of the same village not released until *Saudades*, the formulaic abstraction of the former is fleshed out by the two-dimensional actuality of the photograph. The dividing line through the village indicated in the diagram—which is constitutive of Lévi-Strauss's conception of moiety and

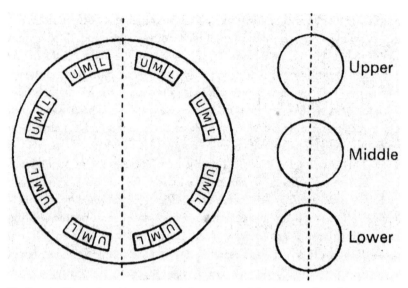

"A diagram illustrating the apparent real structure of the Bororo village." From Claude Lévi-Strauss, *Tristes Tropiques*. Reprinted with permission.

reciprocity and therefore central to the elementary structures of kinship and to structuralism—is "invisible" in the photograph, as he acknowledges in the photographic caption. The photograph returns something of the messy vitality at odds with the pure design of the original. The "unchanging" structure could be perceived only from the anthropologist's "panoramic view," high above the mêlée below. Structure is a property of the real only thence. The charge that Lévi-Strauss overlooked his referent—an overlooking in the sense both of surveying from so far back and of the omission resulting—is thus literalized by the photograph. Pierre Bourdieu highlights the importance of superiority. Lévi-Strauss "takes up a 'point of view' on the action, . . . stands back so as to observe it and, transferring into the object the principle of his relation to the object, conceives of it as a totality intended for cognition alone, in which all interactions are reduced to symbolic exchanges. This point of view is one afforded by high positions in the social structure, from which the social world appears as representation."[20] George Marcus and Michael Fischer write similarly of structural anthropology as "being too distant from the intentionality and experience of social actors."[21] In an essay, "The Scope of Anthropology," a title that like many (*A View from Afar* itself) betrays the essential place of distancing observational metaphors, Lévi-Strauss admits that it is only at a distance, in the laboratory out of the field, that a practice such as face-painting or an object such as a stone axe may be viewed as part of

"Perched on the roof of a cabin like the macaws the Indians bred for their plumage, I took a panoramic view of the unchanging structure of Bororo villages: the men's house in the center and family dwellings, owned by the women, in a circle around it. An invisible line of demarcation cuts across the men's house and divides the village into two halves. A man born in one half must choose a wife from the other half, and vice versa." From Claude Lévi-Strauss, *Saudades do Brasil*. Reprinted with permission.

a system: "it is conceivable that a stone axe could be a sign. In a given context, and for the observer capable of understanding its use . . . even the simplest techniques of any primitive society take on the character of a system that can be analyzed, in terms of a more general system" (*Structural Anthropology* 2:11). The transformation of the real into sign occurs "for the observer capable of understanding its use" and whose observation "has the privilege of being distant" (*Structural Anthropology* 2:28). This distance is emphatically not that of the native, for we should not "confuse the natives' theories about their social organization . . . with the actual functioning of the society" (*Structural Anthropology* 1:130). That would be to get too close up, to look through the microscope that Lévi-Straus rejects in a metaphor as too proximate to its object and hence blurring of difference (*Structural Anthropology* 2:34). The view from close up leads to the *"problem of invariance"* (*Structural Anthropology* 2:24); the metaphor for Lévi-Strauss's view is rather that of a telescope, the view that brings objects close but from afar. Yet it is an irony that "invariance" in the form of the invariants of the savage mind is precisely what the *tele* ("far") view produced. We see at work in Lévi-Strauss, especially when he is at his most structuralist and brilliant, a sometimes excessive reductionism. In his classic statement of structuralist method, "The Structural Study of Myth," he claims that it is possible to reduce "every myth" to a single algebraic formula: "$F_x(a)_y(b) \approx F_x(b):F_{a-1}(y)$" (*Structural Anthropology* 1:228). The mastery of knowledge is total, and it is ineluctable.

Until *Saudades do Brasil,* there are no photographs of Lévi-Strauss himself. And excepting those of face paintings all of the photographs are not taken by the anthropologist but are provided by museums—although *Saudades* is later to unearth a wealth of photographs taken by Lévi-Strauss. The omission of author photographs is true even of *Tristes Tropiques,* the memoir, which was nevertheless considered too autobiographical by some fellow anthropologists when it was published.[22] It was presumably to avert such criticism that *Tristes Tropiques* left out autobiographical photographs in the first place. The concerns about *Tristes Tropiques* as autobiography were expressed before publication of Bronislaw Malinowski's *Diary in the Strict Sense of the Term* in 1967 shocked the anthropological establishment with its revelations of an "I," and not coincidentally with an eye also. For Malinowski revolutionized anthropology through autobiography and photography together. *Participant observation,* the term he introduced into anthropology that has since become a staple, carries in its compound the twin exercises of autobiography and photography. Photographs in Malinowski's anthropology "are used to locate the anthropologist in his field."[23] While his *Diary* doesn't include photographs at all (the success of participant observation has led some critics to believe that the literal figure of the anthropologist-as-photographer was incorporated in the wholly textual figure of the anthropologist-as-participant-observer),[24] Malinowski is conscious there of how anthropology is a function of mediated looking that photography makes manifest: "Photos. Feeling of ownership: It is I who will describe them or create [the Trobriands]"—as if the act of not only taking the photographs but reflecting on it in the autobiography demands that the anthropologist confront anthropology as an exercise, like photography, in taking and creating life.[25] Lévi-Strauss rejected the participant observation of Malinowski in anthropology as too I-dominated (*Structural Anthropology,* vol. 1). In contrast to Malinowski, in *Tristes Tropiques* even those included photographs have an anthropological effect in excess of the personal view sometimes expressed in the memoir. While the body of the text may reveal a personal evaluation inconsistent with objective structural anthropology (for example, of the Tupi-Kawahib chief's primary wife, Kunhatsin, Lévi-Strauss writes in the text that she was—"the native view coinciding with that of the anthropologist—extremely beautiful" [430]), under the photograph of this same woman Lévi-Strauss's caption is now used to elide the personal: "Kunhatsin, Taperhi's chief wife carrying her child" (266). It as if the photograph were not taken by the anthropologist, were not his personal view (although we learn later in the republication of the photograph in *Saudades* that it is and where his personal evaluation is reinstated: "Of his four wives, Kunhatsin was the most beautiful" [194]). Structural anthropology in its methodology depended on a sublimation or elision of self: "the elimination of the subject represents what might be called a methodological need." And here, at the end of the *Introduction to a Science of Mythology* tetralogy in a volume called *The Naked Man,* where he finally reverts from the *nous* form he has used throughout to the *je*, Lévi-Strauss argues that it is only outside the structuralist work proper, in excesses such as prefaces or afterwords that the self can be acknowledged: "If there is a point at which the Self can reappear, it is only after the completion of the work which it excluded throughout."[26] He acknowledges that anthropology "is undoubtedly the only science to use the most intimate kind of subjectivity as a means of objective demonstration" (*Structural Anthropology* 2:15) and that the use of self as a medium to the other makes anthropology at first an autobiographical enterprise: "Every ethnographic career finds its principle in 'confessions' written or untold" (*Structural Anthropology* 2:36). This double paradox, contradiction, or "principle" (*Structural Anthropology* 2:39), as Lévi-Strauss successively calls it, he identifies through Rimbaud's "I is another" (36). This syntax Barthes would use as model in his autobiography, writing of himself in *Roland Barthes by Roland Barthes* in the third person. But Lévi-Strauss suggests that the autobiography or confession must remain untold in ethnography. In order to become anthropology the exercise must disavow autobiography: "To attain acceptance of oneself in others (the goal assigned to human knowledge by the ethnologist), one must first deny the self in oneself" (*Structural Anthropology* 2:36). Even the book intended as Lévi-Strauss's most personal is the story more of the work than of the self; Susan Sontag terms *Tristes Tropiques* an "intellectual autobiography" and—*le revers de la médaille*—Jeffrey Mehlman considers Lévi-Strauss's anthropological other the basis for an intrasubjective voyage.[27] Structural anthropology confused autobiography with biography—to produce *allo*biography: not the story of the self or the story of the other (or the story of the self in open exchange with the other) but the story of the self othered. This paradox or contradiction will become the palinode—as Barthes's initial recognition of a structural paradox in photography becomes his palinode—where, on completion of the methodology, in the photographic memoir, the self returns pictured in relation to the other.

Lévi-Strauss elides not only his self but the technological mediation of anthropology. Structural anthropology, like all anthropologies and photography, is a product of European epistemology at a particular aesthetic and technological moment, modernist and linguistic, or, as some have argued, cybernetic; and structural anthropology does resemble cybernetics's science of perfect control.[28] Myths are a symptom above all of structuralist thought, which was obsessed with mapping relations between textual signifiers and achieving mastery of systems. In a strikingly unreflexive moment in the autobiography during an account of how the Caduveo attempted to compel him to take photographs of them, Lévi-Strauss writes that, while anthropologists are taught that natives are afraid of being photographed and should be economically compensated, "The Caduveo had perfected the system: not only did they insist on being paid before allowing themselves to be photographed; they forced me to photograph them so that I should have to pay. Hardly a day went by but a woman came to me in some extraordinary get-up and obliged me, whether I wanted to or not, to pay her photographic homage, accompanied by a few milreis" (*Tristes* 197–98). Eventually he photographs them with his film unloaded for reasons of expense. Lévi-Strauss reflects not on how his behavior, the presence of his camera, and his anthropology—his technology—might have caused their behavior. Instead he continues anthropologizing even in relating the incident, reflecting that their response "represented the re-emergence, in a transposed form, of certain specific features of Indian society" such as the independence of women, performative behavior, and so on (198). He shows no awareness of his own technique of observation, literalized here by his camera, as mediating. In the "Overture" introduction to *The Raw and the Cooked,* he claims that "it is in the last resort immaterial whether in this book the thought processes of South American Indians take shape through the medium of my thought, or whether mine take place through the medium of theirs" (13)—but the medium surely shapes the message, if indeed it isn't wholly equivalent to it as some critics have braved. Edmund Leach is certainly suspicious of Lévi-Strauss's mastery: "He always seems able to find just what he is looking for."[29] For if pure structures are symptomatic of the primitive mind, they are also a reflection of the structuralist's mind. The structuralist, too, has a savage mind, and indeed in Lévi-Strauss's ideal of the "technique du dépaysement" (*Structural Anthropology* 1:117)—which translates as "homelessness" (1:118, Translator's note 23)—the anthropologist deracinates himself from his culture and seeks to become as primitive as possible in a bid to leave behind his *tekhnē,* his knowledge. Lévi-Strauss practices *dépaysement* in the "chronic rootlessness" of his life in Brazil, sleeping on the ground like the Nambikwara Indians, reduced to eating worm-infested meat and grubs in rotting tree trunks (*Tristes* 459). Becoming the other is the anthropologist's initiation rite into the savage mind he then ordains himself qualified to decode: "Leaving the country, his home, for long periods of time; exposing himself to hunger, sickness and sometimes danger; surrendering his customs, his beliefs, his convictions to a profanation to which he becomes an accomplice when, without mental restriction or ulterior motive, he assumes the forms of life of an alien society. The anthropologist practices integral observation, observation beyond which there is nothing except—and it is indeed a risk—the complete absorption of the observer by the object of his observation" (*Structural Anthropology* 2:15). The assumption of the other through observation has a double meaning in anthropology. The anthropologist can assume knowledge of the savage life because he has assumed (taken on) that life for himself. Yet past and Western self is not wholly absorbed. Lévi-Strauss admits that, especially when he is furthest away from home in the huge alien *sertão* or grassland plateaux of the Mato Grosso in central Brazil, instead of being absorbed by the sights, he hears, tellingly, music from Europe, replaying Chopin and Debussy in his head who "epitomize[d] all I had left behind" (*Tristes* 459).

Music and photography are forms to which time is intrinsic, in the making and experiencing of them. In contrast, in painting time seems almost superfluous, mostly forgotten. Music and photography need time in order to exist. Music and photography carry time's extremes or excesses, its movement and losses; they present us with all that has been left behind, either in the conventional sense of bringing back memories or in the Barthesian sense of *not* bringing back memory. Music, like photography, keeps time to the continual and irrevocable ebb of existence. But in Lévi-Strauss music and photography are, initially, peculiarly timeless forms. Music and myths are "machines for the obliteration of time," he writes (*Raw* 16). And his photographs, too, freeze history and perpetuate the presence of the past rather than acknowledging its loss, in the manner of the photographs criticized by anthropology's historians that manifest "anthropology's atemporal discourse," "presenting a timeless vision."[30] In treating photographs as diagrammatic codes, Lévi-Strauss removes the interaction between self and native from history, and in this his captions, the elision of narrative, are key. It is elimination of historicity that enables Lévi-Strauss to anthropologize, to freeze the real into structure. His captions to his photographs of Brazilian Indians in *Tristes Tropiques* insist on ongoing cultural representativity: "The siesta" (261); "The native method of carrying a baby" (261); "A Nambikwara smile" (262). The article generalizes as it atemporalizes. The native is still doing this, outside of time, has always done it—and yet is already part of the archive, like the artifacts (such as the photographs) that Lévi-Strauss brought back from Brazil. The captioning is consistent with Barthes's analysis in "The Photographic Message" where he wrote of captions: "Formerly, the image illustrated the text (made it clearer); today, the text loads the image, burdening it with a culture, a moral, an imagination."[31] The text is overwhelming in Lévi-Strauss, transforming the realness of photography into code—the raw into the cooked; "for anthropology, photography meant the *necessity* of caption."[32] Stasis in Lévi-Strauss is symptomatically structuralist. His predecessors' documentation of the surface differences of cultures often arranged those differences into an evolutionist narrative in which the primitive was our antecedent in a Darwinian line. Lévi-Strauss opposed narrative organization in anthropology, criticizing what he called "the archaic illusion"[33] or "pseudo-archaism" (*Structural Anthropology* 1:112). In the "Time Regained" chapter of *The Savage Mind*—for he saw structuralism as a Proustian recovery of time for the savage—he criticizes Western civilization's projection of its own origins onto primitive cultures as *"robinsonnades"* (264). Compounded of the romances *Robinson Crusoe* and *The Swiss Family Robinson,* this neologism meant a nostalgic construction of the other. Lévi-Strauss insisted on the simultaneity of the savage mind, and thus structuralism incorporates diachrony into synchrony and event into structure. Stasis was in part methodological for structuralism: "Evolutionism precludes any synthesis" (*Savage* 233). But methodology was also ethical, since Lévi-Strauss sought to bring the preliterate primitive into the linguistic present tense. Yet it backfired. Johannes Fabian singles out structuralism as the most complex contribution to the manipulation of time in his book subtitled *"How Anthropology Makes Its Object."* Structuralism preempts the problem of different times by "packing chronological Time into a spatial matrix."[34] Lévi-Strauss may not assign primitive cultures to archaic times in an evolutionary narrative, but the stasis he devises "to circumvent or preempt coevalness" works "to sustain the new, vast, anonymous, but terribly effective regimen of absentee colonialism" (69). It "calls for a native society that would, ideally at least, hold still like a *tableau vivant*" (67). Structuralism shows not the presence of the past inevitably lost as in a photograph, then, but treats the living scene as if it were already a photograph: the *tableau vivant* holds the natives suspended in what has been called an eternal, "ethnographic present" (Fabian 33).

There is an irony to Fabian's charge of "allochronism" (32) against Lévi-Strauss, though, and that is that Lévi-Strauss was among the first to make it against his predecessors, most famously in "Race and History," where he shows how time is a function of racism. In omitting this and other justifications Lévi-Strauss added to the practice of his structuralist theory, Fabian subjects Lévi-Strauss's structuralism to a similar kind of *tableau vivant.* In "Race and History" Lévi-Strauss shows how "false evolutionism" (*Structural Anthropology* 2:330 and passim) positions the primitive as recessive in a line of development culminating in the observer. Racism "often goes so far as to deprive the stranger of this last shred of reality by making him a 'ghost'" (*Structural Anthropology* 2:329). The ghost, as Derrida says, is "the dead other alive in me . . . a relationship of haunting which is perhaps constitutive of all logics"—and it is so of structuralism.[35] Lévi-Strauss sought to make the ghost live, to bring those who were conceived by his predecessors as dead or dying—"the primitives"—to life. Structuralism is a result of an anxiety about the narrative of progress. But the metaphors and analogies he innovates—spatial instead of temporal, structural instead of narrative—do not evade the problems of history, technology, or observer position of his predecessors. Rather his representation shows the inevitability of the previous frame of representation. Proposing that distinctions between primitive mythic/ahistorical peoples and progressive Western cultures might be rendered as those between "cold" and "hot" societies (*Structural Anthropology* 2:29; *Savage* 233), Lévi-Strauss thereby replaces the temporal metaphor with one drawn from energy. Or, from the discourses of surrealist art and science: primitive societies operate like the "bricoleur," recycling materials that are to hand and working "by means of signs"; the West, working in teleological fashion and "by means of concepts," operates like the engineer (*Savage* 20). And most famous, from the technology of travel: the histories of cultures may be analogized to the course of trains. If the other culture-train is travelling in the same direction as our own, it will appear to be progressing; if travelling differently, to be regressing. And it is only if we are travelling identically that we will be able to "see the faces of the passengers, count them, etc."—to read the culture (*Structural Anthropology* 2:341). While each pair is generated from an attempt to transcend the frame of his predecessors (narrative sequence, technology, and superiority of observer position), each borrows its metaphorical terms from the postindustrial cultures Lévi-Strauss was seeking to demote or at least stabilize in relation to the primitive. Like the too finely tuned cybernetic machine—say the thermostat of a central heating system in which the off and on temperature switches are so closely set that the boiler switches itself off at the very point when it comes on (for how to inhabit the "zero" degree?)—the attempt at perfect control is the system's own undoing.[36] The anthropologist ended up using the means of representation, the technology, that was the product of progress—and that he rejected in his predecessors' photography.

The image of the ghost, or more often of the shadow, encapsulates Lévi-Strauss's agonistic struggle with the frames of representation, and it haunts his writings. Like the ghost, the shadow is a revenant in relation to life: necessarily following and insubstantial.

> One deprives oneself of all means of understanding magical thought if one tries to reduce it to a moment or a stage in technical and scientific

evolution. Like a shadow moving ahead of its owner it is in a sense complete in itself, and as finished and coherent in its immateriality as the substantial being which it preceded. Magical thought is not to be regarded as a beginning, a rudiment, a sketch, a part of the whole which has not yet materialized. It forms a well-articulated system. (*Savage* 13)

The shadow that is finished and coherent in its immateriality; the shadow that *pre*cedes the substantial being from which it *pro*ceeded; the shadow that is not a sketch but a part of what is to follow: the oscillations of time, observer position and referentiality are dizzying. In the autobiography the paradox of anthropological representation—of how to capture an elusive, primitive past within contemporary thought, of how to put the real into his technology—is described in similar imagery of the shadow that flits beyond and before the solidity of his knowledge.

> For every five years I move back in time, I am able to save a custom, gain a ceremony or share in another belief. But I know the texts too well not to realize that, by going back over a century, I am not at the same time forgoing data and lines of inquiry which would offer intellectual enrichment. And so I am caught within a circle from which there is no escape. . . . I have only two possibilities: either I can be like some traveller of the olden days, who was faced with a stupendous spectacle . . . or I can be a modern traveller, chasing after the vestiges of a vanished reality . . . able to glimpse no more than the shadows of the past. (*Tristes* 36)

If the anthropologist "does not journey between the lands of the savages and the civilized [but] returns from among the dead," the question is how to make present, to represent the dead.[37] With his myths and music and his desire to recover lost time, Lévi-Strauss, too, is another Orpheus, as has been recognized.[38] For like Barthes, Lévi-Strauss conceives the choice between the madness of entering into the spectacle, or tameness, representation and code. The real or knowledge. Structuralism sought to avoid photographic texts that aimed "to appease the nostalgic cannibalism of history with the shadows of those that history has already destroyed"; for one cannot use a machine to record a ghost. Or can one?

The Naked Man

The most startling photograph in *Saudades* shows Lévi-Strauss bathing amid the Nambikwara. The anthropologist is naked and uncovering his young white body for view. He looks vulnerable, self-exposed. This photograph must have been taken by someone else, or more likely on a self-timing mechanism by Lévi-Strauss himself, like the one labeled "Self-portrait" that appears on the rear jacket of *Saudades*. The natives in contrast have their back to the camera. They are not really the subject of the photograph, what the photographer or we look at. It is only the toddler's head, so precariously positioned, that covers Lévi-Strauss's total nakedness. The photograph reverses the conventions of anthropological looking. The *punctum* in *Saudades do Brasil,* the photograph encapsulates how this book is the *punctum* in the anthropological *studium* that is Lévi-Strauss's work.

There is much that is new and different in the photographic memoir. The self-exposure. *Saudades* is subjective, a self-declared memoir, the confession untold until this point—not even in the unsubtitled *Tristes Tropiques*. The prologue acknowledges the autobiographical investment: "Let it then be taken for what it is: a testimonial . . . to Brazil and its people more than half a century ago, to whom—as well as to my distant youth—I address a friendly and nostalgic salute" (23). The memoir is referential, revealing

From Claude Lévi-Strauss, *Saudades do Brasil.* Reprinted with permission.

the real place that had made his career, Brazil, his autobiographical investment in it, and making this place and his investment intrinsic to his photography. It was Brazil that made him a photographer. He was "not one until Brazil" and now "I no longer have the interest" (21). (The only other book of photographs Lévi-Strauss published is *Saudades de São Paulo*, a version of this book but focused wholly on São Paulo—and published only in Brazil.)[39] Even *Tristes Tropiques* had interwoven Lévi-Strauss's sojourns in India and Pakistan, retroactively since, taking place in 1950, they were not part of the origins of structuralist theory in Brazil between 1935 and 1939 that make up the entire material of this photographic memoir. In the return photography is embraced to reverse his previous use. Whereas in the oeuvre photographs are subordinated to the text, in *Saudades* the photographs outweigh the text that, after a prologue, is confined to captions and minimal intervening sections. Photography was rejected generically, at least in his art criticism, for its referential realism; Lévi-Strauss's criterion for a successful photograph of his own is reproductive precision. "I think that was our main criterion for a successful negative, for we never ceased to marvel how such a small format, when enlarged, could produce very precise details" (22). More startling in the memoir is the revelation that his father's profession was that of the painter who took photographs on which to base his subsequent portraits—"to guide him in the placement of their principal features" (21): precisely the kind of painting Lévi-Strauss had disparaged for taking the life out of trompe l'oeil. If we accept that the portrait painter was the one victim of photography, as Benjamin writes, we can understand Lévi-Strauss's previously expressed distaste for photography. Lévi-Strauss traces the legacy of the photographic art from nineteenth-century painters to his father, and then from his father to himself. Lévi-Strauss learned photography from his father, a family art. In Brazil, where his parents joined him in 1935, Lévi-Strauss *père et fils* seek out realism side by side, competitive reproduction: "Father and son competed to see who could obtain the sharpest images" (22). It is passed down the patriline. Claude's son Matthieu Lévi-Strauss made the prints for the book; his "decisions were critical" in the selection of the images and he should therefore be considered its "coauthor" (23).

The naked man image as with Bororo village is among 163 of the 180 photographs appearing in *Saudades* that were not previously published, but even those photographs previously published return an excess to the ode. They are "better reproduced, and often displayed differently" from before (9), made possible by new technology. And in the case of the seventeen of the twenty photographs appearing in *Tristes Tropiques* that are republished in *Saudades*, they are all enlarged in a way that undoes the cropping that we can now see was performed on the original. Enlargement, as Benjamin has argued, "does not simply render more precise what was, albeit indistinctly, visible 'anyway': it reveals entirely new structural forms of the subject matter"—or in excess of code/structure, we might say.[40] Subjects are no longer squarely positioned in the frames as they were; the photographs appear more accidental, more untamed. A Mundé woman balancing her child, for example, is now shown off-center, so we no longer necessarily look at the *studium* that Lévi-Strauss would previously have had us see (the eyebrows of the child waxed in preparation for plucking pointed out in the caption in *Tristes Tropiques*) but perhaps the *mato grosso*, the "vast scrub" out of focus and now an irreducible presence behind her (*Tristes* 263; *Saudades* 174). Or, now that it is enlarged, we can see that the odd rectangular object being carried in a Nambikwara Indian basket, catching the sun like a mirror (or sardine can), is a possession of the anthropologist: a fuel can that Lévi-Strauss acknowledges had become part of the Indians' personal possessions (*Tristes* 259; *Saudades* 156). In *Tristes Tropiques*, Lévi-Strauss had criticized the way in which the anthropologist glosses over his approach so as not to spoil our view of the primitives with his presence and that of Western technology, as happens in the photographic memoirs. But "the existence of the latter can be decoded by a practiced eye from small details in the illustrations, since the photographer has not always been able to avoid including the rusty petrol-cans in which this virgin people does its cooking" (31). Enlarging the mediating details in *Saudades* and pointing them out in the caption unlike in *Tristes Tropiques*, Lévi-Strauss turns the inadvertent, mechanical quality of photography and his own mediating presence in his photographs into the subjects of their second publication.

Most interesting, though, are the photographs that were omitted—because they were—and they interweave the eye and the I, the view with autobiographical desire. Many evidence the complex network of looking. In a photograph of a Bororo village ceremony, although the *studium* of the caption points to the villagers watching the spectacle—"At dusk, one part of the population sat down to watch the dance spectacle offered by the other part" (98)—in fact what catches our eye in the photograph are the figures in the foreground who are manifestly not watching the spectacle but watching the anthropologist—watching them. Their consciousness of his observation surely heightened by the presence of his camera, they are refusing wholly to comply with the activity under observation. Other photographs in *Saudades* draw attention to the imbalance and pain of anthropological observation. In *Tristes Tropiques*, Lévi-Strauss had written

"At dusk, one part of the population sat down to watch the dance spectacle offered by the other part." From Claude Lévi-Strauss, *Saudades do Brasil*. Reprinted with permission.

of an eye disease that had broken out among the Nambikwara during his observation of them, causing a very painful temporary blindness that could become permanent. The disease carries to the anthropologist's group, and the first to catch it is his wife, who is evacuated. New photographs in *Saudades* highlight the difference between an I that can be outside of the frame and the natives whose function is to be observed, to remain present. Devastating scenes show women and children lying on the dry earth, their hands raised to their eyes in pain. Lévi-Strauss writes ingenuously, "We witnessed some distressing scenes" (128), and we consider the status of this witnessing. Malek Alloula has written of how, when Western photographers encountered women of Algeria with their veils in the nineteenth century, the screen produced a kind of eye disease in the Western observer, "the symbolic equivalent of blindness: a leukoma, a white speck on the eye of the photographer and on his viewfinder."[41] Photography in the form of semi-pornographic postcards then resorted to stripping the women. Lévi-Strauss's Nambikwara women are already naked, and *they* have the eye disease. But here in returning to the images in his memoir,

Lévi-Strauss articulates his relation to that pain, not in abstraction from it. Photographs now makes visible the penetrating I of the anthropologist in his penetrating eye.

The photographs reveal the anthropologist's look as eroticizing, shaping with his desire. Many of the photographs are of naked young women and girls. Indeed, it's startling to realize how many of the photographs in *Saudades* are of naked women and girls; this degree of exposure had certainly not appeared before. The images have an unguarded, insouciant eroticism to them. Like Sally Mann's snapshots of her children, they make the viewer feel as if it were he and not the subject who projects sexual desire. Through his subjects the photographer-anthropologist is himself exposed, shown off guard. In the case of a photograph of a girl's breasts in which most of her head and torso are chopped off, the shot confronts us not so much with her (she's not a subject) but with him, because of what he is so unmistakably looking at. There is nothing of the anthropological *studium* in these close-ups of naked young women and girls, and the instantaneous, aleatory feel of the photographs wears down the edge of anthropological representativity. The significance is not so much that Lévi-Strauss took this photograph—accidents of course do happen in photography; what's significant is that Lévi-Strauss *publishes* the photograph, the exposure—of himself through the other—now the revelation. The photographic proximity to his subjects undermines his theory's insistence that he viewed from afar. In the autobiographical text, the possibility of a gap between the anthropologist's desire and the natives' culture had been suggested. Of the Nambikwara he had written: "During the amorous fondling in which couples indulge so freely and in public, and which is often quite uninhibited, I never once noticed an incipient erection. The pleasure aimed at would seem to relate less to physical satisfaction than to love-play and demonstrations of affection" (*Tristes* 344). But, he goes on, "It was difficult, for instance, to remain indifferent to the sight of one or more pretty girls sprawling naked in the sand and laughing mockingly as they wriggled at my feet. When I was bathing in the river, I was often embarrassed by a concerted attack on the part of half-a-dozen or so females—young or old—whose one idea was to appropriate my soap" (345). What did being *not indifferent* entail if not *being different*? This is not the ideal of the indifference of the structural anthropologist. Is it possible that Lévi-Strauss was made conscious of his difference—and embarrassed—by his own incipient erection?

So why produce a photographic memoir, why reveal such investment of self now? The turn, while it is implicit rather than acknowledged, is palinodic. For this is a form that Lévi-Strauss recognized—increasingly.

"... most often merry ..." From Claude Lévi-Strauss, *Saudades do Brasil*. Reprinted with permission.

Lévi-Strauss was fascinated by and was repeatedly drawn to write on others' palinodes and to ponder the reasons for returns; this helps us elucidate his reasons for his own return. He suggests a motivation for self-criticism that Durkheim the sociologist performs: "Properly speaking, Durkheim has not changed his attitude toward ethnography. The discipline he had criticized was not that one; at least it was not the same as the ethnography to which he was to rally" (*Structural Anthropology* 2:46). Publishing his photographic memoir in 1994, Lévi-Strauss had certainly seen changes not only in anthropology but also in the conception of photography. They had both moved from their documentary origins to the more linguistic emphases of the mid-twentieth century, when Lévi-Strauss, Barthes, and others were establishing structuralism; the linguistic turn that Lévi-Strauss innovated possibly sustained a suspicion toward photography in anthropology. Finally, photography and anthropology have come to rest in a more ethnographic and cultural point—they are autobiographical and descriptive again. In visual anthropology moreover, Lévi-Strauss saw the coming together of these changes to produce a new interdiscipline, literally a scope of anthropology. Visual anthropology has been described as "a turn from the linguistic to the pictorial, from the abstract to the embodied, from the collective to the individual, from the elaboration of general theory to the sensual evocation of the particular"; and if this is so it represents a recent turn away from Lévi-Strauss.[42] Proposed in the 1960s by John Collier, who came from the tradition of documentary photography which is to be explored in the next chapter, visual anthropology was initially documentary: "The memory of film . . . insures complete notation," Collier wrote.[43] But the most recent writings on visual anthropology argue that visuals should be used to develop a more self-conscious, a more self-reflexive anthropology. For Jay Ruby, the visual allows anthropology to address, literally, the "crisis of representation" that anthropology encountered in the form of first structuralism and then poststructuralism.[44] If we must ask how we look at anthropological subjects at the same time as we attend to the look (mediation) and its source (we), autobiographical visual anthropology proves an ideal hybrid medium for reflexivity, as two instances of self-reflexive anthropology that include photographs show: Nancy Scheper-Hughes's *Death without Weeping: The Violence of Everyday Life in Brazil*, and Marjorie Shostak's *Nisa: The Life and Words of a !Kung Woman* (by a photographer who became an anthropologist)—and Shostak's recent deathbed palinode to this, *Return to Nisa*.[45] Lévi-Strauss's palinode is certainly more in line with these disciplinary developments.

But, on revisions by the composer Rameau and the painter Poussin, he suggests another reason for return. He writes that the latter's return "may have resulted from the unconscious workings of his mind" (*Look* 21). Probably Lévi-Strauss's return is something of a middle way between these alternatives: that reflexive inclusion is made possible by a discipline is not, of course, divorced from the unconscious. He quotes, appropriately, the surrealist André Breton (who made the unconscious his discipline) responding to a critical pointing out by himself of a contradiction between Breton's works in an exchange of letters while the two writers were on board ship. Breton replies to Lévi-Strauss's rather pedantic observation: "Yes, naturally my positions have varied considerably since the first manifesto. One should understand that in such programmatic texts, which do not tolerate the expression of any doubt or reservation, and whose essentially aggressive character excludes all nuance, my thought tends to take on an extremely brutal, that is simplistic character, foreign to its real nature" (*Look* 148). Such doubt in the systematic Lévi-Strauss himself suggests as reason for his own self-reflexive returns; for Lévi-Strauss, like Barthes, was always engaged in a project of return. *The View from Afar* contains reflections on the earlier *Structural Anthropology* 1 and 2, and these are the most reflexive of his works (and he mentions he would have called *The View from Afar* "Structural Anthropology 3" if that didn't give the impression that he merely repeated himself [*View* xi]). "This 'anthropological doubt' does not only consist of knowing that one knows nothing, but of resolutely exposing what one thought one knew—and one's very ignorance—to buffetings and denials directed at one's most cherished ideas and habits by other ideas and habits best able to rebut them" (*Structural Anthropology* 2:26). The doubt of the anthropologist identified by Lévi-Strauss makes him analogous to Lejeune's autodidactic scholar who, in his method of palinodic revision, proceeds through a project of self-correction.[46] And it is with doubt embodied in photography that Lévi-Strauss actually begins *Saudades*.

Tristes Tropiques

In fact, Lévi-Strauss states that he now views photography not as referential but as the real, as failing to recover the referent. The precision that he sought as he took the photographs is no longer their significance in publishing them. The naïve realism he had imputed to and rejected in photography is exchanged for Lacanian—or Barthesian—realism. He opens his prologue contrasting the capacity of his notebooks to bring back the reality of his memories with photography's failure to do this. Significantly, the notebooks return the past anyway not through writing (which is presented as not a means for recording memory in the famous writing lesson of *Tristes Tropiques*), not through their sight but through their smell. This smell, after a Proustian fashion, recalls things past; in *Tristes Tropiques* Lévi-Strauss had written evocatively of Brazil as an "olfactory intoxication," a mixture of "freshly cut tropical red pepper," the "black, honeyed coils" of a Brazilian homemade cigarette, among prime "fruity fragrances" (77–78). In *Saudades* he immediately replaces the smell of the notebooks, which alone have the power to bring back memories, with photographs that do not. There is "nothing Proustian about a photograph" (Barthes, *Camera* 82) for Lévi-Strauss either—

> When I barely open my notebooks, I still smell the creosote with which, before setting off on an expedition, I used to saturate my canteens to protect them from termites and mildew. Almost undetectable after more than half a century, this trace instantly brings back to me the savannas and forests of Central Brazil, inseparably bound with other smells—human, animal, and vegetable—as well as with sounds and colors. For as faint as it is now, this odor—which for me is a perfume—is the thing itself, still a real part of what I have experienced.

Is it because too many years have elapsed (the same number of years for both, though) that photography does not bring any of that back to me? My negatives are not a miraculously preserved, tangible part of my experiences that once engaged all my senses, my physical strength, my brain; they are merely their indices—indices of people, of landscapes, and of events that I am still aware of having seen and known, but after such a long time I no longer always remember where or when. These photographic documents prove to me they did exist, but they do not evoke them for me or bring them materially back to life.

Upon re-examination, the photographs leave me with the impression of a void, a lack of something the lens is inherently unable to capture. I realize the paradox of offering them again to the public, in greater number, better reproduced, and often displayed differently from what was possible within the format of *Tristes Tropiques,* as if I thought that, in contrast with my own case, the pictures could offer something substantial to readers who have never been there and who therefore must content themselves with this silent imagery, especially since, if they went to see it for themselves, this world would be unrecognizable and would in many respects have simply vanished. (9–10)

The paradox lies in producing a photographic memoir once he has recognized the failure of photographs to bring back memory—and beginning the memoir acknowledging this. The photographs are referents, for their evidence of the past is undeniable, as the use of the word *document* suggests: "these photographic documents prove to me they did exist." Yet the referents/memories have cut loose from the signs—so that they are "indices"—signs of lost referents. The Peircean term, *index,* instead of Saussurean *sign* or *code* (these two more common in Lévi-Strauss), suggests the loosening as more traumatic, since for Peirce *index* carries causal connection between referent and sign; Peirce's most frequently cited example is that *smoke* is an index of *fire*. The severing of index and referent is less arbitrary, then, less normalized, than in Saussurean signification. And this loss is not an incidental conception of photography. Rather Lévi-Strauss identifies loss as intrinsic to the camera. Upon his reexamination, upon his return, the photographs leave him with "the impression of a void, a lack of something the lens is *inherently* unable to capture." This inherent inability to capture—or the inherent ability to capture lack, void—is what defines the photographic relation for him now. The thing was there but is gone. *Ça a été; interfuit:* this is a Barthesian conception of photography (*Camera* 120, 121). Returning to photography after Barthes's loss, Lévi-Strauss grasps photography as a form that makes irrevocable the loss of the past. There is no evidence that Lévi-Strauss had read *Camera Lucida,* but since they moved in the same circles and this was the last and most personal work by Barthes it would seem unlikely that he hadn't. After borrowing "code" from Lévi-Strauss, Barthes had made very different kinds of connections between anthropology and photography: mythic, magical. In *Camera Lucida* he describes photography as "an anthropologically new object" because it "divides the history of the world" (88) and shows a world before culture. In looking at a photograph, he writes, "I am a primitive, a child— or a maniac; I dismiss all knowledge, all culture" (51). He writes similarly in *The Grain of the Voice* of photography as "a new iconic phenomenon entirely, anthropologically new," and that before the photograph, "I place myself in the situation of the naïve man, outside culture, someone untutored who would be constantly astonished at photography."[47] Photography locates Barthes in the place of the primitive, which is the native as well as the child. Lévi-Strauss is moved by the same astonishment, though it may be more of the primitive as native—as confronted with the supernatural art that can finally incarnate the ghost—than as child. Annette Lavers suggests that it was the negative reception that Barthes received from admired antecedents such as Lévi-Strauss that made Barthes turn at the end of his life from theory into trying to represent an unspeakable love for his mother, that drove Barthes back, therefore, to the myth that for Lévi-Strauss is foundational of all cultures.[48] If this is so, Lévi-Strauss receives back the gift of his student's work, finding himself in Barthes's same underworld: mythical, precultural, pre-encoded—and photographic.

The referent is gone in the first, most obvious sense because Lévi-Strauss can't correlate it in his memory to the sign. After a lapse of sixty years, he can no longer make contact with his memories through his photographs. This contrasts with the opening of *Tristes Tropiques* that establishes connection between self and experience. Written in 1955 and also retrospective, *Tristes Tropiques* looks back to the same time twenty years before; but here Lévi-Strauss writes that this lapse, "twenty years of forgetfulness were required before I could establish communion with my earlier experience" (37). A sublimation of autobiography into an account of structural analysis and a history of Brazil, *Tristes Tropiques* finds its generic unity in the travelogue. In this the other is remembered in the context, and as trophies, of the travels of the self. Travel, as we know from Lévi-Straus's train metaphor, sees the place/culture as inextricable from time and the viewer's observation: "Travel is usually thought of as a displacement in space. This is an inadequate conception. A journey occurs simultaneously in place, in time and in the social hierarchy" (*Tristes* 86). Others are accordingly *retro-jected* (projection but backwards) into the past from the perspective of the present writing self. In this travelogue Lévi-Strauss follows the tradition of the anthropologist's traveler's tale he began by trying to avoid. Writing back, the *autos* is redeemed in the other's integral, better past to restore something missing in his own present. The recovery of past for present is nostalgic, and *Tristes Tropiques* has been identified as seminal for this most pervasive affect in anthropology. Derrida describes "an ethic of nostalgia for origins, an ethic of archaic and natural innocence" in the book, and Renato Rosaldo condemns its nostalgia as "imperial" and a way to "make racial domination innocent and pure."[49] Writing in 1950s New York after his arrival there in 1941, Lévi-Strauss sees prewar South America as offering the promise of the past lost from the postwar North. Critical of the mass communications and technology he believes are despoiling nature, he presents the Second World War as the catalyst of this monoculturalization and loss of diversity; but the war more intimately spelled the near loss of his own life. Brazil propelled him redemptively into his structural studies. Leaving Vichy France in 1941—as a Jew, "potential fodder for the concentration camp," escaping just in time (*Tristes* 12)—Lévi-Strauss ends up in New York after being refused a renewal of visa for Brazil (for bureaucratic but inexcusable reasons), where instead of living Brazil he writes it, in his first three books, the last of these *Tristes Tropiques*. Brazil comes to be cathected as a way to purify his own terrible time that had brought to an end many parallel lives—including Benjamin's. Brazil is recovered in *Tristes Tropiques* as Eden, which James Clifford identifies as "the ultimate referent" of all nostalgia.[50] On his arrival at his port of entry into Brazil, Santos, just south of the Tropic—"Crossing the Tropic" (92)—Lévi-Strauss remembers the land as "emerging on the first day of creation" (94). The landscape is subject to immobilizing; "the sense of time did not exist in the world I was now entering" (320). His anthropological research is described as going back to find wholeness: "To be the first white man, perhaps, to set foot in a still intact Tupi village would be to bridge the gap of four hundred years" (405). "I had wanted to reach the extreme limits of the savage" (402), he writes, and he finds in the Nambikwara, with their nakedness, their sleeping on the bare earth, and their open lovemaking, the "most primitive" nomads to be found anywhere in the world (327): "The Nambikwara had taken me back to the Stone Age and the Tupi-Kawahib to the sixteenth century; here [coming back from Amazonia] I felt I was in the eighteenth century. . . . I had crossed a continent. But the rapidly approaching end of my journey was being brought home to me in the first place by this ascent through the layers of time" (452–53). The depth of investment of his present self comes through in the language Lévi-Strauss uses to reflect on his anthropological researches. These are not "sequels to colonialism" but "an enterprise renewing the Renaissance and atoning for it" (*Structural Anthropology* 2:32); the modern anthropologist's "very existence is incomprehensible except as an attempt at redemption; he is the symbol of atonement" (*Tristes* 475). The repetition of *atonement,* in French, "expiation"—and with *La fête des expiations*/Day of Atonement as the most religious in the Jewish year—resonates given the burdens of Jewish survivorhood that possibly accompanied Lévi-Strauss, the grandson of a rabbi, from Europe. In describing anthropology as a "collaboration" with colonialism (*Tristes* 31)—or perhaps most pointedly himself as the "one to have brought back nothing but a handful of their [primitives'] ashes" (34) ("des cendres")—Lévi-Strauss bares the life of a French Jew who escaped the Vichy collaborating government and created his discipline out of the irreversible ashes of the Holocaust.[51] No wonder systematically the desire to freeze time, to subject the event to the eternal stillness of structure.

The notion of South America and particularly Brazil before U.S. investment and industrial development as restoring the lost past of the North shapes structural anthropology's conception of the continents. The tropics are *tristes* because they are rapidly passing; the title of *Tristes Tropiques's* first British edition was *A World on the Wane.* In "The Lost World" chapter of *Tristes Tropiques,* Lévi-Strauss moves the history of American settlement back from the then assumed 5000 BCE to 20,000 BCE, and he does so by moving it south, to Brazil—and thus unifies the continents. With his relocation of the origins of American history in Indian Brazil, "The pre-Columbian history of America, like those Japanese flowers made of compressed paper which open out when immersed in water, has suddenly acquired the volume it lacked" (305). The image is straight from Proust: lost time recovered.[52] Written, then, by "an Americanist" (both in disciplinary and geographical affiliation) located in the North (*Structural Anthropology* 2:30), this nostalgic organization between North and South America pervades Lévi-Strauss's anthropology, particularly *Introduction to a Science of Mythology.* In the key transitional volume of the tetralogy that crosses the hemispheric divide, *The Origin of Table Manners,*[53] and in the final volume where North American myths are made to recapitulate those of South America in the first two volumes, *The Naked Man,* South America appears symmetrical to but inverting the North. Thus the loon woman myth of North America's Indians transforms the bird-nester of the Amazonians; the salt in the North is the refrain—but in reverse—of the function of sweet honey in the South. Lévi-Strauss thinks transcontinentally, so that, in places "separated from each other by millions of kilometers, speaking different languages," "there is only one myth" (*Naked* 56, 563). The equator is a temporal mirror. "The Double Inverted Canon" in *The Raw and the Cooked* presents South and North in their respective myths, plausibly because of astronomy, as "form[ing] a chiasmus" (239). In his autobiographical investment in Brazil Lévi-Strauss pursues a desire to inhabit this volumed-out lost past, paradise regained. As he writes of himself in the third person and of the moment of America's discovery: "He would have wanted to live then; indeed, he does so every day in his thoughts. And because, very remarkably, the Indians of Brazil (where I took my first steps in our science) could have adopted as a motto, 'I will maintain,' it happens that their study takes on a double quality: that of a journey to a distant land, and that—more mysterious still—of an exploration of the past" (*Structural Anthropology* 2:30–31).

In contrast, the transgeneric form of *Saudades* as a photographic memoir, photography in autobiography, severs past from present and does not reestablish connection. After a lapse three times that length, Lévi-Strauss can no longer make contact with his memories through his photographs. The captions evidence the I of the memoirist looking back and failing to join with the photographs taken by the eye of the young anthropologist. The photographs were taken in 1934–1939; the text—the captions and the prose interludes—returns to them after a full sixty-year gap (and what a gap). The captions now don't work the images into Lévi-Strauss's broken narrative of lost time. His captions begin in the past tense, with his arrival and acculturation in São Paulo in 1935 (a city which, "still a frontier town, was visibly turning into a financial metropolis" [*Saudades* 26]). As he journeys into the interior, where in photographs of *caboclo* (mixed Indian-Portuguese) farmers colonial "traditional life persisted" (49), and to the Indians and particularly the Nambikwara, though he shifts into the present tense, the subjects appear in the context of his past: "I knew the Nambikwara in the dry season, during a nomadic existence. At such times they live under flimsy shelters made of palm fronds stuck into the sandy soil" (118). Then at this nostalgic origin, Eden, he falls into ellipses that lose the verb tense and indeed the verb. Ellipses pervade the captions in *Saudades*. "Dreamy when the mood struck them . . ." (143); ". . . most often merry . . ." (144); ". . . mocking, provocative . . ." (145): the captions allow the photographs to float free of the anthropologist's project of cultural coding and explaining—and recalling. "The Nambikwara group on the move," in *Tristes Tropiques* (256), becomes, in *Saudades*, "I prevailed upon the Nambikwara to lead me to the site of their winter village. . . . We followed them on horseback" (156). "A Nambikwara smile" (*Tristes* 262) is now instead ". . . mocking, provocative . . ." (*Saudades* 145): all ellipses in original. The syntax of past and present cannot be crossed without omissions, without the syntax breaking down and forgetting, some loss. This elliptical, fragmented narrative is more lyrical (more musical) and suggests the loss of narrative. Clifford explains that nostalgia occurs as the excess when anthropology brings preliterate cultures into writing: "The other is lost, in disintegrating time and space, but saved in the text."[54] In the photographic memoir, in the failure of writing and the recovery of loss as loss, the photographs comprise the ellipses. Black and white, the photographs are imbued with loss. Of course, Lévi-Strauss could only have taken black-and-white photographs given that color was not introduced until 1942, but then the images are held back to be published in the 1990s and so clearly severed from their moment. In our age, color photography is so caught up with tourism it is possibly its principal reason, for the camera has made everyone a tourist, as Sontag writes.[55] Color photography is therefore a cause of the monoculturalization that Lévi-Strauss opposes. Like other contemporary collections, its black-and-white aesthetic appears a resistance to this middle-brow, popularized—domesticated—practice.[56] The stark black-and-white work, for example, of Brazilian photographer Sebastião Salgado in his portrait of his homeland in *Terra* or of the effects of globalization on the world's people in *Migrations,* is at an angle to the photographer-tourist driven by the desire to capture and consume on polychromatic film the others who offer him redemption from his increasingly monochromatic surroundings.[57] Barthes on color in an anthropological film: "colouring the world is always a means of denying it".[58] Lévi-Strauss in *Tristes Tropiques* had condemned brandishing albums of specifically *"colored"* photographs.

The fragmented form to capture loss is like a broken narrative of music, and is echoed in music. In the title of *Saudades do Brasil,* Lévi-Strauss borrows from a composition by Darius Milhaud (also a French-born Jew who fled France for America during the occupation and began his career in Brazil). Particularly in *his Saudades do Brasil,* which keeps disharmonious the African rhythms of Brazilian jazz, sambas and the melodies of Portuguese folk music, Milhaud opposed the systematization and classical mastery of his predecessors.[59] In the one written reference he made to Milhaud before his own *Saudades,* Lévi-Strauss had criticized some fugues Milhaud had composed around 1920 (the date of Milhaud's *Saudades*) as works that fail when they "try to step over the world and the manner of its representation" (*Look* 166). Lévi-Strauss in his musical tastes liked the baroque Rameau, in whose wrought harmonies and chords he had seen a forerunner of his own structuralism. Such music is a model because of its synchronization and encoding, and because it is exceptional in having no presymbolic, no natural referent. Music finds its material wholly in culture: "There are no musical sounds in nature, except in a purely accidental and unstable way; there are only noises," Lévi-Strauss claims, absurdly (*Raw* 19). In *The Raw and the Cooked,* where music is used most fully as Lévi-Strauss tries to write like music, myths and music are said to be "free from those representational links that keep painting in a state of subjection to the world" (22). His earlier conception of music was one that didn't acknowledge loss of the referent. Returning to name his photographs after the previously repudiated composer's desire and failure to join representation and world, Lévi-Strauss now lays claims as guiding to that fugacity. The fugue, literally "flight," is interwoven with loss. The polytonal fugue in its refrain constantly remembers and lets go, recalls and passes on, a melody in successive instruments or voices. In psychiatry, *fugue,* a kind of madness, describes loss of identity, occurring as a reaction to trauma (sometimes involving literal wandering from home). The idealized *dépaysement,* or "homelessness," results, then, not in indifference, but in *saudades*—which can also mean "home*sickness*." Now, like Barthes comparing the Winter Garden Photograph to Schumann's last work (and the last works that Schumann composed as he went mad at the Endenich asylum were, with an exquisite coincidence, fugues), Lévi-Strauss returns to photographs as fugal images. The fugue captures the insanity of photography that is at once named after music and yet claimed "a silent imagery."

What is the death or loss, the *saudades,* that *Saudades* would speak, the silence it would imagize? *Saudades* is in the plural, and there are layers to Lévi-Strauss's retrospection that fail to integrate image into written text, photography into autobiography, and ultimately to redeem self through other. Most manifestly, the *saudades* is for the Indians. The book testifies to their world that has vanished dramatically since the taking of the photographs. For Lévi-Strauss the photographs do not recall their referents not simply because his *memory* is failing, but more importantly because the referents of the photographs really have gone; if we went to see their subjects for ourselves "this world would be unrecognizable and would in many respects have simply vanished." And hence the appropriateness of photography to evidence how the loss of referent became real. Lévi-Strauss's returns are generated from *real* loss. With each return, the photographic referent has receded and has thus become more exigent to show in photography, this form of "melancholy objects."[60] Lévi-Strauss returns to the photographs as if he can't get over the loss—traumatic repetition, not mourning. When Lévi-Strauss first took the photographs in the 1930s, he encountered Indians who had already survived four centuries of colonial decimation and displacement. The Indian population was just 4 percent of what it was in 1500 when the Europeans arrived. In the eighteenth and nineteenth centuries, the *bandeirantes,* or "pioneers," and gold prospectors perpetuated the colonial genocide. Publishing the images for the first time in the 1950s in *Tristes Tropiques,* Lévi-Strauss comments on epidemics and government policies regarding reservations that have continued the loss even in the twentieth century. And when he returns to the images again in 1994, he envisions new threats and further loss: "Before our eyes, a new cataclysm is dispossessing the Indians of this way of life" (16)—a new cataclysm namely in the form of globalization, made up of "giant agricultural conglomerates" (10), the "development of communications and the population explosion" (16), and the plundering of natural resources by the timber and fishing industries, real estate developers—and "organized tourism" (17). Beneath a photograph of a Karaja Indian making a toy for the tourist industry, Lévi-Strauss writes that tourism has expanded the native art but spoiled it, technological advance in proportion to aesthetic—and human—decline. "How can my old photographs fail to create in me a feeling of emptiness and sorrow? They make me acutely aware that this second deprivation will be final this time, given the contrast between a past I still had the joy of knowing and a present of which I receive heartbreaking accounts . . . ." (16). The gap between past and present has widened, the loss of the past now defining the present he would have us see—unclosable, irredeemable. Lévi-Strauss would have us see in his photographs not primitives, Edenic savages, but "wreckage" of earlier civilizations, what one colonial account cited in his prologue describes as "veritable cities . . . each city spread over several leagues along the banks of the river and comprised of hundred of houses of a dazzling whiteness. . . . A very dense population . . . fortifications adorned with monumental sculptures and the fortresses built on the heights. Well-maintained roads, planted with fruit trees, crossed cultivated fields" (11). The reason for Lévi-Strauss showing these photographs is not because he believes they will offer something present or integral to his readers. Quite the opposite. They will offer us loss of this substance. Here photography is embraced for its association with death—Barthes's "literal death"; for it is death, Barthes writes, that makes photography anthropologically new, the rites of death having transferred from religion to photography: "*Life/Death*: the paradigm is reduced to a simple click, the one separating the initial pose from the final print" (*Camera* 92). The loss is nowhere more shocking, more apocalyptic, than in the images of the Nambikwara who, naked and sleeping on the ground and with their eye disease, appear the embodiment of absolute human indigence.

> In those who, among the Indians, strike us as being most destitute, we must therefore see not examples of archaic ways of life that have been miraculously preserved for millennia but the last escapees from that cataclysm that discovery and subsequent invasions have been for their ancestors. Imagine, keeping everything in proportion, scattered groups of survivors after an atomic holocaust on a planetary scale, or a collision with a meteorite such as the one that, they say, caused the extinction of the dinosaurs. (*Saudades* 15–16)

The enjoinder to keep this holocaust in proportion can only be self-conscious and deliberately contrary, given the effect of the photographs (and the analogies) is to blow up the proportion.

Into the Indian loss Lévi-Strauss weaves not only his autobiographical loss, the *saudades* for Brazil and his own lost youth. In the loss Lévi-Strauss would have us see ourselves. Speaking "No longer as an anthropologist, but as a member of my civilization, I feel this dispossession profoundly" (19)—returning to the self after the methodology, Lévi-Strauss makes us the subject and would have us enter into the spectacle. Before the photographs, particularly of the Nambikwara, that most primitive of nomads, Lévi-Strauss would have us see our own losses. He writes that he could show pictures of contemporary Paris, Tokyo, New York in order to match the devastation of his past photographs of the Indians.

> As for progress, it is devouring itself. More and more, the advances of science and technology, including medical breakthroughs . . . have as their principal objective, often used as a pretext, the correction of harmful consequences of previous innovations. And when that end is achieved, further ill-fated consequences will result, for which it will be necessary to devise other inventions as a remedy. Dispossessed of our culture, stripped of values that we cherished—the purity of water and air, the charms of nature, the diversity of animals and plants—we are all Indians henceforth, making of ourselves what we made of them. (18–19)

We, our civilization, are the subject of loss. Now, at the turn of the century with globalization defining, it is we who are *tristes, our* world on the wane. And here, Lévi-Strauss produces a palinodic reversal of time. It is our civilization that has brought about the loss of theirs: our drive for progress has effected their regression, their loss. But now they, in the form of Lévi-Strauss's photographs from the '30s of a vanished world, bode our future. Brazil is no longer the North's past but our possible future. And new to Lévi-Strauss is a recognition in *Saudades* of the Indians as not simply elegiac but adapting to technology. The way of life in the photographs is almost gone, but, on the quincentenary in 1992 of the "discovery" of America, the Nambikwara travel as representatives of Brazil's Amerindians to Mexico City. "They went back home delighted by their trip and bringing with them transistors, which they said were cheaper than those available in Vilhena . . . where the shops are full of Japanese products" (10). In museums across the Americas, Indians place next to traditional masks a mask of Mickey Mouse. Even "the Amazon forest is not as 'primeval' as people liked to think," Lévi-Strauss admits here (13). At the mouth of the Amazon, evidence is being uncovered of multiple man-made flood defenses to protect cultivated fields covering 50,000 square kilometers and to maintain a population numbering seven or eight million—proof that there never was an Eden and the suggestion that this was the possible birthplace of technology in America. Photography's role in this temporal paradox is perfect. It brings apocalypse. New aerial photographs are being used to sell off and destroy more land, to forge unimaginable roads (the Trans-Amazonian highway) into the rainforest in order to encourage more prospectors—loss "caused by the development of communications" (16). But it is the same aerial photography (invented, by the way, by Nadar) that is helping to recover the prehistory of the Amazon. Lévi-Strauss's photographs from 1935 show "a prophecy in reverse—like Cassandra but with eyes fixed upon on the past" (Barthes, *Camera* 87). In evidencing the apocalypse that happened between this prehistory and the present, photography becomes a way, in Lévi-Strauss's photographs, to avert our own future apocalypse.

And this, then, is the reason for publication of these photographs now. Not nostalgic cannibalism of the other—for Lévi-Strauss can now show the true complexity of primal cultures *and* their loss: photograph ghosts—but consumption of ourselves and of the world resources (globalization, the form that world civilization takes, Lévi-Strauss describes as "a body without flesh" [*Structural Anthropology* 2:358]). The photographs urge our awakening to loss. For *saudades* is not equivalent to the backward-looking restorative and mournful nostalgia. It's significant that Portuguese has another word for nostalgia, *a nostalgia,* which *is* nostalgic mourning over a personal or a national loss—*as saudades da pátria, ou de casa, ou da familia,* "mourning for country, home or family." The yearning in *saudades* is unqualified, immeasurable: foundational. *Saudades* is, as Lévi-Strauss says of the French *tristes* in his *Tristes Tropiques,* an untranslatable word (*Tristes* xix). *Saudades* acknowledges and sustains loss. Why the retraction of hated photographic memoirs in the past in *Tristes Tropiques,* then? Ultimately for ourselves. For our future.

CHAPTER 3

GORDON PARKS'S TAKING A LIFE

CHOICE OF WEAPON

If the unconscious of the anthropologist is revealed through photography, the photographer is also something of an anthropologist. Photography is in its origins a work of anthropological documentation, of curiosity about the world. Nadar was a documenter of Paris and its people, and Barthes writes that great photographers like Nadar, or August Sander in his photographs of Weimar Germany at the beginning of the twentieth century, are like mythologists because they give the face a mask, which for Barthes means they give the referent a signified—for "the mask is the meaning."[1] These photographers turn the photograph into a project of social and historical encoding. Works of photographic social documentation, instances of documentary photography then, treat photography as cultural record. From *documentum*, the medieval term for an official paper, "'document' means 'evidence,'" and documentary photography makes the photographic referent proof of a meaning.[2] This is why photography is intricated in the service of anthropology, for anthropology too reads from evidence code. Documentary photography emerged as a named genre as a kind of visual anthropology in which it cultivated an anthropological style. John Collier's term for photography as "visual anthropology" grew out of his training in the early 1940s with Roy Stryker.[3] Stryker was the head of the Farm Security Administration (FSA), where he had the effect of making photography *the* medium for social documentation. The FSA embraced photography as a chronicling of reality and canonized documentary photography as a mode of witnessing. Reflecting on the remit of the photographic project, Stryker suggests photography as a compilation of social facts. "I wanted to do a pictorial encyclopedia of American agriculture."[4] The FSA was premised on the belief that photography was the best form for that encyclopedic record, more transparent than any other medium, and that the photographer in the field could work as comprehensive recorder. Stryker often loaded his photographers up with "shooting scripts," which not only directed them to certain subjects but gave information about the profile, economic, political, and social context of their photographic subject.[5] Stryker believed that photographers should research a story thoroughly before shooting. The photographers, he said, "must be something of sociologists, economists, historians."[6] This total immersion was intended to subordinate the photographer as controlling auteur, to make invisible the photographer's subjectivity.

Recording life as it is, documentary photography appears to be a take on life, photography at its most realistic. Yet the aim of these photographs was not to record reality but to change it. Documentary photography was intrinsically political, its mythology national. The agricultural aid and resettlement unit of F. D. Roosevelt's New Deal program, the FSA was set up to combat the Depression specifically in the rural United States. It was directly sponsored by the U.S. government. Its brief was to support the Democratic president's New Deal, to justify his program of reforms and projects that sought to alleviate the plight of the U.S. poor. As Lawrence Levine has written of the documentary era, "Photography was not merely a mechanism for depicting these changes, it was simultaneously their product and their agent, their creation and their creator." As offering the rationale for and producing rather than transcribing social change, documentary photography romanticized and idealized certain subjects. What got to count as real in Roosevelt's New Deal United States was politically overdetermined. People were selected as representative, in this case of Depression America, and the entire documentary tradition, both photographic and literary, is bound up with mythologizing the masses. U.S. writers and artists documented this side of the United States because they "preferred the struggling poor to the genteel affluent: the former were more 'real.'"[7] Documentary photography did not portray victims then; it created them. The photographs have a point of view, that of myth-making, and this non-neutrality is what makes a good documentary photograph. The successful documentary photograph convinces us of its vision. Propaganda works by direct appeal to the viewer, and by seeking to effect this documentary photographs were not unmediated. The documentary was not such at all: "Many people would now acknowledge that a work of social documentary, whether or not they agree with its message, is, or originally was, propaganda."[8] The point of the photographs was to propagate in the viewer approval for the New Deal in support of the U.S. government. There is a paradox of time here. In order to justify social change, documentary photography had to present in a rosy, nostalgic light the very conditions it suggested as outdated and in need of change. It had to present a harrowing experience, but not in so alienating a glare that the viewer immediately turned away. Documentary photographs had to convince us that the suffering were worthy of redemption, that there was nobility even in abjection. In this documentary photography bears comparison to the contradictions of photography in salvage anthropology condemned by Lévi-Strauss as consuming the people the combination of forms sought to preserve. The missionary role, the zeal of documentary photographs is also undeniable.

In this moment of the 1930s also lies the nationalization of the genre of documentary photography. Roosevelt was himself something of an inveterate documenter, relying on factual reports for all his political changes. The notion of documentary traditions and above all photography as the best means for bringing about change to U.S. reality (U.S.-)Americanized documentary photography. The form enabled ideals the nation had about itself. Recent work has begun to unpick the ideologies and constructions that lie behind documentary photography.[9] Dorothea Lange's "Migrant Mother," one of the most famous documentary photographs and the archetype not only for this moment but perhaps of a turning-point in American modernity, worked because of its apparent unmediatedness, because the viewer is supposed to have an immediate and compassionate political response to the distressed-looking mother and her three filthy, reticent children. But the revealed context of Lange's taking the photograph compromises documentary photography's claims to attest to the real on several fronts. It shows Lange's construction of and distance from her subject. Lange selected this image of the family because it fit the social subject (poor U.S. farmworker in need of aid or resettlement, migrant mother without father) that she was being directed to see by the FSA. She chose the most devastating shot from her roll of film and left unpublished many others that showed the family smiling, more relaxed, and considerably less harried. And Lange's comments on taking the photograph, that she just happened on her subject and did not ask her name or any information about the family, undermine the anthropological ideal of Stryker's informed sociology and reveal the photographer as opportunist. More than any this photograph made Lange's career. The photograph tells a story, but it may be more of the life of the photographer and less of her subject's. The photographer controls the subject as image, and the purported real in the photograph may consist in the photographer's autobiography. One of the most problematic aspects of documentary photography is that by definition it occults the photographer's (autobiographic) investment in her subject, as opposed to the pictorial tradition in which the point of the photograph is the photographer's conceit. As Clive Scott has written, documentary photography is voyeuristic, "breaking down responsibilities connected with the *continuity* of experience and *one's own visibility;* the camera, one comes to believe, conceals the photographer." In this documentary photography "dramatizes our problematic relationship with photography generally," by keeping out of the picture the location of viewers in relation to subjects.[10]

Gordon Parks is the key documentary photographer of African American lives. Parks followed other, more famous FSA photographers, such as Lange and Walker Evans, in travelling the United States and documenting the American oppressed, but Parks's main concern is African Americans. Parks has photographed crucial moments in the history of African American life in the second half of the twentieth century, including the rise of the civil rights movement and the Black Muslim movement. He has also photographed the quotidian details of ordinary African American lives, what he calls "moments without proper names."[11] His signature photograph, entitled "American Gothic" (1942), shows an African American woman, "Mrs. Ella Watson, Government Charwoman," in front of a huge U.S. flag in the federal government offices she cleaned. In the juxtaposition of this thin woman, holding her bathetic mop and broom, and the grandeur of the Stars and Stripes, Parks evokes in a small human document, with irony, the place of African Americans in the U.S. institution. Parks's documentary skills had been honed by his training starting out as a photographer with Roy Stryker and the Farm Security Administration in the early 1940s. He then worked for the Office of War Information, which was what the FSA became after the Second World War broke out and, as is obvious from its name, was the war's propaganda unit. During this time Parks produced a photographic project, *Midway: Portrait of a Daytona Beach Neighborhood,* which is perhaps his most anthropological. Like the anthropologist, Parks with his camera provided a meticulous record of all aspects of a Florida community, an encyclopedia of this time African American life.[12] He also innovated and made his own the technique in which he would focus a series on one person or a small group of people to tell, in a kind of biography, a broader story of humanity. His series in 1948 of Red Jackson, a Harlem gang leader, or of the Fontenelle family in Harlem in 1968, both first published in *Life* magazine, are exemplary and as such were landmarks in documentary photography.[13] Parks was the first African American photographer at *Life*, where he worked for over twenty years. It was at this magazine that his documentary photography really came to fruition. *Life* was the institution that inherited the documentary tradition in photography and conveyed it to the larger public in the form of photojournalism—the telling of a current-events story in photographs. Famous documentary photographers had contributed to *Life* before Parks, such as Margaret Bourke-White and Lange. Parks was inspired to become a photographer when he found a photojournalistic magazine while working as a waiter on a Pullman train and saw photographs of dispossessed migrant workers in the Dust Bowl and California. Lange's and Evans's are among the images, and while Parks doesn't mention its name, given that it led both in publishing FSA photographs and in the U.S. photojournalistic market in the 1930s, more than likely the magazine was *Life*. Parks's project of representation and representativity has extended to other media. He is known as a filmmaker and directed the seminal and popular blaxploitation film *Shaft* in 1971, an attempt, he has said, to give blacks a positive role model. He also wrote and made a film of *The Learning Tree*, his previously written autobiographical novel.[14] Parks's style across his oeuvre is consistently documentary. Michael Torosian has termed his crisp, clear prose "telegraphic," its short, punchy sentences serving to communicate in minimal form a powerful message apparently culled from reality.[15] It is not insignificant that Parks's greatest writerly influence—and the work to spur him to write—was Richard Wright, with his *Twelve Million Black Voices*. A collection of documentary photographs of African Americans made in 1941, this greatest of mid-twentieth-century African American realist writers used the FSA files.[16]

Parks's photographic witnessing of African Americans is enabled by his conscious use of his identity as an African American; he is an observer who is nevertheless participant. Photography is significant for African Americans because, as bell hooks writes, "For black folks, the camera provided a means to document a reality that could, if necessary, be packed, stored, moved from place to place. It was a documentation that could be shared, passed around" and that thereby "offered a way to contain memories, to overcome loss, to keep history."[17] Portable, migrational even to the most uninhabitable of communities, yet allowing a record or testimony of those conditions to be made, the camera for African Americans was a "choice of weapons" against poverty and bigotry, to use one of Parks's own descriptions.[18] With Parks's work the camera passes from the anthropologist to the native—or rather the native becomes a self-reflexive and political anthropologist, documents his own life to record and challenge adversity. Parks's oeuvre repeatedly seems to stem from his proximity to and involvement with—identification with—his subjects. He was able to photograph intimately, because he was actually with, the family of Malcolm X the night the activist was assassinated. He photographed—while sharing a hotel room with him—Muhammad Ali on the night he became heavyweight boxing champion of the world. He was invited by Eldridge Cleaver to join the Black Panthers as "Minister of Information" on the strength of his photographs, though he refused because of his commitment to "objectivity" in documentary photography.[19] Nicholas Natanson argues that Parks's work represents the most sustained engagement with African American subjects in documentary photography. Parks was exceptional in the documentary tradition in his intimate photographs of African American subjects because, "consistently able to gain his subjects' cooperation for close-in, low-angle shooting, [he] achieved a considerable degree of immediacy." But in line with the FSA's "photographic 'constructing'" of reality, Parks "fell short of a full documentary encounter with urban conflict and change," precisely because of the national mythologies in which documentary photography was enmeshed and in whose tradition Parks followed: "these shortcomings reflected a long-standing weakness in FSA documentation of the deepest class and race divisions in American society, the fissures that could not be healed with New Deal initiatives."[20] Parks's photographs do not live up to the ideals the photographer himself might have had about race and equality in the nation but are instead co-opted by the institutions and cultural frameworks in which documentary photography was produced and distributed—mythologies not altogether realized in the consciousness of the photographer. In his analysis of the series of images surrounding Parks's "American Gothic," Natanson reveals that Parks rearranged certain objects in the surroundings in order to intensify the impact of the photograph, and he argues that this compromises the photograph's documentary quality and objectivity. Parks in his autobiography *Choice* writes of posing Mrs. Watson with broom and mop and admits that he "overdid it." And his initial request to photograph her pops out because he can think of no way to help: "I was escaping the humiliation of not being able to help."[21] Photography is the inadequate and artificial recompense for help. Like the anthropologist whose mission to bear witness to threatened lives is inextricable from those lives, the documentary photographer is inevitably entangled with and adjusted the lives of those he photographed, however subtly and unconsciously.

For Sontag, the photographer is "an extension of the anthropologist" not so much because he can live up to the ideal of recorder—"The whole point of photographing people is that you are not intervening in their lives, only visiting them"—but because he fails.[22] "To photograph people is to violate them," to turn them into "objects that can be symbolically possessed" (14). The "predatory" aspects of photography are that, although the photograph records for posterity, it at the same time steals—"loots and preserves" (64). This is particularly so in America, she suggests, where links between photography and tourism meant that pushing back the frontier and the genocide of North American Indians were coincident with the popularization of the camera. Nature was domesticated, and the primitive or original "cannibalized" in photography: "In America, every specimen becomes a relic" (65). The loss in photography is similar to that she has already recognized in Lévi-Straussian anthropology, which she calls a "necrology," since it, too, is implicated in the death it seeks to recover its subjects from.[23] Documentary photography may be similar to anthropology in this much more problematic sense. It opens up the language of what it means to "take" or "shoot" a photograph, the terms we use for capturing on camera that bring to the surface the injurious effects even in documentary photography. Or, in the French *tirer*, which means not only "to draw," "to draw back" (as in curtains), and "to photograph" but "to take away." Portuguese for taking a photograph of a person has even more resonance. In *Tristes Tropiques* Lévi-Strauss describes some young boys in Brazil who urge him to "Tira o retrato! Tira o retrato!" of them instead of begging money from him.[24] *Tirar* has the sense of the French *tirer* of "to take away," "to take out forcibly"—but also "to earn." *O retrato* is "a portrait" but also "a likeness," "an effigy"—the essence, as if it were the life itself that is taken. It is this same primitive conception of photography—living in the myth as reality; not making the myth and controlling code—that leads Barthes to write that "young photographers who are at work in the world, determined upon the capture of actuality, do not know that they are agents of Death." Apparently preserving life, they take it: "in this image which produces Death while trying to preserve life . . . the simple click."[25] The primitives' belief about photographs stealing the soul seems to be borne out in the case of Parks's most famous subject, celebrated in his day but now forgotten—taken. But as to whose life the camera takes, and where life has particular resonance given the role played by *Life* magazine, is unclear, in this two-part, extraordinary story of the involvement of a photographer in his subject's life.

EVIL EYE

Parks had been given an assignment for *Life* magazine in 1961 to document poverty in Latin America. The original plan was to get Parks to represent poverty by one photo in seven separate Latin American countries. The mandate to Parks on setting out was "Find an impoverished father with a family of eight or ten children. Show how he earns a living, the amount he earns a year. Explore his political leanings. Is he a Communist or about to become one? Look into his personal life, his religion, friends, his dreams, frustrations. What about his children—their schools, their health and medical problems, their chances for a better life?"[26] This proves too impersonal for Parks. Parks actually finds as his single subject Flavio da Silva, a twelve-year-old boy who lives in a Rio slum *(favela)* with his family of seven other children, an out-of-work father who sells kerosene, and a mother who

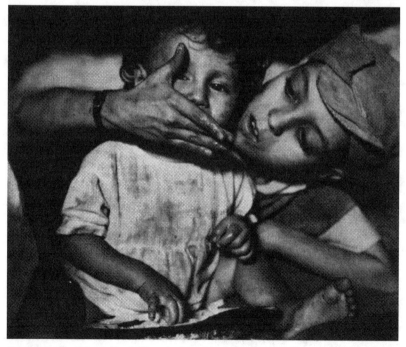

Gordon Parks, "Flavio Feeds Zacarias" (1961). Copyright Gordon Parks. Reprinted with permission.

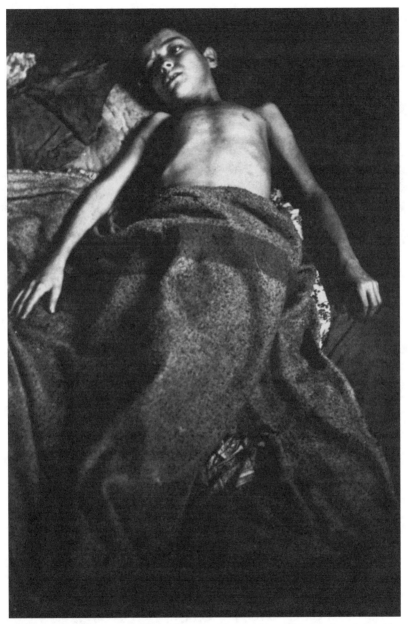

Gordon Parks, "Flavio da Silva during an Asthmatic Seizure" (1961). Copyright Gordon Parks. Reprinted with permission.

washes clothes, immigrants from the northeast of Brazil. Sick with bronchial asthma and malnourished, Flavio according to Brazilian doctors is on
the point of death. This seems to be Parks's initial draw to Flavio: "Death
was all over him" is one of the first things Parks notices about Flavio (14).
Parks's photographs bear all the signs of Stryker's training. They use classical documentary techniques to represent and attest to reality. Their theme
is social, that of poverty and starvation, recalling documentary photographers' favorite subjects of thirties United States. It is embodied in a human
subject. Parks's close-ups reveal a detailed realism, so that we see the dirt
in the child's clothes, the roughness of the blanket, the thinness of Flavio
in his rib cage. The social context is given, as the unremittingly poor shack
on the Catacumba ("Catacomb") *favela* is shown cluttered among other
makeshift homes but crouched symbolically beneath the Cristo Redentor
("Christ Redeemer") of the Corcovado hill, Rio's most famous landmark.
And the assignment is marked by Parks's trademark biography. He moves
from *Life*'s instruction to represent poverty generically to representing
Flavio biographically. Flavio's story is told as representative, with occa-
sional statistics about poverty in Brazil given in parentheses in the text
accompanying the photographs. The series follows a day in Flavio's life,
from getting out of the bed that he shares with his parents and four other
children, to doing chores, to preparing the supper and struggling to feed
the other children. Though clearly the sickest, as the eldest child Flavio is
his family's mainstay. The photographer's proximity to his subject creates
an intimacy. The point of view the photographs want us to have is that of
compassion, to feel involved and empathetic. They idealize their subject's
unquestioning fulfillment of duty and hard work. The photograph of
Flavio in his bed, originally captioned "Sick and exhausted from week's
care of the family . . . ," iconizes the boy as a Christ-like figure with his
arms outstretched, like the Cristo Redentor, who Flavio's father says has
deserted the *favela*. The layout and caption similarly manipulate this response in us. The photograph of Flavio sick in bed appears on a page facing
that of an actual dead child—as if this is what Flavio could be. And the
caption goes on, presenting Flavio as martyr: "'I am not afraid of death,'
he explained to Parks. 'But what will they do after?'" The chiaroscuro
style of the photographs emphasizes the dark more than the light involved
in photography; the photographs enter into a horrifying, very dark underworld. Parks's account of taking the photographs, excerpts from his diary
at the end of the series entitled "Photographer's Diary of a Visit in Dark
World," works to draw out the Hadean journey.[27]

If social change is the aim of documentary photography's recording of

Gordon Parks, "The Catacumba *Favela,* Rio de Janeiro" (1961). The da Silva shack is near the top, just beneath the Christ figure (Cristo Redentor). Copyright Gordon Parks. Reprinted with permission.

reality, this is what the publication of Parks's photographs in *Life* magazine achieved, perhaps more dramatically and more completely than any other documentary photography. As a result of the photographs' publication, *Life* received and three weeks later reported back on a "uniquely urgent and moving response," in the form of donations and letters from its readers.

Among some of the letters it publishes: a widow promises Flavio an allow-
ance from her monthly sum; offers are made of a home and an education
for Flavio; money has been collected in a school, and other children have
arranged a yard sale to contribute; there are gifts of bicycles, of an inhaler
for Flavio's bronchial asthma—and most crucially the pledge of a compli-
mentary place for Flavio at the Children's Asthma Research Institution
and Hospital in Denver. At the bottom of the page *Life* announces that
it is setting up a "Flavio Fund," calls for further donations, and suggests
that with the money Flavio would be brought to hospital for treatment
and the Da Silvas relocated from their slum.[28] Combined with the initial
donations, this call produces what amounts to an unprecedented flood of
$30,000 from readers. Channeled into the fund, the money allows Parks
to return to Brazil and collect Flavio to be brought to the Denver asthma
institute. There is no doubt in *Life*'s mind that Parks's photographs and the
response of *Life*'s readers have saved Flavio's life. Another two weeks later
shows how effective the original documentary photographs were. "Flavio's
Rescue: Americans Bring Him from Rio Slum to Be Cured," the July 21,
1961, cover of *Life* beams, with new Parks photographs of Flavio in new,
clean pajamas and proper, clean bed. The color images of Flavio the smiling boy relocated in the United States in this issue are in stark contrast to
those of him reprinted here in its "Story of the Week" in his dirty bed in
a "Rio de Janeiro hovel, wasted by malnutrition and bronchial asthma,
with only a few years to live": "Today he is in Colorado, and his smile, his
new clothes, his Hopalong watch flopping down his skinny wrist and his
chance to live—all are the work of hundreds of generous, compassionate
Americans." The juxtaposition dramatizes the transformative effects of this
relocation. In this issue we see Flavio in his first shoes, Flavio in Denver
learning English ("such basic American words as 'baseball,' 'television,'
'food'"). He "symbolized the enormous problems of Latin America's impoverished millions." His family, too, have been relocated, and the issue
includes photographs of the Da Silvas moving from the shanty town to a
proper, stone house.[29]

Flavio spends two years in the United States at the institute. His bronchial asthma is treated and apparently cured, and he grows eight inches and
gains twenty-two pounds. But his treatment is as much psychological and
cultural as physical. On arrival and repeatedly during his stay, he undergoes intelligence and psychological tests; there's apparently one theory that
asthma has psychosomatic dimensions. He's found—and repeatedly—to
be maladjusted and falling short. He's seen to have emotional and social
problems. After his asthma is resolved, according to one report Flavio re-

mains "belligerent, resistant to discipline, and uncontrollable," although Parks senses in his withdrawal, silence, and lack of communication that he is depressed because he is isolated and misses his family (*Flavio* 102). He becomes a social experiment, and the cure corrective. He is taught the wrongness of stealing, better eating habits, and correct table manners. He undergoes cultural assimilation as part of his improvement, is given an ideal American life. He lives with a Portuguese American family, and his foster mother, Kathy Gonçalves, an American married to a Portuguese, teaches him not simply English but better Portuguese, instead of the *favela* slang they think he comes speaking. The photographs of this two-year period, when he is out of Parks's life, show Flavio experiencing Thanksgiving turkey dinner with his new family, his first Christmas, his first fishing trip with the Gonçalves boys, all of these taken by foster father José Gonçalves. These photographs are family snapshots and they paste Flavio firmly into the family album, a form that does not reflect family life but, as Marianne Hirsch has written, "perpetuates family myths while seeming merely to record actual moments in family history."[30] The white nuclear family was a particularly favored subject of *Life*'s: it "symbolized the United States," was an "imagined community" for the nation.[31] Flavio is a tabula rasa according to Kathy—"He's like dry soil soaking up everything around him" (*Flavio* 105). He is a symbol or metaphor—better yet, given that in the eyes of North American readers his existence originated in and is confined solely to photographs, an emanation of Brazil. So his eventual adjustment to his new life is seen as successful Americanization. "We'll soon have a number one American boy at Willens," his house parent at the institute promises (111–12). Not surprisingly, the result of this adjustment is a gap for Flavio between his Brazilian past and his U.S. present. He rejects all things Brazilian, refuses to speak Portuguese and insists on only English, stops writing to his mother, and loses touch with his family. "I don't want to go back" (131). *Life*'s involvement not only with Flavio but with his family and the *favela* of Catacumba may have exacerbated these rifts. With part of the Flavio fund, *Life* not only relocates the Da Silvas out of the *favela* to a suburban house, bringing about a remarkable and immediate—and very photogenic—transformation, as the family are kitted out with new toys, clothes, and furniture—courtesy of Sears Roebuck. *Life* helps create a means of work for the father, in trucking. The *favela*, too, undergoes a project of development, with access to drinking water provided and a process of building and the introduction of services such as power supply and waste disposal. These adjustments result in differences in degrees of poverty and security and introduce the sense of envy and alienation:

between the Da Silva father and his eldest son, between the Da Silvas and their neighbors, and between Catacumba and surrounding *favelas*. Flavio's "rescue" from Brazil is so successful that "Flavio da Silva had, after twenty months, grown to love America. It had given him more than most children around the world ever get—a small fortune, a house for his family, a chance to learn, love, and to live a full and healthy life. It was a place where he had been close to complete happiness, and he did not want to leave it" (130). Dread of return to the *favela*—that underworld—and the recurrence of the illness and everything that had characterized Flavio's life there, hangs over the whole episode—for Flavio and for Parks.

Why the unprecedented generous response by *Life*'s readers to the original Flavio photographs, and what lies at the heart of the episode? The event is a good deal less redemptive and more appropriative than may initially seem from the story of compassion and salvation. The historical moment is key. The episode is actually in line with postwar American policy, spread from McCarthyism to inform foreign policy—toward Korea, Latin America, and soon Vietnam—an expression of containment of the subversion of communism. *Life*'s readers are not seeking to eradicate poverty for its own sake but are responding inextricably to *Life*'s presentation of Flavio's poverty in the context of the fear of communism. As so strongly but oddly indicated in Parks's initial instructions from *Life* ("Find an impoverished father. . . . Explore his political leanings. Is he a Communist or about to become one?"), his assignment for *Life* is thoroughly embedded in U.S. politics toward Latin America. Parks's photographs appeared as part of a five-part series in *Life* in the summer of 1961, entitled "The Crisis in Our Hemisphere"/"Crisis in Latin America." The exchange in titles between what appears on the cover and what appears inside the introductory issue suggests how U.S. anxiety about the fifth column within its own borders in the fifties extended to the continent in the south in the sixties. The titles and headlines in the series are equally evocative of the Red Scare in Latin America of the moment: "The Menacing Push of Castroism" (front cover: "Exclusive Photo Report Shows How Castro and the Communists Are Working to Seize Latin America"); "Freedom's Fearful Foe: Poverty" (front cover: "Shocking Poverty Spawns Reds"), in which Parks's Flavio photos appeared; "Bolivia: U.S. Stake in a Revolution"; "Latin America's Story of Turbulence"; "Prisoners of Our Geography—The Races and the Terrain, a Mixed-Up Inheritance."[32] In the early 1960s at the height of the cold war and after the Cuban revolution of 1959 (but populist reforms in Guatemala had already caused U.S. concern about communism in Latin America), Latin America, the United States' own "backyard," was the main battleground between the "Christian free world" (capitalism) and the threat to the free world (then, communism). The year 1961 when Parks published his photos and the Latin American series ran was particularly pivotal. In April the buildup of tensions between the United States and Cuba resulted in the failed, U.S.-sponsored invasion of Cuba, the Bay of Pigs fiasco. And in March President Kennedy had announced his Alliance for Progress in the Americas, a policy to develop continental links as another strategy to combat communism, the goal to eradicate the poverty that "produces" communism. In the words of one history of the messy U.S. politics toward Latin America, in adherence to the Monroe Doctrine of right to intervention in Latin America that has characterized U.S. policy for almost two centuries, following Cuba "Latin America's economic development became an obsession in Washington."[33] The Alliance for Progress echoed the political intervention hiding behind economic and cultural development in F. D. Roosevelt's "Good Neighbor Policy" in the thirties and forties; and the Good Neighbor Policy was itself an exportation abroad of Roosevelt's New Deal at home, with all its attendant national mythologies about poverty and social and economic stability.

Brazil was particularly significant to the United States. Historically it had been the only Latin American nation that had fought for the Allies in the Second World War; and in its geography it was equivalent to the United States without Alaska, as comparisons of the time repeatedly stress. But Brazil was most important politically in the bipolar vision of communism-versus-the-free-world of this moment. The Kennedy government desperately wanted new Brazilian President Jânio Quadros's regime to succeed, since the suicide of longtime dictator Getúlio Vargas in 1954 had produced a series of fast-shifting and unstable governments in Brazil that swung the pendulum with regard to cooperating with their relations in the north. The forces of communism and nationalism often formed uneasy alliances in Latin America and always resulted in anti- (North-) Americanism, as they were in Brazil especially in the late 1950s-early 1960s, its modern period of greatest political uncertainty—and possibility. The United States was willing to pour finances into the Brazilian government to ensure stability and friendly relations—in other words, anticommunism and openness to U.S. corporate investment. In May 1961, weeks before Parks published his photographs, a communiqué from the U.S. government announcing loan arrangements to Brazil "emphasized that Brazil's future was vital to the future of the hemisphere and that the maintenance of free government in Latin America was dependent upon the success of Brazil's economic development."[34] In the early 1960s, the United States was the biggest foreign investor in Brazil, begun in industrialization in the Second World War. Half of foreign investment in Brazil was from the United States. By 1961, a summer of what turned out to be a period of transition but not crisis in Brazil, Quadros (described by *Life* as "radical")[35] both played the United States for financial support *and* courted the new Cuban government. He visited Cuba in March 1960 and in August awarded the Order of the Southern Cross, Brazil's highest honor, to the Cuban-Argentinean Che Guevara, refusing to comply with the U.S. demand for sanctions against Cuba. While he accepted their aid, Quadros was less pro-American than any Brazilian president since the Second World War, preferring instead to pursue "independent foreign policy" alliances with other Third World countries.[36] This autonomous, ambivalent policy so far as the United States was concerned would only end with the right-wing military coup in Brazil in 1964, which would rule Brazil and suppress democracy for the next twenty years. The coup delighted Washington. The U.S. government supported the coup militarily, dispatching warships to Brazil in March 1964, and financially, skyrocketing aid to 600 percent after the coup's success. Brazilian police, who proved so efficient at rounding up intellectuals, left-wing activists and anyone who objected to the military regime, continued to be trained at the Washington Police Academy through the 1970s even once the brutality of the regime was internationally well known. "Clearly involved in the military overthrow of the constitutional and democratic government of Brazil, the United States became intimately associated with the military dictatorship that followed." In the summer of 1961 when *Life* magazine ran its stories and when the United States "bore the brunt of [Brazil's] attack on imperialism,"[37] it was crucial for the United States to justify its ideological and economic investment in Brazil and to portray a cause-and-effect relation between poverty and communism. In the concluding editorial in the last of the *Life* series, *Life* journalist Robert Coughlan argues in support of Kennedy's Alliance for Progress that pouring money into the continent would battle anti-U.S. stance and communism.[38] And if we have any doubt about how anticommunist belief insidiously informs the overwhelming response of *Life*'s readers to Parks's photographs of Flavio, the letters page provides adequate testimony. "Let us first beat the Russians to the distant star in Flavio's eyes," as one reader manages to put it both whimsically and bellicosely.[39] In writing of his decision to focus in on a Brazilian *favela* in his assignment, Parks initially saw his story within the anticommunist remit: "During a trip to Rio de Janeiro several years before, I had seen poverty at its worse in the infamous favelas ringing the city. The poor there were a large part of those already ripening for the sharpest danger facing the Western Hemisphere, a Communist take-over" (*Flavio* 58). Flavio's fund is "With President Kennedy's Alliance for Progress as a model . . . a pilot *project for progress*" (91). Flavio's life becomes the choicest weapon in this moment of the cold war.

Life was particularly significant in the nationalist politics of the moment and the war against communism. John Tagg insists that to evaluate documentary photographs' realism we need to look at the "institutional frameworks within which they are produced and consumed," for documentary photography functions "within certain ideological apparatuses."[40] *Life* magazine was a propagandistic institution, inheriting the mantle of documentary photography in unabashed function as a U.S. nationalist mouthpiece. Conceived as the United States' first truly national magazine, it was targeted at every American, and it decided America's issues. Its emergence and success were interdependent with the emergence and success of U.S. technology and economy. Technology made possible not only good media photographic reproduction but the mass distribution of *Life*—first nationally, then globally. Economically, *Life* was funded initially and at different points sustained by advertising revenue from expanding U.S. companies.[41] Coughlan goes on to underline the part that communications should play in similarly priming the U.S. population for the government's message: "merely to make the facts available—as our present information agencies mostly do—is far from enough. What are needed are the tactics of full-scale psychological warfare, for we are dealing not simply with an information gap but with an empathy gap, the production of long condition and deeply set emotional attitudes."[42] *Life* explicitly performed this function. The publisher's mission statement for the magazine, in the first of the series on Latin America and thus in the issue just before Parks's initial photographs of Flavio, presents *Life* as a nationalist tool, not merely reflective but creative of national goals. "For the next 25 years, therefore, what better dedication could there be for *Life* than the fulfillment of National Purpose and the pursuit of excellence in our American civilization? . . . LIFE dedicates itself to being a lively instrument of the National Purpose, to helping the people of America recognize their deepest aspirations and work increasingly toward that fulfillment." The "National Purpose" is summarized as twofold. "1) Win the Cold War. 2) Create a better America."[43] *Life* magazine was proclaimed the "pictorial window on the world" by Henry Luce, its founder and head of media empire that also included *Time* and *Fortune*; but "The outlook was relentlessly American. . . . Time[-Life] was more an exporter of American ideas than a global publisher."[44] From his initial vision to "get the photographers into the byways of America"[45] when the magazine was set up in 1936, Luce, by 1941 in his famous editorial essay "The American Century," was writing that the United States "must undertake to be the Good Samaritan of the entire world," which meant exporting not just economic aid and American ideals but a system of free economic enterprise led by America and American technical and cultural expertise. Noting that American artifacts were the one thing world communities had in common—the one thing that could unify the world in a time of division, of self versus other—Luce dreams, under the guise of America as global redeemer, globalization, *avant la lettre*.[46] As William Stott puts it ironically, "Our [U.S.] sympathy had grown beyond all boundary."[47]

It was impossible for *Life*'s photographers or journalists to be critical of the United States. *Life* photographer, German Edwin Rosskam's challenge to the U.S. position in Puerto Rico previously had only resulted in "incurring the wrath of *Life*'s conservative editors."[48] And the pattern was repeated, for even Barthes remarks of *Life* that its editors rejected the images of one photographer "because, they said, his images 'spoke too much'; they made us reflect" by distracting us from the message that *Life*'s editors would have us see, something other than the authorized code.[49] *Life* had served a major propagandistic function in Brazil before. In 1941 its editors helped launch a South American version of *Life, En Guardia*, under the auspices of the Office of Inter-American Affairs (OIAA) during the war and at the time of Roosevelt's Good Neighbor Policy. This office sponsored the work of Parks's closest predecessor in Brazil, U.S. photographer Genieve Naylor, who was sent to Brazil with a mandate by the OIAA to convince North Americans that Brazil was a "Good Neighbor," a trustworthy ally. Her recent commentator suggests that *she* deliberately failed in this duty, and in accordance her photographs are a good deal more open in their meaning, less nationalist in their mythologies—and therefore less documentary than Parks's.[50] The Office of War Information where Parks began his documentary career effectively made irrefutable the political bonds of documentary photography. And then it got too much even for its chief proponent: "When the object of the pictures changed from essential 'truth' in the old FSA sense to the outright manufacture of propaganda for the OWI, it became offensive to Stryker."[51] In war and especially in cold, virtual ones, photographs are ammunition. Photographs of the Cuban boy Elian Gonzalez, which recently played a similar role to Flavio's, demonstrate this. Photographs released, first in the U.S. press of Elian waving an American flag, and then by the Cuban government of him happily reunited with his Cuban national father, caught the boy in a crossfire of information/

disinformation.[52] Flavio was subjected to a similar propaganda battle. On initial publication of Parks's photographs, the Brazilian magazine *O Cruzeiro,* recognizing the documentation of Brazilian poverty as politically laden, "rushed one of its own photographers to New York City to do a similar story on a Puerto Rican family in the Wall Street district, and it depicted a sleeping child with cockroaches crawling over its face, and another child crying from hunger" (*Flavio* 91). *Time,* sibling to *Life* in Luce's media empire, quickly countered and revealed the *O Cruzeiro* story as fabrication. Parks remarks the irony that "O Cruzeiro had felt it necessary to go to such lengths. If it had gone to New York's Harlem or Chicago's South Side, they could have found a story as genuinely tragic as the one of the Catacumba" (*Flavio* 91–92). Or it could have gone to Parks's own rural Kansas.

Life's photojournalistic format is key to its place as propagandistic institution. *Life* is celebrated for taking documentary photography into a photojournalistic format, and its combination of photographs and text was groundbreaking at its launch. Photojournalism sought to bring to a mass audience a reflection of current events in photographs with few words—to report through pictures. *Life* was the most successful of photojournalistic magazines from the 1930s because in its photographs, apparently "for the first time, the real world was depicted realistically, aided by rapid technological advances"; and its minimal prose narrative catered to the U.S. public's perceived lack of time to read the news in full, as story.[53] In its quarter-centenary anniversary issue, in which the mission statement appears and which serves as an introduction to Parks's photographs, *Life* announces that it has revamped itself in order "to quicken and sharpen communications between printed page and reader's eye." The publisher touts his magazine's attributes and makes clear what is different about photojournalism: "In its first 25 years LIFE has dedicated itself to enlarging communication among the American people through the revealing power of picture journalism."[54] *Life's* editors rightly attributed its success to its "'new picture-and-word editorial technique' which 'makes the truth about the world we live in infinitely more exciting, more easily absorbed, more alive than it has ever been before.'"[55] The text-photograph combination that was the hallmark of *Life* ensured both the apparent comprehensiveness of the picture—we seemed to be seeing the facts, the event itself—and yet at the same time a narrow, even coercive, what Barthes called a coded point of view, the meaning. The photographs enlarged the details. The text underwrote these with the national line. And the combination of forms gave a sense of instantaneity in keeping with modern mass media, of making issues alive and bringing them home, of news in the making or changing. Prose was factual but typically emotive. The whole focus was on simplification, on direct and unmediated communication. In his autobiography *A Choice of Weapons,* Parks recounts that in his training Stryker insists that text must "underscore" photographs, that images and words must be "fitted together properly." The text and photos should appear to literalize each other, so the reader has instant apprehension and instant response. Stryker looks at Parks's initial prose and rejects it: "you have to simplify all this material. It would take many years and all the photographers on the staff to fulfil what you have put down here."[56] Parks studies other documentary photographers—Lange, Collier, Evans—and realizes that what he must aim for is conveying contemporary disasters literally, with no ambiguity about their message. *Life* magazine as photojournalism spelled the end of an era of documentary photography because it was undeniably propaganda, making a parody of whatever documentariness there was in documentary photography. The documentary photograph had a title. Photojournalism provides the photograph with a caption and accompanying editorial text, with the result that the meaning of the photograph is anchored down. And captions or editorial text are often used in photojournalism as part of the image, turning photographs into mythologies.

Thus in the introductory issue of the Latin American series, a whole page is given to the hideously enlarged eyes of Fidel Castro, dark-ringed, out of focus, with nothing else of the face visible. Text is used not only to underscore but as part of the face. "The editors of LIFE present a New Series"—and then massively enlarged, too, and in between and below the eyes instead of the face, "CRISIS in LATIN AMERICA." The lower part of the page is used to literalize the image: "The messianic eyes of Fidel Castro," as the text declares, preside over what determines the content of later *Life* issues. He is the "face of the troubles of Latin America."[57] In the upcoming issues *Life* would show photographs of banners of Castro surrounded by firebrands at protest rallies across Latin America—as if Castro's face was incendiary, prefigurative of continental communist revolution—and add other faces, among them that of the popular land reformer Francisco Julião from northeast Brazil, who was organizing the first landless movement in Brazil and who suggested the Cuban Revolution as precedent. And in Flavio *Life* finds another face that, as "poverty always has a human face" the presentation urges, could become Castro's if his poverty was not alleviated. Faces are given masks, meaning, especially with the success of Parks's own technique in photobiography which is exceptional in these issues in representing poverty instead of through several Latin American countries by a single boy in Brazil. After his contravening their instruction, *Life* initially decided to reduce Parks's photographic-biographic record to a single photograph. But then, with a transitoriness that is how photojournalism works, the magazine changed its mind when Dean Rusk, Kennedy's secretary of state who worried that Quadros was making a populist Peronist turn in Brazil, made clear the inexorably engendering relationship of poverty to communism, warning that very week in the *New York Times* "that if our government didn't give immediate and sizable aid to the poor of Latin America, Communism would surely spread rapidly throughout the hemisphere" (*Flavio* 65). This pronouncement is key to why the story does get published, and Parks personally writes to thank Rusk. Under the title "Freedom's Fearful Foe: Poverty," the colon making simplistically clear that what precedes it is equivalent to what follows it—that "freedom's fearful foe" or communism is a result of poverty, that there is a direct causal relationship—Flavio's story in photo-text format expresses Rusk's worst nightmare. But the effect of Parks's photographs of boy Flavio fulfilled unwittingly the propagandistic remit beyond Rusk's or even Coughlan's and *Life*'s editors' wildest dreams. Embodying his theme in a single boy, Parks makes Flavio a symbol of poverty and saving his life a test case for the U.S. war against communism. From leaving Brazil until Denver—when he made the cover of *Life* magazine—Flavio is according to Parks the most celebrated, mediatized boy in the Western Hemisphere. For a moment.

According to the good old contradictions of the U.S. immigration service and with the very success of the experiment (the U.S. courts reached similarly contradictory decisions regarding Elian Gonzalez's patriation, first that America should save him from Cuba, and then that he should be sent "home" to his father), Flavio is eventually compelled into leaving the United States. Parks seems to sense the contradictions of prematurity and belatedness, the limitations of the project: "we had dreams for Flavio da Silva that were hopelessly beyond his reach. It was as if we expected abundant fruit from a sapling already gone barren" (142). Returned to Brazil in the summer of 1963 when the increasingly left-wing and nationalist successor to Quadros, President João Goulart, was busy fostering new alliances "between the undeveloped nations of Latin America, Africa, and Asia" and pointedly ignoring the United States—when Brazil was most on the verge of a popular social democratic revolution[58]—Flavio no longer serves a useful, elucidatory role for North Americans and the media circus vanishes. Yet Flavio, though back in Brazil, cannot go home again. Initially sent to a boarding school in São Paulo as a kind of halfway house between U.S. affluence and his *favela* poverty, even then Flavio says "America is the only place to be. Brazilians are awful and this school is awful" (159). He is expelled from the school. Attending another school in Rio, his desires for America alienate him from neighborhood boys. He rows with his father and invokes *Life* as a buffer or salvation in his arguments. Flavio's visit to the Time-Life building in New York—where he saw an image of himself and asked for a job—inserted him into the heart of the institution. And his family's experience is no longer the fairy-tale world of *Life*'s rescue. The family still owns the house, but it is a shambles and in disrepair. The contrast between what was and what is Flavio finds traumatic, experiencing "embarrassment at his family's situation" (155–56). And when Parks returns in 1976 after Flavio inherits the remainder of the *Life* fund at twenty-one, we see the horrible irony, the provisionality and regression of the whole project. The mother ends up back washing clothes, the father loses his trucking business, and Flavio feels like they are back in the *favela* again: "Fifteen years of failure showed there beneath a dripping wash. The throwback to a state so close to their former one was hard to accept" (189). Parks "felt as if I were escaping a disaster" (189). Even on Parks's return when Flavio is living poorly but in employment and supporting his family, Flavio is still hankering after a return to America as a way to rescue him from problems—even at the airport as Parks leaves for his flight: "'I think almost every day about going to America, Gordon, to see the places that I once passed and to find all the friends that I know. It would be so good to have a job and live there again. Please, Gordon, see if you can get me back there.' The longing in his eyes was unbearable" (197). Parks wants to say, stop dreaming, those places are passed, but instead is still making promises. "His yearning was honest, poignant. He would go on believing that only in America could he have another chance" (186).

At the time of 1961–63, only José Gallo, a Brazilian working for *Life* in Rio and thus at the border of two national mythologies, recognizes the current of bereavement, of deprivation underlying the whole project—although Flavio's father is suspicious and distrustful of *Life* all along. When Flavio returns to Brazil Gallo "complained that some of the Americans had done more harm than good by spoiling Flavio. He hoped that no one from the States would write him, and that Flavio would forget his whole experience there" (152). *Life* produces no real follow-up story though, amazingly, continues to publicize its role. Flavio-as-Christ is reproduced in a 2000 edition of *"Life" Classic Photographs,* in which we are told that a house was purchased for the family in Brazil and that, in 1986, Flavio had steady jobs, his own house, and a color TV: "Thank God," Flavio is quoted as saying, "dreaming isn't prohibited."[59] There's a shocking editing-out of the dilapidation of the Da Silva house, the failure of the father's job and the reversions that Parks finds in '76. We do not see the loss or the failure to realize dreams that Flavio himself will realize by 1998, when British newspaper the *Guardian* found Flavio to do an update on the boy. At last, he has given up his driving wish and no longer wants to return to the United States. Thirty-seven years later, he is unemployed, divorced, and living in a shed in the back of the house bought for him by *Life*'s readers. The house is now a slum: "he has slipped back into the poverty from which *Life*'s readers thought they had saved him. His life has come full circle." Flavio recognizes that, instead of being given a life, he has had his life taken from him. "As well as feeling he was a foreigner in his own country, Flavio's sense of disillusionment and disorientation was accentuated by having seen the prosperous western world and knowing that he would probably never see it again." He returned home a foreigner. He could no longer speak Portuguese—"I could hardly speak to my friends. . . . I felt that everything had been stolen from me"—and he talks now in broken sentences of English and Portuguese. The trauma was that of being extirpated from his community and thrown back. The Da Silva family talk about how Parks's book *Flavio* was not translated into Portuguese—they never knew what was written. The *Guardian* correspondent (who lives in Brazil) uses the story to deconstruct Western mythology held even to the present day. "Far from being a symbol of how to help the third world, Flavio is perhaps a better example of the difficulties—some may say irresponsibility—of spontaneous acts of charity."[60]

When Parks first takes his camera to the slum, the *favelados* (*favela* inhabitants) seek to dodge his lens. His informant tells him that they believe the camera is "an evil eye that brings bad luck" (28), and in *Flavio* Parks reveals how, in the destructive potential of his "choice of weapon," it does. Flavio as symbol or sign does not get a better life. As foster mother Kathy Gonçalves says, "he couldn't even realize what he was meant to symbolize" (133). The most remarkably interventionist effect of Parks's photographic witnessing is that Flavio is removed from his family and sent to a Denver institute and home for two years. While this might clinically save his life, it also steals his cultural life, and the sacrifice of the son takes on other, irremediable dimensions. When he is taken from his family home, Flavio's mother, Nair, views his departure as loss and, enclosing him in her arms, weeps in grief: Pietà. Ultimately what Parks's photographs "take" from Flavio is Brazil; his photographs initiate the (U.S.) Americanization of Flavio. Flavio is led the American way, which is not so different today. There are always losses entailed in manifest economic and political redemption. With

Flavio's ingenuity, it is likely that he would have got out of the *favela* himself, given evidence of his hard work, as he holds two jobs for years. Perhaps he would even have got further. These *favelas,* historians of Brazil have written, are set up as a route for migrants to better things, to improvement; people struggle out. But what does it mean to photograph someone's life and to change it? What of self-consciousness and after-effects—remorse, atonement for sacrifice of other—in the photographer?

GHOSTS OF MY OWN PAST

The other intriguing aspect of the story concerns the other player in it. What was Parks's role, and especially why the return to write about it seventeen years after taking the photographs? By 1978 Brazil had a change in government, with a military dictatorship in power. The gap between rich and poor had grown and there were new *favelas* sprouting around the country. But the United States is no longer interested to the same extent. The Carter years beginning in 1976 practiced a deliberate policy of non-intervention in Latin America following post-Vietnam remorse (though it was not to last long—Reagan in the 1980s, in the Iran-Contra affair, reverted to U.S. custom). Parks discusses none of these political changes. His decision to go back is made, according to *Flavio,* apparently on impulse. In '76 he decides to visit Brazil and seek out Flavio on a trip back from Argentina, when asked by a clerk in a Buenos Aires shoe store about Flavio's current welfare. The return to Brazil may be to satisfy his curiosity. But one doesn't write a book—and indeed what is a biography—on impulse, or to satisfy one's own or a reader's curiosity. Instead "confusion and guilt" (51) seem to be at work. Guilt is one of the most repeated affects of Parks's text, a regret tied up with displacement, dislocation, and Americanization. A photographic memoir, what *Flavio* adds to the original assignment is, in fact, autobiography, the life of self interwoven around (in exchange with) the story of the other in photographs. Released from a photojournalistic context, *Flavio* is less a simple social document of Flavio's life than it might initially seem. Only the middle section is mostly documentary, in the account of Flavio's life in America for two years when he's at the institute and not part of Parks's life—when Parks is out getting a life, getting assignments, and getting known as a result of the Flavio story. Even then Parks writes of his guilt for not giving Flavio personal attention. In the tradition of documentary photography the impression is of an omniscient camera with the photographer invisible. In the photographer's autobiography Parks includes his self, his presence as part of the story of his subjects' lives, and perhaps in terms of revelations this is his most autobiographical text. The chronic distance on the assignment allows Parks's anxious reflections to come to the fore. Retrospective as well as self-conscious and reflective, Parks's palinode *Flavio* encourages Parks to assess his own role in the story. Like Lévi-Strauss he returns, in relation to photography, to the problems of witnessing and observation. *Life* magazine has gone, made obsolete possibly by television, Parks thinks. From this point on, Flavio "would be keeper of his own memoirs" (168). Yet Flavio is not so, and Parks continues to record and to entangle Flavio's life in his own—and to write Flavio's memoir. What is at stake in the autobiographical element of this entanglement? In the return, in the palinode, the photographer expresses doubts about his profession. *Flavio* is more about himself and the subsequent effects of his photography. *Flavio* shows how Parks becomes too involved in Flavio's life. The realization and renunciation are perhaps not always conscious, but they are what come back belatedly.

What returns in *Flavio* is the remarkable intrusion of a photographer's self into his subject's life far in excess of the participant observation of his documentary photography. Parks writes in *Flavio* of how his engagement with Flavio quickly moves beyond that initial photographic assignment to record and beyond politics. He recognizes that as a photojournalist he should be emotionally disinterested. "I tried to be objective. The fact that I had become deeply attached to Flavio was irrelevant. After all, his real importance was not this personal bond, but the fact that he was the medium through which I could show the ugliness of poverty to millions of people. For a moment, I was like the man who is proud of his inability to shed a tear—free of any sentimental attachment to an experience. I would be a tougher, better reporter for this" (51). But he experiences real conflict. After three weeks, New York *Life* is concerned about his silence, and he is concerned that perhaps they'll feel he's changed the story and got too close to it. His account of taking the photographs is a paradox: "Flavio's predicament was my story" (24), but he can't simply witness the predicament. The point is that he can't leave Flavio simply as a story. How wonderful to change the life: to rescript the story. Becoming more and more immersed, he enters into that other world—that underworld. We see the contrast between Parks's world and the photographed, as Parks is increasingly unable to spend time at his Copacabana hotel—with its food and perfection and beauty and the size of his room—after the shack. He goes to the *favela* at night, ignoring advice not to risk his life thus. He enters into their lives. He holds Flavio when he coughs, he removes a nail from the younger child's foot, he stops the children fighting and brings them gifts of food concealed in his camera case so as not to upset the economy. But he does upset the economy, and on their moving the Da Silvas incur the wrath of the other *favelados*. They need to move because of the effects of outside intervention, because they have no answer to the others' question: why not us?

And at the time of taking the photographs in 1961, although he had been at *Life* magazine some twelve years, when the editors of *Life* decided to publish only one photograph of Flavio in keeping with their initial instruction and limited space—and then opposite a fashion shoot—Parks compromised his career. Furious and emotional, he dashes off his letter of resignation. He was prepared to give up his professional life at *Life* magazine over Flavio's representation, no negligible sacrifice given how hard he had struggled as the first African American photographer there. And even after he realized that with his initial visit he had fulfilled his assignment as a photojournalist, Parks nevertheless wants to save and intervene in that life but is constantly drawn up short by his ability and the ethical rectitude of his attempt. The regret and guilt follow him even seventeen years after the assignment—for planting the dream and then realizing its impossibility.

> I couldn't respond to his desire to return to a place that only existed in his memory. I felt that I had already shuffled his dreams too much. Those of us who had in some way touched his life witnessed an incredible experience. But now I was asking myself what that experience really meant. The miracles of energy that took place on Catacumba were dissipated; it was as though they had never been. The Da Silva family was better off, but their experience was precarious, in fact tragic. Flavio had survived the Catacumba. But it looked as if he had gone as far as he could go in his lifetime. Now that his life had been saved, I hoped that he would not waste it chasing a futile dream. (197)

One situation illustrates the remarkable intervention and shuffles Parks's own dreams. Wracked by the guilt of his distance from the situation he is photographing, he travels one night from his beachfront hotel to the *favela*. It is well past midnight but, he writes, he lets himself into the Da Silva one-room shack, where the family sleeps crammed on one bed, and settles down to watch, not photographing but an observing presence. "I sat in the strange darkness watching the embers cooling and falling into ashes, unable to find my place in such an experience" (49). He remembers the dream he had in the shack—and it is remarkable as the one dream in *Flavio*. The passage continues: "Eventually I fell into a nightmare of sleep. The great concrete statue of Christ tumbled backward into the favela crumbling the hills and its shacks into a river of terror. There were coffins filled with garbage and human limbs" (49). He had visited the Corcovado that morning, intending to photograph it but unable to because it was covered in a heavy fog; he returns in the afternoon to Flavio, whom he does photograph and who becomes his subject. Flavio, the substitute Christ symbol, is here destroyed by the Christ of suffering and redemption so important to the book—the Cristo who not only hangs over the *favela* but figuratively over the whole narrative. About the destruction by a Christ who is meant to be a redeemer—*redentor*, this zenith of redemption—the dream suggests the disturbing effect of redemption, of intervention on the *favela*. Does the dream betray Parks's anxiety about the potentially devastating effects of his own "evil eye"?

With Parks focusing on the boy, instead of the father as he was instructed to do by *Life* magazine, at first Flavio seems like Parks's surrogate son. Parks is a substitute parent in place of negligent parents too distracted by poverty or their own suffering. Flavio asked Parks to keep him as a son before returning, and Parks even considers adopting Flavio. In a slip in the text he refers to Flavio as his natural father José da Silva's "troublesome stepson" (168). (A current Web site states that Parks, in effect, adopted Flavio and still calls him in Brazil "to this day").[61] Driving back and forth from his hotel in Copacabana to the shack in Catacumba, Parks forms, in his account of the assignment in *Flavio,* a potential paternity: "I could not help but compare the good fortune of my own children with the fate of these others. Fate might have so easily reversed the circumstances" (51). Parks's dedication of *Flavio* to his own daughter seems to underline these lines that cross and diverge in the narrative but only by chance. Yet more profoundly there is a generational slip. It suggests his continuing uncertainty about his autobiographical place in relation to his photography. Parks himself begins with a life almost identical to Flavio's, that had a good deal more in common with the Da Silvas' fight for survival in a Rio *favela* than does his own children's comfortable middle-class life on their Long Island home. Parks's mandate from *Life,* "Find an impoverished father with a family of eight or ten children. Show how he earns a living, the amount he earns a year" could be an instruction to return to his own past. Parks departs early on, to make a better life from a poor Kansas childhood, a family of fourteen brothers and sisters, and an apparently uncaring father for whom he appears to have as little sympathy as he does for José da Silva. He experiences periods of homelessness and moves into the ghetto in Harlem during the Depression where he describes being surrounded by squalor. In his account of Flavio's circumstances, he constantly interweaves his own identification. His own poverty and Harlem and Chicago's South Side seemed "pale by comparison" to the poverty and hunger of the *favela* (19). His desire to make things different for Flavio is to fulfill, he says, the wishes in this child he himself had as a child for things he could never have. His *Choice of Weapons* chronicles in detail the context of exclusion faced by a young boy and his family growing up amidst segregation and lynchings in the United States, with Parks torn between absorption by national mythologies and opposing them. "I stood before the cracked mirror in our house and wondered why God had made me black, and I remembered the dream I once had of being white, with skin so flabby and loose that I attempted to pull it into shape" (8). "At fourteen, in the black-and-white world of Kansas, anyone whiter than I became my enemy" (8). The struggle is in identification. In *Moments without Proper Names* he reveals autobiographical origins for photographs. "I was born to a black childhood of confusion and poverty. The memory of that beginning influences my work today. It is impossible for me now to photograph a hungry child without remembering the hunger of my own childhood. Time has taught me that it is not enough to look, condemn, or praise—or to be just an observer. I must attempt to transcend the limitations of my own experience by sharing, as deeply as possible, the problems of those I photograph. . . . We must give up silent watching and put our commitments into practice" (7). And the point is that his photographs are beyond testimony and that he can't just watch. As if, as another critic writes of a documentary photographer who was a precedent for Parks, "The story that seeks to 'know' through what it can 'see' of the other finds, not the other, but itself."[62]

Parks punctuated his work with reflections on his photography and makes repeated returns to consider his own place in relation to his subjects. His oeuvre is marked by serial autobiography, which suggests something unworked-through about the life and his career. He wrote his early life as "a novel from life" first in 1963, later as a screenplay for the film *The Learning Tree* in 1968; this was recast as autobiography in *A Choice of Weapons* in 1965, and part two followed as *To Smile in Autumn: A Memoir* in 1979. Finally—but is it?—the life was integrated in *Voices in the Mirror* in 1990. Such repeated revisions constitute constant self-assessment and betray anxiety about self-representation and self in relation to representation. *Born Black* for instance, a collection in 1971 of assignments Parks took for *Life* magazine between 1960 and 1970, intercalates moments from Parks's life with classic photographs, not as if they were identical but as if he were trying to close the gap between self and other, personal and career: past and present.[63] Parks personally got involved with and tried to help several of his subjects, long after he took their pictures. Next to Flavio the most prominent story is that of the Fontenelles. The Fontenelles were a poor

African American family living in Harlem whom Parks photographed for *Life* magazine after Flavio. Assuring the family the community would benefit from the photographs, Parks was allowed to live with the Fontenelles and to photograph them for one month. Parks faces the same struggle over objectivity and remaining outside. "It was difficult not to immediately, being in my position, take money in, take food in, to ease their situation. Because the minute you do that you've lost your story. So you pray and hope that you can get your story over as quickly as possible, and that there will be a response from the public." There was a response and with readers' donations again *Life* enables the Fontenelles in '68 to move to a house on Long Island. But this help, too, might be seen as containment, since *Life's* editor had asked Parks to explain why black people were rioting through urban areas and *Life's* answer once again is economic. The father came back drunk one night, caused a fire—and died in the fire with one child. The end of it all, at least for Parks, is that the mother wants to go back to Harlem, and Parks pays for the mother's funeral. "The whole family was destroyed," Parks sighs. "The problem in documenting a family like that," he explains, "is that, you wonder, in the end, whether you should have touched the family, or just left them alone."[64] This assignment in turn becomes cause for anxious return, a canvas for many of the same ph/autographical doubts that surround Flavio—"Perhaps I shouldn't have touched that family, I thought to myself"; "it's impossible to detach yourself. You become a part of the family. They become a part of you. I am still a part of the Fontenelles."[65] Indeed it is the Fontenelles who are evoked at the beginning of *Flavio*—"a private tragedy at once very public—and I became caught up in their struggle to survive it" (7).

But although the Fontenelle story is more dramatic—a literal loss of life for which Parks cannot exonerate himself—and has more in common with his own black rural Kansas childhood, Flavio's is the most returned to and elucidated, for himself, the most returned to, compulsively, irrepressibly. After initial publication on June 16, 1961, was followed up by an update on July 21, 1961, Parks made a film of his assignment in 1964, shown on NBC in 1966.[66] In 1974 his collection *Moments without Proper Names* republished Flavio's images embedded in a poem. In 1978 we have *Flavio*, his autobiographical memoir account of photographing. And in 1990 Parks reflects on Flavio in two chapters in his latest autobiography, *Voices in the Mirror*. What is a puzzle is why it should be Flavio who becomes vehicle for Parks's palinode, why he should devote to him his only book-length account of photographing one subject. Flavio is the one white subject and the one non-U.S. subject whom Parks has focused on in his documentary photography (he photographed some fashion models for *Vogue* and poverty in Portugal in the fifties before joining *Life*). The choice might seem all the more surprising given that the book *Flavio* itself opens not with Flavio's story but an account of the Fontenelles. In the foreword to *Flavio,* which considers photojournalism as destructive, Parks suggests why this Brazilian boy fascinates. There are two stories, the Fontenelles and the Da Silvas. Parks tries here to differentiate the Da Silva story from the Fontenelles, the success of the first in contrast to the disaster of the second—but *Flavio* contains precisely doubt and uncertainty about the involvement of the photographer. *Flavio* begins with an autobiographical reflection on a photojournalist career—and regret: "As a photojournalist I have on occasion done stories that have seriously altered human lives. In hindsight, I sometimes wonder if it may not have been wiser to have left those lives untouched, to have let them grind out their time as fate intended" (7). He sets out his belief that "The condition of anyone hopelessly ensnared in such misery and poverty could only be helped, I thought, by its exposure in such a great magazine" (8). He then takes his photography into his self and expresses uncertainty about its beneficial role. "From the outset of each assignment to its very end, I reported objectively. But in the end, my emotions, which are by nature subjective, took over. Disguising these emotions in objective clothing I dug deeper and deeper into the privacy of these lives, hoping, I realize now, to reshape their destinies into something better. Unconsciously, I was perhaps playing God. I hold a fierce grudge against poverty because I was so desperately poor when I was young" (9). And it is in giving his account of this assignment that in his autobiography *Voices in the Mirror* he explains his autobiographical involvement in his photographic subjects thus: "I have for a long time, worked under the premise that everyone is worth something; that every life is valuable to our own existence. Consequently, I've felt it was my camera's responsibility to shed light on any condition that hinders growth or warps the spirit of those trapped in the ruinous evils of poverty. . . . To me, they were ghosts of my own past" (179–80).

In confessing in his autobiography that he photographs ghosts of his own past, Parks finds in the image not only not the other and his self but his past self; the images are ghosts of his own past, and in this sense the photographs are a haunting of the present by the past (the dead past self of me alive in the other). It casts documentary photography as a much more ominous—and literal—taking of a life. The racial and national complexities of African American photographer identifying more with the white Brazilian boy than other poor African Americans might be the key to the conundrum. Parks remarks more than once in *Flavio* that his assignment and his photographs are facilitated by his "dark skin" (42), which allows him to blend in with the Brazilian poor amongst whom Flavio lives and who are themselves mostly black. A local television cameraman, blond, comes to film Parks photographing Flavio. Oddly Parks feels the need to "shield" Flavio and the Da Silvas from the local filming (41). Some *favelados* notice the white cameraman and rough him up. African American Parks is seen as insider and the (white) Luso-Brazilian as an outsider/ intruder. But Parks feels shame: "I felt deeply ashamed to have been spared their spittle. My dark skin had saved me—and I wasn't very proud of it" (42). When marked out as different among the white Da Silvas, in his initial account of his assignment, Parks is seen not as black but as American. He gives the children cruzeiros, and they still want more money, forcing their hands into his pockets: "Americano, mawny, mawny, mawny, Americano!" Here, it is his language and his camera that set him apart, not his skin—as American.[67] Unconsciously but inevitably perhaps, he is drawn into a history of African American ambivalence toward Brazil, which has mythologized itself as a color-blind nation, whose central mythology perhaps is that it has no color line.[68] One can be definitive of, represent, the nation, but at the expense—in sacrifice—of what? Why, after all, does Parks choose a white subject when *favelados* tend to be darker than most Brazilians, and certainly darker than the apparently white *Luso* Flavio?[69] Is it to encourage identification among *Life*'s readers? One wonders if the same amount of money would have flowed in had Flavio been in Brazil *and* black. There is a deep irony in Parks's disturbing of Brazil in *Flavio*, given his critique of America and his combating of racism and poverty in the United States—and at this time he was photographing the rise of Black Nationalism in the United States. This irony corresponds to splits in racial and national institutions in Parks's life. He achieves a Rosenwald Fellowship which starts his career photographing Chicago's South Side and African Americans. But to fund this work he photographs fashion assignments and white society ladies. As a *Life* photographer he documents racism. But out on *Life* assignments he is himself confronted with racism and segregation. Writing in a collection that brings together his classic photographs of African American life, Parks wonders if his career has required him to leave black culture. "I wondered whether or not my achievements in the white world had cost me a certain objectivity. I could not deny that I had stepped a great distance from the mainstream of Negro life, not by intention, but by circumstance. In fulfilling my artistic and professional ambitions in the white man's world, I had had to become completely involved in it."[70] While Parks's identity with his subjects enabled his photographs, his success in institutions interposed a distance. It is in relation to Flavio that the contradiction between outsiderness and opposition, and belonging and assimilation is dramatized. He is most insistently Americanized in this assignment, not only part of the national mythology. The publication of these photographs, in *Life* magazine, makes Parks purveyor of the national mythology. Caught up in *Life*'s propagandistic machine, in his Flavio assignment Parks's eye is strategically white, his I—worried, regretful. Flavio represents his palinode as an inverted (negative) reflection of his own departures. Photography has propelled Parks into a white man's world; Flavio as a poor white boy living in Brazil is a ghost of his own past. The text *Flavio* is less an attempt to recover the life than, through retelling Flavio's loss, the echo of a melancholic doubt, not till then expressible about his subjects, about whether Parks saved the life and indeed lost his own. Flavio's story repeats his own loss—but without the mythology of redemption of *Life* magazine. *Life*'s photographs took a life. But as to whose life has been taken and in what sense they have taken a life remain—open.

In one of his reflections on Flavio in his collection *Moments without Proper Names*, Parks writes a poem about a stranger watching a sick boy.

> A stranger, uninvited but expected,
> Coming from a distance
> That only a mind could travel
> Sat silent outside the door,
> Patiently feeling the pulse
> Of this stilt-leg house,
> This minute scrap
> On a mountain's festered side.
>
> Inside, crumpled in his fevered bed,
> A boy lay, silent too, thinking,
> Trying not to remember much,
>
> Knowing that there wasn't much to remember,
> only that
> His knees stood just above the weeds,
> only that
> His shadow still slanted short
> Beyond the hot glow of late suns that
>
> Cut across steaming paths
> (Dung paths of man and dog alike)

Where only beasts should have to climb.
Why then, asked this boy of so few moments,
Should this stranger have come so soon
To sit uninvited at his door?[71]

We only know that the boy who tries not to remember too much is Flavio because the poem is reproduced amid images of Flavio. But there is confusion about who the uninvited observing stranger is. By the end of the poem it turns out to be death, who then waits for another night. But at the beginning of the poem the reader, especially the one who knows the Flavio story and *Flavio,* thinks that the stranger could be the photographer. Does Parks's encounter with Flavio rescue Flavio from the underworld or condemn him to it? Does Parks's involvement with his subjects represent the photographer's redemption from his underworld or his return to it? Is it coincidental that, since *Flavio,* since about the late 1970s, Parks has retreated from his career as a documentary photographer and laid aside that weapon increasingly to take photographs instead of nature—more painterly and abstract images, consciously poetic and less realistic? He has also worked on his music as well as his poetry, for he learned piano from his mother, and has gone on to compose a symphony, sonatas, concertos, and a ballet on the life of Martin Luther King. In interview in 1998, Parks, then almost of an age to rival Lévi-Strauss's venerable years, states "You know, the camera is not meant just to show misery. You can show beauty with it; you can do a lot of things. You can show—with a camera you can show things that you like about the universe, things that you hate about the universe. It's capable of doing both. And I think that after nearly 85 years upon this planet that I have a right after working so hard at showing the desolation and the poverty, to show something beautiful for somebody as well. It's all there, and you've only done half the job if you don't do that. You've not really completed a task."[72] This trajectory, from photojournalism to art photography, tells of disillusion with documentary photography and the approximation of a poetic conception of photography, one that doesn't insist on revealing truth or perhaps offers a different kind of truth—allusive, lyrical, missing: losing. In one of Parks's latest books, *Arias in Silence* published in 1994, his foreword draws our attention to the fact that this is a collection of photographs not of crime, racism, and poverty but of nature.[73] "Arias in silence" also poignantly suggests the necessary limits on speech and the powers of communication. Nevertheless, like photography conceived through music as silent imagery, there is a paradoxical and rather mad recognition—the recognition of the palinode—of the need to say this.

The final chapter of *Flavio* is where Parks really confronts what has been the effect of his photographs. He returns in 1976 with the adult Flavio to the site where he first photographed the boy. Skirting the Lagoa or "lagoon," where in 1961 "the lovely sweep of water . . . divided the shacks of the favelados from the radiant white homes of the rich" (191), Parks writes that now as he looks to the Catacumba the *favela* has gone along with all *Life*'s improvements to it. Closed by the state governor Carlos Lacerda who used funds from the Alliance for Progress, for his "Battle of Rio" declared that the *favelados* needed to be evicted "before the Communists get to them"[74]—or moved to other parts of Rio depending on the extent of your vision—the Catacumba hill in 1979 opened as a park with sculptures. For Parks, the *favela* and its struggles had reverted to an original state of nature. "I got out and looked skyward. Cristo Redentor was still there, strongly silhouetted against the darkening clouds. Now I looked just below it. The favela of Catacumba was no more. Where once there had been thousands of shanties clinging to the mountainside, there were now only acres of unkempt tropical foliage. It was staggering" (192). They climb. "The silence of those who had died on Catacumba mingled with the silence of those who had escaped it. . . . And why had we come back to this tomb of bad memories, other than to recall its misery?" (193). Why indeed resurrect this tomb of the Catacomb, ascend to a place to which one ought in the scheme of things descend—a world as topsy-turvy as Toni Morrison's Bottom at the top of a hill?[75] Actually, it's as if the slum had never been there. "As we drove away I turned for one final look, still amazed at how nature had so thoroughly reclaimed the poisonous mountainside" (194). The closing motif, Parks tries to see this forgetting as hopeful and to take the story forward, to the next generation. He concludes that, if we are unsure about the success of Flavio's life, the juxtaposition of Flavio adult with Flavio's own son, Flavio junior—enabled by a photograph of the new Flavio falling out of a billfold Flavio senior gives him before Parks boards his plane and placed next to an old Parks photograph of Flavio at the same age—provides the movement of desire, of Parks's desire: "I stared at the two faces for several moments, realizing suddenly now what the point of Flavio's story was—it lay in this boy" (198). The mood is propulsive but the direction of *Flavio* has been all retrospective, to take us back. The most poignant photograph in the republished *Flavio* is perhaps the final, of adult Flavio looking at photographs of *himself* as a child taken by Parks. I'm not sure that, in *Flavio,* Parks lays to rest his own ghosts. And certainly in his adulthood Flavio remains haunted by his past experience and by Parks.

CHAPTER 4

ELIZABETH BISHOP'S ART OF LOSING

LOOKING FOR SOMETHING, SOMETHING, SOMETHING

In her explicitly autobiographical poem "In the Waiting Room" (the only place where she names herself), Elizabeth Bishop describes the sense of loss that comes from looking at photographs in the *National Geographic* magazine. What the child Elizabeth "carefully / studied" are the ethnographic photographs, particularly of "black, naked women with necks / wound round and round with wire / like the necks of light bulbs. / Their breasts were horrifying." The child reads the magazine straight through, "too shy to stop." In the poem's lack of narrative transition our eye travels with Bishop's. "Suddenly, from inside, / came an *oh!* of pain." The cry, which Bishop first thinks comes from Aunt Consuelo but then is surprised to discover comes from her own mouth, appears to issue from inside those photographs. Bishop writes of the effect of the moment as "I—we—were falling, falling, / our eyes glued to the cover / of the *National Geographic*, February 1918." The "we" must include the women in the magazine. In the midst of "the sensation of falling off / the round, turning world," Bishop realizes "you are an *I*, you are an *Elizabeth*, / you are one of *them*"; but *what* this is she scarcely dare look at. She knows that "nothing stranger / had ever happened / that nothing / stranger could ever happen." What the child awakens to, in the real of the photographs, is the loss of mastery that underlies every moment of self-knowledge.[1]

Throughout her life Bishop was reluctant to be photographed or to send photographs of herself. In a letter to a photographer renowned for her work of authors, Bishop shied at once from photographical and autobiographical exposure. "Maybe one has no right to one's own life or looks."[2] Bishop's reservations about the autobiographical, tied here to the photographical, distinguish her poetry. Her contemporaries of the 1950s and '60s—Robert Lowell, Sylvia Plath, Anne Sexton—took themselves as subjects. Whereas the confessionalists went public with the private, ironically a trajectory that goes from inside to out, Bishop moved from the outside in: from geography to the self as in "The Waiting Room" to produce a geography of the self. She can seem the more introspective and self-reflective poet. She insisted that her poems were "almost invariably just plain facts" about a place (*One Art* 621). Yet like the twice misreferencing of photographs that critics found her doing in "The Waiting Room" and after (there are no photographs of African women or babies in the February 1918 issue of the *National Geographic,* nor in the subsequent issue as Bishop claimed in interview),[3] it is the wavering around the referent, the *almost* invariably that is striking. Can facts ever be variably plain? Can the photograph, this most referential of forms, represent something that's not only no longer there but that's never been there? At issue is how forms such as poetry and photography capture fact. Can one ever represent the facts of a place, of a life, above all in poetry, which is surely the most mediated literary form, the most linguistically self-conscious: one that—particularly as Bishop practiced it as an expert and committed metrician—depends on the "mastery of . . . art"?[4]

The visual, long recognized by critics as prominent in Bishop's poetry, is an attempt to get at the facts but with an awareness of mediation. Bonnie Costello calls Bishop's "a poetry of looks." Harold Bloom says of the "reality of Bishop's famous eye" "it confronts the truth." And Adrienne Rich finds that in Bishop's poetry "the eye of the outsider" enables an identification with other outsiders—but this is too unmediated, as the shifting, thwarted glances and the broken phrasal lines of "In the Waiting Room" show.[5] The perspective that Anne Stevenson notes in Bishop's poetry, what she later calls Bishop's quality as a "word painter," needs to be taken literally and therefore meticulously and poetically.[6] Bishop saw herself as more visual than most poets; she was flattered by the early comment that she was a poet with a painter's eye.[7] Her painterliness has been brought out by the recent publication of her watercolors, which are characterized by their minuteness of observation and self-consciousness of perspective.[8] Like her poetry they show the facts and the problems of representation. *Anjinhos* ("Angels") is inspired by the drowning of a young girl in Rio de Janeiro. As a collage it is made up of detritus of the fact, flotsam of the real: a sandal, shells, a child's dummy, dead butterflies. But these objects are framed in a glass box, Cornell-like: "Objects and Apparitions," as Bishop titled the poem she translated by Octavio Paz about Joseph Cornell. *Cabin with Porthole* similarly documents a ship's cabin during a journey—suitcase, notebooks; fan, flowers—with an exactitude and simplicity of the primitives she so admired, like Gregorio Valdes (who did his best work copying from photographs).[9] But the open porthole again inserts a frame and suggests the difficulty of distinguishing inside from out. In her notebooks Bishop wrote that on board ship, especially with the cabin's lens-like window, travelling produced "some physical shift . . . in one's self," and because of the round porthole the sensation is "of being in a box-camera, of being 'exposed' to the sea & sky—*(camera obscura)*."[10] In the dark room of the ship's cabin an acutening—or rather an *acutance* (photographic sharpening)—in the self's consciousness takes place. We might compare this click or shift to "that sense of constant readjustment" which is loved by the acutely self-conscious early "Gentleman of Shalott" and found throughout Bishop's poetry. The poems like the artwork see the thing but never quite fixedly and never finally. Of oil hitting water Bishop searches out the best way to describe the color produced, and the poem becomes a record of not resolving that search—adjustment in punctuated aside: "like bits of mirror—no, more blue than that: / like tatters of the *Morpho* butterfly." Substitution, or repetition (the latter anaphora), is typical of Bishop. An art of self-correction, it suggests not approximation of perfection but the failure of getting it right. The thing itself, like a butterfly, just escapes. Doubt is intrinsic to Bishop's unbelieving art.[11]

As the cabin/camera analogy suggests, the lack of settling representationally is enfolded in Bishop's work with an unwillingness to settle geographically. Travelling is what shifts perspective. The other place makes you look, makes you notice things, Bishop is remembered by friends as discussing.[12] The visual text that is the consistent analogy for and often subject of Bishop's poetry is the map. Mapping transcribes real space into cartographic representation. As she says in the opening "lessons" of *Geography III* just before "In the Waiting Room," the map is "A description of the earth's surface," "A picture of the whole or a part of the / Earth's surface." But mapping as a form of mastery loses the real. The *National Geographic,* for which mapping remains a principal vehicle of representation, casts its masterful eye over the world. (In its hallmark shots in the vault of Bishop's memory, "Thousands of young boys viewed female breasts for the first time in its pages, a display considered, curiously, not indecent, because they belonged to women of another race."[13] In her letters Bishop called the *National Geographic* "silly"—although she says "I'll buy it just for the photographs" [*One Art* 341].) In *Geography III* in the epigraph, Bishop's proliferating questions override any didactic conclusions we can draw from the opening lessons of her mock childhood primer: *Geography III*. Travelling posed questions for Bishop in excess of answers. Her volume of poetry *Questions of Travel* begins with an awareness that there is a "childishness" in rushing "to see the sun the other way around," to shift perspective through travel. Her notebooks remark on how this desire can become "the god-like ambition to see what something looks like from *there*—or what 'here' looks like from 'there.'" But it is also possible in the process of travelling to find oneself as exposed as a child, inside that camera, not mastering the other but feeling uncertainty about, even losing, the self. "One holds on to the child's sides of one's berth—as if one were going somewhere," Bishop notes, still on board ship. And on arrival in her strange city she writes this is how the world must seem to a child. The child's sense of wonder, seeing for the first time, doesn't translate the seen fully.

Questions of Travel is Bishop's book of poetry about Brazil and this is where she was headed, for the first time when writing these notebooks. To "see the sun the other way around" is of course to cross the equator, which Bishop did, in her voyage from Brooklyn to Brazil in 1951. Brazil especially brought out her "acutance" of observation and compelled her to ask questions. She found a culture overwhelmed by detail to which she, as an outsider, was attuned: "a good place for the keen observer. It is teeming with particularities," as a friend who also spent much time there commented.[14] Settling in Brazil—at least the longest she settled anywhere in her life—Bishop translated a child's narrative, Helena Morley's *Minha vida de menina* (My Life as a Little Girl). What she liked was Helena's precision of observation; as she puts it in the introduction, "*it really happened*; everything did take place . . . just the way Helena says it did."[15] She later attributed realism as a Brazilian characteristic (*One Art* 434). Marianne Moore, the poet with whom Bishop had most in common in her precision of observation, in her review said that Bishop as translator was attracted to qualities she shared with her Brazilian subject, in particular a "hyper-precise eye."[16] *Minha vida* was also an autobiographical work: both the original narrative and Bishop's act of translating it.

Brazil drove Bishop at this later stage of her life to recollect her own childhood. *Questions of Travel* contains in a section titled "Elsewhere" poems about her early life in Nova Scotia. It was also in Brazil that she wrote many of the prose pieces about her childhood, including "In the Village" that sits between the "Elsewhere" and "Brazil" sections of *Questions of Travel*, neither separating nor connecting them. If Brazil posed travel as a question for Bishop, she never quite answered fully, and the significance of that "almost invariably" is that she doesn't close the gap between origin and destination—though her desire is surely there and evident. *Questions of Travel* begins with poems that see Brazil through the self-conscious, self-questioning tourists' arrival. Geography is the subject but mediated. The most realistic poem, "The Burglar of Babylon," retells an event from the *favelas* of Rio: the police shooting of a young *favelado*. When it was originally published the poem was prefaced by Bishop's insistence that everything in it, "often word for word," is true.[17] Bishop watched the episode through binoculars and included this detail in the poem: "Rich people in the apartments / Watched through binoculars." Hers is *a* perspective, not necessarily *the*. Her longest poem accumulates other voices including that of the burglar, his aunt, residents—and the soldiers who shoot him.[18] In the form of a ballad moreover with its origins in the folk song, "Burglar" is particularly responsive to its probably illiterate subject. (Bishop had the poem published as a book for children.) In other Brazil poems Bishop describes Brazilian realities with similar consciousness of perspective. In "The Squatter's Children" the children at first are "specklike" from the point of view of the "sun's suspended eye" suspended in the lines below them. In "Going to the Bakery (Rio de Janeiro)," the moon's gaze takes us down a columnar poem to the "glazed white eye" of the sickly cakes on sale in inflation-stricken, rationing Brazil.

If painting is an analogy for mediation of reality in Bishop's poetry, photography as in "The Waiting Room" draws our attention to what gets lost in mediation, what can't be caught; for that "almost" of the invariable proves a chasm. Photography appears elsewhere in Bishop's poetry and prose. In "First Death in Nova Scotia," one of the poetic returns to childhood enabled by Brazil, little cousin Arthur is "laid out" dead by *her* mother, beneath the chromographs (early color photographs) of the current royal family. At the end of the poem they "invited Arthur to be / the smallest page at court," to enter *into* the photograph. For the child Elizabeth the photograph is the place where the dead go. In a childhood prose memoir again written in Brazil, "Memories of Uncle Neddy," the arrival in Rio of two painted portraits of her uncle and mother as children, "these ancestor-children," sends Bishop back to the family album to compare "tintypes" (photographs on tin plate)—"And although she has been dead for over forty years," to look at photographs of her mother as a child.[19] For less metropolitan Brazilians, she writes of the arrival of photographs, "all portraits apparently strike them as being of dead people" (*One Art* 346). Photography sets up another encounter with death and dying, and tellingly more explicitly this time her dead mother. Her memories of Neddy are recollected in place of those of her mother, because her mother's madness and confinement to a mental institution when Bishop was five meant her early and final absence from Bishop's life. Bishop never saw her mother again. But she lived until Bishop graduated from college. Finally in a poem translated by Bishop but included in her own *Complete Poems*, "Retrato de Família" ("Family Portrait") by Carlos Drummond de Andrade, the photograph is not simply frozen in lost time but its personages could still fly from the portrait, hide. The portrait does not communicate. It does not distinguish the living from the dead. There is only through it "the strange idea of family / travelling through the flesh."

Bishop worked on two collections of photographs in her life. One was published, the other not. When the photographer turns to poetry he retreats from documentary truth. What happens in the inverse? Why would the poet turn from her most linguistic medium of poetry to this message without a code? Bishop likened her observational eye to her intently focused "Sandpiper": "Yes, all my life I have lived and behaved very much like that sandpiper—just running along the edges of different countries and continents, 'looking for something.'"[20] If she never quite found it—probably a home inside and outside herself: a geography of the self—or if, rather, she found she had repeatedly lost what she'd found, her engagement with photographs propelled her each time more deeply into that missing.

Why Not Tell the Truth?

Seen as an authentic representation of Brazil and an addition to Bishop's oeuvre if read superficially; shunned as superficial and incongruous with the oeuvre when read thoroughly: Bishop's published volume of photographs, *Brazil*, has had a mixed critical fate.[21] Appearing with Time-Life publications in early 1962, it was the one book she regretted in her life. As late as 1977 two years before her death, she said she chose not to remember much of the book.[22] She had troubles with the form, particularly with the journalistic brief. "Probably no one reads the text, anyway, just looks at the photographs. . . . that kind of writing is hard for me to do and I have to cover the whole country . . . *everything*, even if superficially" (*One Art* 399). She also hated the institution of *Life*. The reason for her taking on the project is that they could afford to pay her as no publisher could for her poetry. She received $10,000 plus expenses, three complimentary weeks in New York, and an excuse to travel in Brazil. "I don't like the magazine and don't like *them* much—these high-pressure-salesman types—but I am doing it for the money—and I do know a lot about Brazil by now, of course, willy-nilly" (399). What she feared is that they would put her knowledge "through their own meat grinder, lawfully, and it will come out sounding like them no matter what I say"; "It is really more like manufacturing synthetic whipped cream out of the by-products of a plastic factory than anything remotely connected with writing—even journalistic writing" (399). It turned out as she feared. After the New York trip to do the final editorial work she was exasperated beyond redemption: "I wouldn't work for them again for $50,000 a book—honestly. . . . And the poor little book isn't going to please anyone—me, LIFE, nor the Brazilian friends I did hope to please—don't judge my prose style by it, for heaven's sake—and I am awfully disappointed in the photographs, too—after all their boasting they had almost none when I got there—and I fought a bloody fight for everyone you will see" (400). Though we are right to read *Brazil* as contentious, we are wrong to read it as Bishop's. We recover Bishop's voice, the significance of *Life*'s manufacture, and the bloodiness of their fight if we go back to Bishop's drafts and her correspondence.

The form of the book is superficial and generalizing. *Brazil* closes down questions of travel. "That *Life*-slicked book" (413), as Bishop execrated it, took its place in the Life World Library series. It was the book version of *Life* magazine—or rather it moved the news stories of *Life* toward the geographic overviews of the *National Geographic*. The *National Geographic* began publication, also in America (the "national" was U.S. American), in 1888, but it was only successful when twentieth-century technology made possible travel to ever remoter places and the reproduction of photographs. In a slogan that would be harnessed by *Life* decades later, it was declared by its founders "America's first window on the world"; yet as one of the most profitable publishing companies and the largest purveyor of maps and globes in the world, the *National Geographic*'s camera lens like that of *Life*'s has been less than transparent. The *National Geographic* was as much an advance arm of globalization as *Life*; it brought the world to America and, by mediating every corner of the globe, exported America to the world.[23] The invention of the illustrated magazine, as one astute contemporaneous commentator said in a criticism that anticipated those made by Lévi-Strauss and Benjamin, was "a strike against understanding"; for illustrated magazines made the world mass reproducible and instantly accessible.[24] The Life World Library cast its standardizing eye on others. Before beginning writing, Bishop was advised to peruse as models those in the series on Japan and Germany. Intended as authoritative, comprehensive and for mass distribution ("sold through the mail" as her literary agent Carl Brandt conveyed the commission to Bishop), *Life* was looking for something that "would, in a sense, sell the country here," and it shouldn't be too factual. The follow-up from Oliver Allen, editor of Life World Library with whom Bishop would have an increasingly antagonistic and eventually furious correspondence over two years, elaborates that the text is neither a guidebook nor exactly a history, a "textbook." It is instead meant for the reader who is "extremely intelligent but not necessarily very well informed, who has a consuming desire to understand the important countries of the world but who may never have the opportunity to visit more than one or two of them." It is in short the ethnography for the armchair traveler scorned by Lévi-Strauss. Above all *Life* want "a readable . . . picture," "for the country to come alive on the pages."

The combination of photographs and text makes *Brazil* a readable picture. The photographs were not Bishop's. She wrote the prose, and the photo-essays inserted between her prose were written by someone else, the book's publication information tells us. The photo-essays, along with intermittent boxes of data about language, history, geography (Allen's idea), emblematize how Brazil is turned into immediate, digestible nuggets. *Brazil* deploys photography in the manner of *Life* magazine as in Parks's assignments. In a photo-essay summing up the Amazon the compressions produce a single, hackneyed message: "the Amazon forest rises, inhuman and repellent, an appendage of wilderness occupying almost half the area of Brazil" (32). This is clearly not Bishop's voice. Contrast Bishop's Amazon in "Santarém," where the "dazzling, watery dialectic" makes this a place from which the poet "really wanted to go no further." The outsider's perspective is embodied in the retiring head of Philips corporation "who wanted to see the Amazon before he died" but, of the wasps' nest admired by the poet and given her by a pharmacist ("small, exquisite, clean matte white"), can only ask: "What's that ugly thing?" The photo-essays echo but monotonize Bishop's prose. It was here that she lost most control. But the process of writing over her in relation to the photographs is typical of the whole book. The photographs-plus-prose format produced confusion from the beginning about the authorship of the book. While Allen says in his commissioning letter that her text is the "guts" of the book (his word) and that Bishop would appear to be the author, what the reader sees on opening the book are the pictures. Allen promised "you can correct us at any stage," and this covered both prose and photographs. In her copy of the letter Bishop underlined and put a check by this assurance. In fact she lost control of both aspects. By the end of the project Allen will acknowledge that what lies behind their misunderstanding is the book's joint byline. Bishop would be so unhappy with *Brazil* that she rued even that her name came first in the dual authorship declared on the title page: "by Elizabeth Bishop and the Editors of *Life*" (3).

The photographs were an important part of the appeal for Bishop. At the beginning she gave Allen a list of "ABSOLUTELY IMPORTANT PICTURES" of what she wanted to show—"new" material including wildlife, such as parrots, monkeys, a toucan, the ant-eater, termite nests, the Brazilian Morpho butterfly; as well as slaves and "Indians with pets." In her choice she wants to give the reader "a fair and up-to-date picture" of Brazil and to avoid the "ephemeral and flashy." They mostly ignored her suggestions and at the same time managed to include what she didn't want. On the cover they placed a photograph by Dmitri Kessel, the fashion photographer whose work Parks refused his photographs of Flavio to appear opposite and who is credited with many of the photographs in *Brazil*. Bishop specifically stipulated that she didn't want a picture of the Sugar Loaf, but their choice of Kessel's of the Rio bay includes it. Their photographs skim off the most obvious of Brazil's geography, contemporary society, architecture. They also ignored her request to write captions. She wanted to "point out the thing that is interesting to have *seen* . . . and avoid *clichés*, preconceptions." Her increasing anxiety about the photographs was not helped when Allen wrote to her toward the end of the project, in an apparent attempt to reassure her in the face of the erratic photographers they were sending out to her in Brazil, that he as picture-editor had final say: "I not only have complete supervision of all copy but of all pictures too." This proved true yet in complete contradiction of his earlier promise that she would be able to make final revisions. For Allen as editor of the Life World Library series it was essential that they produce *Brazil* as readable picture. He stated they needed to strike a balance between pictures that "are purely spectacular, with not very much content" and photos that "are extremely meaningful but perhaps not very appetizing photographically." His commitment to balance was not so ingenuous. Even from this stage in his correspondence we can see on which side *Life* truly weighted the scales: "We feel we must not put out a book that is uninteresting to look at."

One of the few photographs that make it into *Brazil* that Bishop did suggest is Parks's *favela*/Corcovado shot, which in a handwritten postcript to one of her responses to Allen she calls "superb." Clearly she must have seen this issue of *Life* magazine. The juxtaposition in Parks's photograph would have appealed to her. In the notebooks for *Brazil* Bishop remarks on a similar yoking of the beautiful and the terrifying in the film *Black*

Orpheus: "the horror concealed lightly decorat[e]d," she writes of this retelling of the myth of Orpheus set during the Carnival in Rio's *favelas.* The
paradoxes of Parks's photograph have been flattened by the final version of
Brazil. Where she and we and Parks might see at once the redemption and
trauma, the beauty and horror, *Life* overwrites the irreconcilable real with
their code. Their caption would have us read simply that "The blight of
poverty, increasing in spite of industrial growth, is taxing the capabilities
of free institutions" (138). The caption is remarkably similar in meaning to
those that accompanied Parks's photographs and that produce equivalence
between poverty and political threat to freedom, in other words communism. That Bishop's book of photographs of Brazil for *Life* was published at
this particular moment, in 1962, so soon after Parks's *Life* magazine assignment in 1961, is not coincidental. As Bishop is written over in the process
of producing *Brazil* a theme emerges that is the same as that underscoring
Parks's photographs. The theme, a political one, is that Brazil is a "land
of unfulfilled promise"—as Allen proposed it in his commissioning letter (every book has to have a theme, he said). At the same time he offered
topics that would enable the theme's progression, enclosing sample chapter
outlines from two other Life World Library books.

The photographs with the editors' captions narrate the theme of
promise. *Brazil* reenlists several photographs published previously in *Life*
magazine. The notion of how "radical movements" "feed" on poverty is
embodied in two now-facing images that appeared in *Life* June 2, 1961.
One of "militant marxist, Francisco Julião" speaking to workers, another
of Castro's face on a banner held aloft at a demonstration again suggest an
incendiary political situation (142–43).[25] At the same time the book must
evidence potential for fulfillment, the open-endedness of the words of the
title of the last chapter that Brazil is "A Nation Perplexed and Uncertain."
Toward the end of the book, particularly in the photo-essays, the narrative
becomes entirely futural, speaking of the "critical role ["the new middle
class"] will play in the new Brazil" (119). The tense of the book is that
Brazil is emergent but not enough, that progress is incipient: that Brazil
is "under-industrialized" (97). We are not surprised then when the book
concludes with a direct appeal for financial aid, which we are told will lead
to strong, in other words U.S.-friendly government. Brazil is presented as
developed and stable enough to deserve financial aid but undeveloped and
unstable enough to need it. Particularly in the northeast and with the growing *favela* problem, poverty is related causally to communism: a narrative
that can be redirected given sufficient financial investment. The rewriting
of Brazil's contemporary history for the United States is the rationale of

the book. This theme—and its theme is its *studium*—is revealed in the introduction to the U.S. edition by John Moors Cabot, a former U.S. ambassador to Brazil. Sounding suspiciously like the mission statement that preceded Parks's photos in *Life,* Cabot emphasizes Brazil's importance— and *Brazil*'s importance—in achieving the current U.S. administration's "inter-American ideals" (7). "The magnificent picture essays [and] . . . Miss Bishop's brilliant text . . . bring the reader a better understanding of our South American sister republic. . . . For . . . understanding and cooperation between Brazil and the United States were never more necessary than they are today" (7). This introduction is quite different from that to the British edition that, by a British professor of Portuguese, presents *Brazil* as helping redress readers' poor knowledge of Brazil.[26] Bishop says Cabot's introduction resembled nothing that Cabot wrote (*One Art* 405).

In fact particularly Bishop's last two chapters resemble nothing *she* wrote, at least not in the records we have. And in her list of corrections to the revised galleys that she got back from *Life,* chapters 9 and 10 are most subject to her rejections of their revision, rejections that were not accepted of their revisions that therefore eventually got published. *Brazil*'s narrative and its politics are not hers. The titles of the last two chapters were published as "Struggle for a Stable Democracy" and "A Nation Perplexed and Uncertain." In Bishop's drafts her title for chapter 9 was first "A Golden Age of Republicanism," later changed to "The Republic"; she had no title for chapter 10. Her chapter 9 is designed to give a much fuller, more complex, less linear account of the politics of contemporary Brazil embedded in the context of the history of the Empire and Republic. While in the published version some of the historical material has been moved to an earlier chapter that would now be recognized by *Life*'s readers as "historical," most of Bishop's writing has been omitted or condensed. In the place of the excision the editors reduce four to five pages of detail to a platitudinous sentence: "Although the young republic had yet to produce a body of statesmen, matters gradually improved" (128). What was not included from Bishop's drafts complicates the politics of the book. An account of the politicization of communism in Brazil, "which provided the pretext for setting up the Vargas dictatorship," is much reduced in the final version. Bishop's drafts call Vargas's regime a dictatorship with consistency. While *Life* occasionally use the word *dictator,* they mostly perform substitutions: "Vargas era" for instance (130). Bishop is much more critical of the brutality of Vargas's rule and reveals its political allegiance. They cut her description of his crushing communism "with great severity" and its effect on intellectuals of arrest and exile. By the same token *Life* inserts into her prose for

Vargas's opponents the labels "Communist" and "hard-core Communists," which would seem to justify his nondemocratic government (147). And whereas she says that Vargas allied himself with the fascist party during the Second World War and was forced to fight against the Axis powers only after popular demonstration, they say he made "friendly gestures to both sides" (130). "Under the name of the 'New State,' fascism began in Brazil," Bishop wrote. Allen deletes and inserts passages that describe how with the help of U.S. aid, Vargas "laid the foundations on which a strong economy could eventually be constructed" (131).

Far from the theme of financial aid in current U.S. relations with Brazil, Bishop is *critical* of loans. In the drafts she speaks against the concentration of policy on financial aid. She writes that it is not just money Brazil needs—"far from it"—and suggests that U.S. aid to build Brasilia fed a cycle leading to inflation. Allen's inserts are thus all the more brazen: "To alleviate the ills besetting it and to enable it to maintain its economic growth, Brazil needs financial aid" (147–48). Her chapter 9, on recent politics in the context of Brazil's history, is open-ended: "It is still too early to foresee the results of the change." Their substitution draws the chapter to an alarming close by connecting Brazil's increasing foreign debt, inflation, and the need for electoral reform. Crucial in the difference is a passage from chapter 9 discussing the awarding of the Order of the Southern Cross to Che Guevara by Brazil's President Quadros, which had just taken place. This passage is entirely missing from Bishop's draft where there is simply a gap and a red question mark. Allen notes that Bishop promised to cable a new version of the Guevara passage later but they never received it. Yet in her later correction notes on the galleys Bishop charges them with leaving out the word *communist* for Guevara, which indicates that she did at one point produce the passage, whether from Brazil or written in New York. If Guevara, just given Brazil's highest prize, was a communist, then Quadros too would appear communist and *Life* had to be careful in justifying the worthiness of financial aid about making Brazil seem too red. At the same time Goulart, the replacement populist president, *Life* presents as regarded as leftist. Bishop writes that he was regarded by military heads as leftist. These subtle changes—variations—are crucially loaded. She foresees problems with the military that are again cut: "the very expression, ["spirit of compromise" between the left and right] like 'land of unfulfilled promise' is almost a red flag to a Brazilian at present." If the former phrase had always meant the excuse for a military coup, and the latter an excuse for foreign intervention, Bishop in one sentence speaks against both and warns at the dangers of relying on truisms. While it is not true to say that Bishop's and *Life*'s anxieties about Brazil's future lay in antithetical directions, certainly Bishop's drafts evidence that her political outlook is less fixed and secure than the published version would have us believe.

In Bishop's drafts the "theme" is how the United States looks at Brazil. Though *theme* is the wrong word since she says in conversation that unlike many she has no theories of Brazil.[27] The published book, therefore *Life*, stress how a shift to the left in Brazil "would have far-reaching repercussions throughout South and Central America" (146). Bishop in her corrections insisted that they make the change back to her original, that it would have "repercussions for the USA." Allen replaces all of the comparisons Bishop makes to the United States with "any other part of the world" or "any other country" (146, for example). But this is not Bishop's point. She's working as a comparative Americanist. They repeatedly neutralize the concerted and evident effort she makes to perform comparisons at almost every turn. In her notes for chapter 10 for example, she writes that Brazil is "Undoubtedly the most important country for us to deal with." In her corrections she accuses *Life* of being "pretty condescending" about Brazil and clearly her desire is to highlight this lack of U.S. knowledge. She calls for more education of Americans in relation to Brazil. She begins her draft of the contentious chapter 10 with lack of perception on both sides: "The United States and Brazil have many things in common. . . . It is time we got to know and appreciate each other better; time that the United States gave more to Brazil than loans and those less attractive features of our culture that, rightly or wrongly, are thought to be 'Americanizing' the world. The United States and Brazil have more in common than coffee and Coca Cola."

Bishop's comparisons result in a sometimes impassioned and certainly prescient criticism of the United States. She hopes that the "harsh industrialization" of the United States may be avoided by Brazil. The "United States should be careful of what it exports." And she recollects all that the United States doesn't know about Brazil that may be a precedent for the United States. She presents the "Indian problem" as better managed in Brazil (as it might have been then) and likewise racial problems following slavery. Her *Brazil* contains a good deal more on racial mixing (one can imagine how this would have gone down in civil rights–riven United States) as definitive of Brazil and she is keen to detail racial typology—"caboclo," "claro." Allen is determined to whitewash this with his substitution— "With each new census an increasing proportion of the total population is classified as white" (114). Bishop details an advertisement for a gas range of a black cook kissing her white mistress, which for her illustrates Brazil's characteristic racial tolerance and which she states would never have been shown in the United States. When this description was first published in her article on Rio for the *New York Times* in 1965, she was dragged over the coals by a Brazilian critic for being patronizingly American by treating Brazil as a country of underdevelopment awaiting U.S. development.[28] But the passage was omitted from *Brazil,* one imagines, for suggesting the opposite and what Bishop had intended—that Brazil was progressive in race politics compared to the United States. Bishop's suggestions of what the United States can learn from Brazil cut from publication are consistently subversive: Brazil has no death penalty, no real enemies, has never had a war of conquest, atomic bombs ("and so far has never expressed any desire for them") and "no industries that circle the globe." She is much more critical of tourism, capitalism, and commodification. "Progressive" and "modern" appear in quotation marks in her drafts, removed for the published version, with the attitude to development a big difference between her and Allen. Allen's inserted calls for financial aid seek to further industrialization and building in the interior. Surviving in *Brazil* is Bishop's discussion of the effects of commercialization on the sambas. Radio technology and Hollywood have homogenized their poetry, she writes, producing from Carnival a monoculture. And—although she doesn't seem to have any self-consciousness when she writes this; or none survives—photographers, including tourists, interfere and change the nature of the activity by trying to get good shots. In her criticism journalism is implicated in this commodification, for Bishop writes that in Brazil writers must often resort to journalism for financial reasons, to "deadening effect" and the "deterioration of writing": again, of course, cut.

The notion of perspective and the sense of where we're looking from so important to Bishop are cut from the published version even on the level syntax. Allen has replaced every "we" in Bishop's drafts to produce passive sentence constructions or simple statements—no longer "we think" but "it is." Predicates: every subjective has been objectified out. Her personable "you" addressed to the reader has also been cut. In this "you" she had conjured her reader into perspective in Brazil. Her notes for chapter 1 multiply points of view so that "you see" Brazil from various times and places, as she asks us to make one "shift in angle of vision and imagination" after another. She describes Rio de Janeiro as it would be seen by "A foreigner lying in the old Strangers['] Hospital" (where Bishop had been to dry out, placed there by her partner Lota for whom she decided to settle in Brazil); and from a plane; and from a skyscraper penthouse; and from a boat approaching part of a coast that had barely changed since 1500, reliving the sensation of the Portuguese as they approached it for the first time:

a complicity of perspectives Bishop would take up in her "Brazil, January 1, 1502" poem. The whole draft is much more like *Questions of Travel,* with the writer indicating that this is what "the average North American" would see, parenthetical asides reminding us that these are an outsider's observations of Brazil and therefore limited and subject to adjustment—pointers to what has been left out which have all been deleted by Allen. This loss of perspective is perhaps what Bishop means when she accused them of "telescoping" her sentences. In radical revision of Bishop's descriptions of paintings of Portinari compared both with the actual Brazilian landscape and what the stranger on arriving in Brazil might be struck by, *Life* cut the double frame, making Portinari's images simply reflective of Brazil. They do this by compressing her sentences, flattening her focal shifts. They slide together her perspectives on Brazil to produce generalization and cliché—forcing them into one another like the tubes of a hand-telescope; or, taking the view from afar but using the telescope, eliding or belying the distance. Bishop, who writes the anecdote without generalization, the quirky concrete without conclusion, somehow manages to be closer up while indicating her viewing distance.

Bishop's protest—"Why not tell the truth?"—comes in response to *Life*'s leaving out "communist" for Guevara. They are "*lying* like RUGS" she wrote to friends (*One Art* 400). Their suggestion had been "communist-leaning" and eventually they decided on the awkward and dangling "believed to be a Communist" (133) (by whom? Again perspective is cut). "It is a very severe thing, Elizabeth, to call someone a Communist," Allen scolds. "How would you define the truth in this instance?" In response to Bishop's accusation on their tiptoeing around the Vargas regime that they were "whitewashing dictators," Allen wrote that although she may find it hard to believe there was no editorial slanting in an "operation" run by "Time, Inc." These political details are important because as Bishop's draft recognizes they set the stage for Brazil's volatile contemporary politics. For Bishop in the draft, Vargas's suppression of left-wing activity was an excuse to bolster his own dictatorial powers. It was to be—and Bishop's insistence on the perspective of political and other judgments is historically farsighted—a precedent for the military dictatorship that would justify its coup of 1964 by pointing to the increasingly socialist politics of first Quadros, then Goulart. The political changes in Brazil in turn set the stage for Bishop's life. The key connection for Bishop is Carlos Lacerda (the same governor of Rio and Guanabara state whose effects are encountered by Parks and who was himself a newspaper man), in whose circle Bishop increasingly moved in the '50s and early '60s. An assassination attempt on Lacerda in 1954 was the main factor in bringing the end of Vargas's regime. Lacerda had eyes on the presidency himself, but after the coup he capitulated to the military government.[29]

At the end of 1961 Bishop went to New York to do the final revisions on *Brazil*. The trip was already three months late and what is clear from Bishop's drafts is that the book, particularly those all-important chapters 9 and 10, was patchy and incomplete. She apparently didn't have time to check that final chapter. In the dispute that continued even after the project Allen says that it was because Bishop was "unable to do the revisions on chapter 10" that he did them himself—and apparently therefore almost conjured the chapter from scratch and in the course turned the book into its plea for American governmental financial aid for Brazil. What happened in late 1961 that Bishop proved unable to finish the project, particularly that final chapter, the most important and the one that surely most led to Bishop's repudiation of the book? In 1961 Bishop's Brazilian partner, Lota de Macedo Soares, an architect, received a job from Lacerda to direct the design of a park for the poor on the reclaimed Flamengo landfill, something of a counterbalance in Rio to the Lagoa for the rich besides which rises the hill of Catacumba and (before Lacerda) its *favela*. At the time Lacerda was speaking out against communism, Castro, and in support of the U.S. invasion of Cuba. Relations between him and the then president, Quadros, who had just decorated Guevara, were strained, a tension that did not make Lota's work on the park any easier. Bishop's letters, which were responsive initially to Lacerda's obvious intelligence, found him increasingly the political opportunist, egoist and hysterical. Conversely she at first didn't trust Goulart and his politics but then admired his calm. When Bishop was supposed to be finishing *Brazil*, Lota was preoccupied with the park and increasing bureaucracy. Bishop's letters in turn are preoccupied with Lota. Work on the park would change Lota and their relationship irreversibly. The park with its backdrop of the changing politics in Brazil would not only prove key to thwarting Bishop's work on *Brazil*. It would carry over as trauma from this photographic book on Brazil to the next one.

Bishop notoriously hated politics, and in extensions of the Brazilian journalist's criticism of her previous representation of Brazil she has been charged with being patronizing and even racist, as having a detached if not reactionary stance. But new readings of Bishop complicate the received idea of her as conservative. Camille Roman argues that Bishop moved to Brazil in part because she dissented from U.S. cold war militarism and she seeks to highlight dissenting politics in her poetry. The paradox is that Bishop had not escaped the military conflict at all but becomes more immersed in it, with Lota's park, Lacerda, the military coup—and *Brazil.* For Roman's reading as for Sandra Barry's, it is important that Bishop is outside of American culture.[30] She was not of course U.S. American but three-quarters Canadian, born in Nova Scotia, and only moved to the United States when her mother was institutionalized. Her mother was diagnosed permanently insane and confined to a public sanatorium in Nova Scotia, moreover, after the death of Bishop's father—who was half American—removed from her mother the right to U.S. citizenship and the private treatment she had to date received. In the notes for *Brazil* Bishop was consistently critical of nationalism. Her articulated comparisons of Brazil with America make us conscious of the limitations of national perspectives. Bishop was certainly not cognizant of the contemporary U.S. propagandistic context in which her prose would appear. At the beginning of the project she is telexed from *Life*'s New York office to ask if she'd ever been a communist, which at this point causes her much mirth and incredulity. Yet *Life,* she intuits in her letters, behaves exactly as does the U.S. embassy in Brazil (*One Art* 400). It may look like conjuring a conspiracy theory to suggest the connection between Allen's cuts/substitutions and contemporary U.S. politics toward Brazil but they do produce a consistent line. And we can't believe it is just the process of edition as Allen tells Bishop.

Bishop can't tell the "almost invariable" truth in their format. The different political conceptions of truth intersect with truths in different genres: narrative, prose, and photography lined up as documentary or absolute on one side; fragments, poetry, and a notion of photography as more variable and losing on the other. Truth fixed and revealed versus a form that allows truth to escape, or rather recognizes truth as that which escapes. The joint authorship of Bishop and the editors of *Life* was a remarkable mismatch. He is full of flattery for her writing when he commissioned her but one wonders if Allen had ever *read* Bishop. She's an appalling choice for this book given that she was a poet not a journalist, that she had published very little, and that she was terrible at meeting deadlines and letting go her writing. He gave her very little time to write the book, commissioned as it was in June and with the bulk of it expected by September. The pace of the project was so against Bishop's nature. Her notebooks for *Brazil* are telling. One titled *"to be used"* is empty other than a single address on the first page. In another, scrappy and fragmented, one phrase is repeated throughout and concerns a *Life* photographer with whom Bishop was apparently drawing a contrast to the traveler—something that a traveler could do or see "(always excepting / a LIFE photographer)." As not prose and thus not usable in *Brazil* the poem is working out her frustration with, rather than furthering, the *Life* project. Bishop's drafts submitted to *Life* suggest she struggled with the writing. "I gave up here," she hand-annotates the end of one chapter draft.

Bishop anyway found prose more difficult than poetry. In correspondence with Lowell she wrote that poetry allows her a truth that prose doesn't: "somehow—that desire to get things straight and tell the truth— it's almost impossible not to tell the truth in poetry, I think, but in prose it keeps eluding one in the funniest way." Lorrie Goldensohn comments that it is precisely the ellipses and gaps of poetry that allow Bishop to shape a truth.[31] Whereas taking prose to its most prosaic, *Brazil* demanded that she document everything and do so in a narrative with a theme. It is significant in this regard that Bishop objects to Allen's use of the term *verse* as interchangeable with what she had written, *poetry*. *Verse*, from the Latin for the turn that comes at the end of the line of the plough and now synonymous with that line, is more narrative than *poetry*, from the Greek for doing, making. Bishop's voice is heard in *Brazil* most recognizably when she speaks about the untranslatability of nineteenth-century Brazilian romantic poets. She evokes their "*saudades* (melancholy yearnings)" (103)—though in an earlier draft she had glossed this as "nostalgia tinged with despair," struggling to translate as if to emblematize this non-translatability. In interview soon after her anthology of translations of Brazilian poets, Bishop said that Brazilians were given to depression;[32] her biographer believes she equated melancholia with homesickness, but her balancing both terms in the drafts suggests she wanted to keep open a gap—a gap that *saudades* perhaps occupies (but doesn't fill).[33] Bishop rejected the line about "unfulfilled promise" in a letter to Allen. She acknowledges this to be true of Brazil but wants to make it secondary, include other things, less line. Her early drafts after the notebooks make clear what these other things were. Her *Brazil* would have been much more fragmented, more like her poetry with the gaps showing. She wanted not a unifying picture but a broken, composite collage, holding at a distance certain generalizations about Brazilians: "familiarity" and "laziness" appear in her chapter outline in quotation marks. She wanted to illustrate Brazil through the anecdotal, as depressed but humorous, made up of quirky details and quotations—bumper stickers ("Woman, still the best Brazilian product"), sambas (which she called "a real living poetry of the people"), folklore, jokes, and sayings, which do make it in but thinly. Bishop's book on Brazil would have been much more pointed, much more in perspective.

Allen also changed her prose style and this is why *Brazil* reads so clunkily and it's obvious that this isn't Bishop. Reading the drafts one realizes that in the cutting of details all the life has gone. There's very little call for this because though they are clearly written fast the later drafts are as coherent as Bishop's prose ever is. The cuts matter because Bishop cared so much about *le mot juste.* She agonized over precision, over every aspect of production, finding the act of writing very painful, and alternated between putting her writing away, destroying it, and rewriting it.[34] Bishop was the arch self-critic. "I supposes no critic is every really as harsh as oneself" (*One Art* 146). When asked if she thought someone had too many defenses she responded, surprised, "Too *many*? Can one ever have *enough* defenses?"[35] As *Life* make prosaic, the beautiful balance and rhythm of Bishop's prose that reads more like poetry is thrown off. "A hand's-breadth is often more than a day's work" on the art of Portuguese women's lace-making becomes Allen's "A hand's breadth often takes more than a day to do" (84). Allen U.S.-Americanized Bishop's prose. "Manioc" becomes "tapioca"; "sweets," "candy"/"confections" (54). *Life* wanted to render the other perfectly trans-latable, to master. In debates with Lowell about translation Bishop said that, though one must be faithful to the original, the translator can never get it exactly: "probably at least 50% is always lost, in another language."[36] While there's no record of whatever Allen and Bishop agreed in person in their meeting in New York, the violence of *Life*'s overwriting can be felt in her response to the galleys sent her once she had returned to Brazil. "Please don't put in that cliché," she begs, accusing them of "ignorant chauvinism" toward Brazil. And repeatedly she writes "I corrected all this in N.Y.," "I re-member correcting this satisfactorily in N.Y." She was a distressed reader of the galleys and became more so, particularly of the crucial chapter 10, with question marks and underlinings and asterisks culminating in a frustrated *"No!"* and a plea: "Please . . . my words and phrases." Of the photographs apparently Bishop didn't see these with the proofs at all.

In response to her corrections Bishop received back from Allen's of-fice a telegram rejecting them, defending their changes, and turning the criticism back on beleaguered Bishop, even to grammar; key for them is narrative, transition, down to sentence: "PLEASE DONT CALL US IGNORANT CHAUVINISTS . . . WHAT YOU TERM CLICHE IS RESULT OF MY ATTEMPT TO SHORE UP TRANSITION AT THAT POINT AFTER YOU CONFESSED INABILITY TO DO SO." This was followed by a nine-page letter. Beginning with none-too-carefully-disguised impatience at how "fascinating and challenging assignment it was for us all. Each one of these books turns out to be exas-peratingly different from the last, and each one turns out to be a great deal more difficult than we had anticipated, and all that was particularly true in the case of *Brazil"*—Allen goes on: "It came as something of shock to me to read, 'I beg you not to change my words any more. If necessary omit phrases but please don't distort or iron out what little life they have left.'" He proceeds to give her "a point-by-point explanation" of why they failed to meet her request that they not make changes. Given that the book was now in final proofs and was anyway beyond change, particularly Bishop's, it is hard to understand why Allen undertakes this, other than to pour out his defensive, at turns offensive, stream. It must have been a crushing letter for Bishop to receive. Allen is at turns "amused," "confused," "surprised," "irritated," "puzzled," and "disagreed" with her reaction to their changes, which he would "defend vociferously." His refusal to meet her requests saved her from foolish errors, he writes, and he throws back at her the charge of "condescending," which they fixed through their editing and revising. He simply understands meaning not style. Though the style was changed, he says, to put in transitions, the meaning was not changed. "But for goodness sake *[sic]* what difference does it possibly make?" he writes, illustratively. For him they are "bickering over these microscopic points." Yet for her they had telescoped her in style, views, perspective and hence in her Brazil. She, like the sandpiper, wants the detail.

Bishop came out of the battle absolutely ambivalent about revision. She clearly wanted to wash her hands of Time-Life. In her letter to Lowell coinciding with the book's publication she writes, "Well, as Ginsberg put it so brilliantly: 'Are you going to let your emotional life be run by *Time* magazine?'—it seems to me I have been, lately" (*One Art* 406). She uses *Time* magazine as exemplary of the globalization happening all over the world, which she sees as leading to the "dying out of local cultures . . . one of the most tragic things in this century" (408). In her old home of Great Village, Nova Scotia—as in her new home of Rio de Janeiro—"trucks arrive bringing powdered milk . . . and *Time* magazine" (408). U.S. Americanization is taking place in the continent north and south and *Time* is inculpated. Yet what's striking is that in the same letter Bishop does not wholly disown the *Life* book. She is still wanting her readers to go to it, to get something of her ideas about Brazil. "The *Brazil* book is awful; some sentences just don't make sense at all. And at least the pictures could have been good. Maybe, if you can read it at all, you will find a trace here & there of what I originally meant to say" (405). Before Bishop signed a copy of *Brazil* for at least one friend she went through the book, "every line of every page making changes in the text back to the way she originally had written it," obsessively looking to return her work to her work to regain some sense of her truth lost from representation. Yet when Time-Life asked her to revise and update certain sections formally for a second printing in the autumn of 1962, she flatly refused.[37] What's marked about the *Brazil* drafts in fact is the very little correction that appears on them. Bishop was in her poetry a serial reviser. It took her sometimes decades to perfect a poem, and her numerous drafts and corrections show her struggle with completing, show that for her writing was struggling. "Nature repeats herself, or almost does: / *repeat, repeat repeat; revise, revise, revise*," Bishop wrote in "North Haven." But unlike Lowell, for whom "North Haven" is an elegy, Bishop never revised her poems once they were published, the only exceptions being when she had been pressed too soon to a deadline. Nature almost repeats herself. Like the "almost invariably" the almost makes all the difference and makes for not a repetition but a return.

Repeat, repeat, repeat; revise, revise, revise

Three years after publication of *Brazil,* in a letter of 1965 Bishop writes to Lowell about a notice of a Rockefeller award she had received. The Imaginative Writing and Literary Scholarship required initial nomination by a committee, to be followed up by an application from the candidate, and Lowell, who was then an adviser for the Rockefeller Foundation, had put forward Bishop as he did for many of her fellowships and appointments. Saying that she guessed he had something to do with it, Bishop declares that she was "delighted" to receive the invitation.

> IF you can—I know you're in Maine—will you tell someone or other that I DO WANT ONE (desperately, but don't say that!) It fits in so well with a scheme I've been working on lately—I haven't time to go into details now, but I want to put a book together—prose pieces—about Brazil—and in order to do it I shall have to make a good many rather expensive trips by air and boat. I think writing on S[outh] A[merica]—and Brazil—has declined sadly since the days of the great naturalists—for a 100 years, that is—and the run-of-the-mill book is written, badly, by someone who has been here three months. . . . I have three pieces more or less done— before I heard from the Rockefellers.—My idea is to mix places, a few life-stories, short stories more or less, a piece on Aleijadinho probably— perhaps popular music, etc.—and the places will be those where the journalists don't go, or rarely—Where life is pretty much unchanged but bound to change very fast very soon. I shall try to do all this, of course, in the most beautiful prose imaginable—and with photographs—for which I shall have to buy a new camera;—& films are very dear now, etc. . . . So

far I'm calling it (all this was in the works, so to speak before I heard from the Rs at all, so it isn't made-up specially) the old title I wanted to use before: BLACK BEANS AND DIAMONDS; (tentatively).[38]

From 1966 to 1968 Bishop received $12,000 from the Rockefeller Foundation, successful with the full amount she requested for the full time. Her application outlines in more detail what she had in mind in putting together this other book on Brazil. She begins by mentioning Lévi-Strauss's *Tristes Tropiques* as the exception to her century's writing about Brazil that is "vulgarly written, extremely superficial, and frequently inaccurate as well." She, in contrast, "fond enough of the people to have made a home here" for fourteen years, knows the language and has visited most of the better-known sights. And with the money and the time she planned to travel further, to the more inaccessible parts of the country, to see the upper Amazon and the Rio São Francisco. She had already "completed, partly completed, or outlined" a dozen chapters: an account of a voyage down the lower Amazon, another to the Amazon delta; an essay on Aleijadinho, Brazil's greatest artist; an article on St. George's Day in Rio; a study of Noel Rosa, the most famous of samba composers, the life story, "a typical one, of a servant of mine from the northeast, etc." She also planned to include some poems "that would seem to go better in such a book than in a volume of verse." And she wanted to use her own photographs to illustrate the book. She already had a few "considered good enough to use for reproduction." The book would be 400–500 pages. She was sure that she could complete it and had a publisher already interested.

Undoubtedly Bishop had been planning such a book on Brazil for many years. Her letters reveal the trail. Even before *Brazil,* in 1960 she had written to Lowell—and this may have planted the seed in his mind for the nomination—"Rockefeller has long been interested in South America, and I have an idea for getting money to see more of it and finish up a book of stories about Brazil" (*One Art* 383). In 1956 she noted that she had "planned out a special book of travel sketches about Brazil" (327). And in 1946 even before she went to Brazil she wrote to her publishers Houghton Mifflin seeking an advance for "a book of travel essays about certain parts of South America" (142). She didn't get it, but the request raises the question of to what extent she went to South America with such a book in mind. Hence when she wrote to Lowell about his nominating her for the Rockefeller fellowship in 1965 that "It fits in so well with a scheme I've been working on lately," the scheme was late not so much in the sense in which she meant it of "recent" as late in "already overdue." It was also overdue following *Brazil,* for what is clear is that this was going to be corrective if not retractive, to replace not only "the run-of-the-mill book . . . written, badly, by someone who has been here three months" but also her own previous book on Brazil, and its "places will be those where the journalists don't go, or rarely." This critical comment reveals that Bishop had obviously been smarting since her involvement with *Life* and that she bucked against the journalistic directive of *Brazil.* The "working title" she proposed in her application, "Black Beans and Diamonds," is at the pivot of this old-but-new, originary but revisionary project. Bishop considered "Black Beans and Diamonds" at one point as the title for her *Minha vida* translation. (She sent her introduction to *Diary of Helena Morley* as a sample of her prose about Brazil with her grant application, and she sent her translation of *Helena Morley* originally to publishers with photographs) (*One Art* 301). But the words also appeared together in the drafts of *Brazil* in a passage about *"futebol"* that is among those that get cut. In some lovely, lyrical details Bishop writes that the Brazilian team in the 1958 World Cup were allocated a supply of black beans, the staple dish of Brazil. Pelé, who changed the face of world football (and race in the football world),[39] was known as the "Black Diamond." When proposing "Black Beans and Diamonds" as a title for *Minha vida,* Bishop was aware that she would have to wait and "see what the publishers think" of it (*One Art* 316). Obviously they didn't think very much. "Black Beans and Diamonds" would appear to have been dropped from both projects as being untranslatable, not recognizable. In choosing it as title now Bishop redeemed something of that untranslatability and made it her subject.

The title "Black Beans and Diamonds" also captures the mosaic nature of the book. Its fragmentedness, ellipses, or compressions were instrumental in making Brazil *un*translatable in this work. *Black Beans and Diamonds* was to be unapologetically not a narrative. "This may sound like a grab-bag sort of book—and that is really what I have in mind," she wrote in her application. Made up of fragments and observations, not only in different genres but different media—text and photographs; prose and poetry; memoir, essay, and fiction—the book would have been multiperspectival. For all its fragmentedness much of the material Bishop promised is remarkably complete. Even the more sketchy pieces give us a consistent sense of her shifting perspective, not only from piece to piece but within pieces. Translated newspaper quotations jostle alongside sambas. A recipe for the beautifully named Brazilian sweet *baba de moça* ("maiden's drool"), with grated coconut, sugar, egg yolks, cinnamon, wonderfully intersplices the political history of sugar in an account of plantations given by Gilberto

Freyre. As non-narrative but also photographic-textual *Black Beans and Diamonds* was to be *Brazil*'s mirror image. (The only other transmedia text Bishop had produced was *Brazil.*) The photographs were again fundamental. In a 1966 interview given at her home in Brazil and much about Brazil but that conspicuously fails to mention the *Brazil* book, Bishop says *Black Beans and Diamonds* is to be "a combination of a travel book, a memoir, and picture book. I am quite interested in photography. I'd like to make Brazil seem less remote and less an object of picturesque fancy."[40] Part of the reason why she needed so much money, she writes in the budget section of her grant application, is the expense of a camera, the film, and development.

That Bishop budgeted for and did indeed take her own photographs shows a very different relationship to photography from that we have seen her take in *Brazil*—to others' photographs, detached, written over by *Life,* apparently objective. Bishop's letters reveal that she took photography into her life, from 1938 when she enclosed her "best snapshots" of Key West and planned to take still "many more pictures" of local life (*One Art* 67). Once she was in Brazil references to enclosed photographs increase, presumably because she was further away from her correspondents but also perhaps to convey the real difference of her life there. Her written comments on the rear of many of her photographs, about the mechanics of a water supply or the exact location of a perspective, as well as annotations and arrows on the front indicating what she wanted her recipient to notice, show she used photography to detail the facts about a place. Or rather the almost facts of a place, because that she couldn't quite cede text in her annotations suggests that she didn't quite trust photography to do the truth-telling. Yet her photographs are remarkable on initial viewing because they corroborate her poems of *Questions of Travel.* It really did happen just as she wrote it. There really are "too many waterfalls" in her home with Lota, Samambaia, Petrópolis; there really are "clouds putting pressure on the mountaintops." In an ornate birdcage one can see the "whittled fantasies of wooden cages." There, in a canoe, is the "riverman"—though Bishop had yet to go to the Amazon when she wrote this poem. Bishop's collection holds a wealth of slides and photographs, a wealth not only in quantity but quality. She was a prolific and good photographer, not surprisingly given her eye in painting and poetry. She cared about photography as form. In her letters she remarks on a man who could write about Brazilian flora and fauna, "although he was a dreadful photographer, you'll see" (*One Art* 280). In what appears to have been at the time just a happy juxtaposition, in that same 1960 letter in which she first mentions her plans for a book via Rockefeller on Brazil, Bishop writes excitedly to Lowell of her growing photography collection: "Did I tell you that I have been taking photographic slides? . . . I have a small Amazon lecture and a small Cabo Frio lecture, etc. Lota does the machine part. . . . Who is ever going to look at these, and when, I can't imagine" (383). The excitement is contagious to any researcher looking at the photographs now. This is particularly the case with the slides, which one must view through Bishop's own projector, since their frames now measure too large for modern projectors; we take the machine part of Lota. The plans for *Black Beans and Diamonds* suggest that Bishop had found a place for her photographs.

Several of the prose accounts that Bishop planned to include and wrote show how she would have punctuated her writing with her photographs. She notes when and where she took photographs with regularity, often then with these placed in her typescript into handwritten parentheses, as if in a later drafting the photographs would replace notes. On her promised

Elizabeth Bishop, photograph taken in the Amazon, February 1960. From Special Collections, Vassar College Libraries. Reprinted with permission.

account of her trip to the Amazon finally made in February 1960, she details taking photographs in Manaus, the Amazon's main port, of the fountain in the city's square, the Praça de Matriz; and we see it just as she describes it, "a magnificent affair" with its life-sized cherubs and hexagonal base pool. We see described and photographed the poorer section of the town, the bright colors of shutters, the men with their white pants sitting outdoors eating dinner, with *cafezinho* cups arranged on bright, oilcloth table covers—photographs that are painterly for, as Bishop says, the scene is "all very much like Brazilian primitive paintings." We recognize the hub of that city's life, the huge elegant *Mercado* or market on the docks with its wrought iron and glass roof (designed by Eiffel and based on Les Halles). She records in writing and photography the traffic of the river, villages passed through, the process of their boat taking and in return receiving supplies. She notes and photographs their boat being loaded up with meat, great hunks of raw carcass carried by brown-skinned boys red against the verdant shore. And we recognize the huge open seas of the Amazon itself with all its life. "I have never seen a lovelier wild sight," Bishop writes of a flock of 150 white herons, luminous with an "electrical effect" against a sky darkening with an Amazonian storm. Released from her photojournalistic context like Parks in *Flavio*, Bishop produces a form that is photographic travel memoir, with the I and the eye, the perspective returning. In an account of another river trip better drafted this time and (with notes to herself about editing) clearly for publication, "A Trip on the Rio São Francisco," the personal journey is interwoven with a history of navigation that she was obviously reading at the time. She visited this river in 1967, alone this time on the advice of Lota's doctor. Bishop says the voyage acted as "a sort of eraser" for the political and personal turmoil of the moment (*One Art* 463). On a boat named Wenceslau Braz of which she has a photograph, she evokes the quietness of the stern-wheeler, the way in which it seemed to be symbiotically blended in with the river life through which it passed: It went "*ppph . . . ppph . . . ppph . . .* softly, rather like a seal coming up for air." The simile puts one in mind of Bishop's comparably cross-species seal of "At the Fishhouses." *Black Beans and Diamonds* would have been—as she noted in her notes for a plan of one chapter—a "sort of prose poem."

Bishop's eye in writing and photography notes quirky details. Her observation making its way from the foreground of her poetry to behind the camera, the photographs contain none of that lumpen, *studium* quality of the photos of the *Brazil* collection. She is conscious of perspective, angles, shapes, movement, juxtapositions. At Pirapóra (which means "'jumping fish' in the language of the Cariri Indians"), she photographs the fishing nets she had seen used on the São Francisco, interested in how the light she describes as fading creates from the nets silver patterns against the water and soft sand. In Ouro Prêto where Bishop bought her own house as things began to get difficult with Lota in Rio and Petrópolis, she photographs the baroque architecture that she so loved, particularly the town's famed churches and its terra-cotta-red roofs. She took many photographs of the sculptures by town artist Aleijadinho ("little cripple"), their bodies with oversized heads startlingly vital and misshapen as though picking off his own crippling deformity. Bishop asks questions in photography, catches the *punctum*. Two boys squat in a road. The shadows are long, the light soft and golden. Is it evening? The street is almost deserted; a woman walks away from the camera, a man walks toward it. Here is no theme, no revealed message. In a photograph that looks like a Bishop watercolor—actually better than one—a rust-colored wall sprouts a dark, ivy-like plant with red, perpendicular flowers. Next to it a cracked, red-brown wooden door has been

Elizabeth Bishop, photograph taken during travels in Brazil, 1960s. From Special Collections, Vassar College Libraries. Reprinted with permission.

decorated with pink flowers in the shape of a cross. In other photographs women and children stand in long queues. In the poor northeast? Or somewhere in Minas? An old woman dressed in a large mackintosh holds a red flag with "Scotch" written on the side. The flag appears homemade. Scotch what? Is this a public ritual? Or the private habits of an eccentric? Behind an old man are some political posters. He carries a massive tray of—parasols? political streamers? These are places journalists and *Life* photographers don't go. Like paintings, like poetry, they are mediated. Unlike them the photographs catch a reality that we can see really *was* there—but that still goes unanswered.

In many of the photographs Bishop's subjects return her look. They are conscious of the photographer's presence and she is interested in this. Back in the *praça* in Manaus Bishop photographs a photographer photographing. He has his back to us. A woman to his right, and a girl to the left in a turquoise dress giggling self-consciously, look back at Bishop and us. Bishop writes that the photographer was annoyed because he had wanted

Elizabeth Bishop, photograph taken during travels in Brazil, 1960s. From Special Collections, Vassar College Libraries. Reprinted with permission.

to photograph her. She finds her "beady-eyed" proxy in him. Nowhere in Bishop's unpublished prose is self-consciousness of what it means to look at Brazil better caught than in her account of a trip to Brasilia in August 1958. "A New Capital, Aldous Huxley, and Some Indians" was rejected by the *New Yorker*—not to her surprise: "the material just didn't go together," she realized (*One Art* 369). In fact the forty-five pages of completed typescript constitute a wonderful poised memoir that is also an essay on the building of Brasilia and its effects. It is exemplary of the kind of work that might have been included in *Black Beans and Diamonds*. One of the few critics interested in *Black Beans and Diamonds* searched for but didn't find this piece, writing that "Hundreds of pages of prose about Brazil have never been found; unless one includes her drafts toward *Brazil*, the extant material amounts to few dozen pages."[41] It is quite likely that Victoria Harrison mistook this piece for a draft of *Brazil*, since Bishop's annotations written over the typescript show where she culled from it for material on Brasilia in *Brazil*, taking all the facts, shucking like corn the variation, the memoir. The design of the essay was to show how the material it describes doesn't go together. How to reconcile, even see side by side, the development of Brazil's new capital in the interior with the survival of the Indians surrounding it? The founding of Brasilia and the industrialization of which it was the most visible symbol promised to alleviate poverty and bring workers from the northeast to stem the tide of migration into *favelas* like those in Rio. But the government "Palaces" are erected by workers who camp in a "free city" of wood shacks that themselves are growing like *favelas*. The pool at the presidential palace is bigger than an Olympic pool. But the builders and the employees are housed inadequately below ground, the architect Niemeyer "like a lazy housewife shoving household gear out of sight under a deceptively well-made bed." Above all the development has brought the selling and development of Indian lands much closer to the Mato Grosso where the Nambikwara live. Bishop's account travels from the most modern and extravagantly designed city in the world to "the most primitive people left in the world."

Or putatively, because Bishop doesn't reconcile and narrate since she's so conscious of where she and we are looking from. Writing for an audience of which she demands greater responsiveness to nuance, she unravels expectations we might have of both an overreaching South American government and "primitives." Bishop ends with a comparison between Anthony Trollope's cynical remarks about the development of Washington in the United States in the middle of the nineteenth century and

Elizabeth Bishop, photograph taken during travels in Brazil, 1960s. From Special Collections, Vassar College Libraries. Reprinted with permission.

what Americans might think of Brasilia now. This time her comparativist approach—English author/United States; American perception/Brazil—stands. Traveling in an international party Bishop is as much about observing them as observing the sights; this generates the greatest juxtapositions. From others' reactions to Brazil she produces satire: the Polish countess who, on her hunting trip, thinks Brazilians have the killing instinct; the English Cambridge anthropologist studying the effects of contact; the reserved Huxley and his Italian wife, Laura. Their looking is as prismatic as all the glass Bishop describes has been used to build Brasilia. Images of tools of observation pile up, not only in the descriptions of that glass that acts as an "aquarium" (though who exactly are the fish?). Huxley is key to her looking at looking, accruing as he does an entourage—her included. She notes how he was fascinated by instruments of observation, with his magnifying glass, miniature telescope and special lensless spectacles ("These, he told us, were an ancient invention of the Chinese, useful for both near-sighted and far-sighted eyes. Laura remarked that she also found them very useful for going to sleep, and when we finally got on the plane she put them on and promptly did so"). Huxley's book on vision, *The Art of Seeing,* though not mentioned by Bishop, shows the extent of philosophical, psychological, and cultural investment her writerly other recognized in looking.[42]

The inclusion of photographs in the piece above all reveals mediation and in the process the loss of the real or primitive. The appearance of cameras, hers and Laura's, highlights the canniness of the Indians—this most "primitive people left in the world" are already touched. When Laura takes pictures with her Polaroid "these Indians knew all about cameras and were happy to pose, in rows, with their arms about each other's necks." One Indian in pants and a shirt when asked to pose for a photograph "politely removed his clothes," and puts his trousers back on to cook the lunch (the sausages they'd brought). "The Indians loved the Polaroid pictures (in fact a Polaroid camera and a large supply of film should see one through the jungle), almost tearing them apart to see the results." Bishop photographs Laura preparing to take a photograph among the Indians. With Huxley discreetly in the rear, the Indian woman with the child, and the young white woman on the right (probably the Huxleys' interpreter whom Bishop mentions) all looking off in the same direction possibly at some Indian activity, the focus of the photograph is not obvious. It is in fact, *Las Meninas*–like, the photographed camera's lens. Only Laura looks back at Bishop. Laura the photographer mirrors Bishop the photographer. The effect is endless reflection, and the white woman photographer (both of them) is the subject rather than the Indian woman—who somehow becomes at the edge. Bishop's self-consciousness in shifting perspective includes, in her prose too, the Indians. From the Indians' point of view "Huxley did appear, not homely, but exceedingly long, white, refined, and misplaced."

Bishop too was intrigued by optical instruments. Living in Key West before she went to Brazil she worked in a factory that made lenses for binoculars—a job that, ironically, gave her eyestrain. She read Newton's *Opticks,* and when given a pair of binoculars by her doctor Anny Bauman she wrote, "The world has wonderful details if you can get it just a little closer than usual."[43] The interest in optical instruments that we also saw in "Burglar" makes it elsewhere in *Black Beans and Diamonds.* In "Rio de Janeiro, 1565–1965," two pages of rough typescript that promised to reinstate that overlaying of historical moments and of perspectives cut from *Brazil,* she borrows a pair of binoculars from an officer as she returns to the coast of Brazil by boat. But she says here she is "far-sighted" and could anyway see miles and miles, a beneficial hypermetropia (the inverse of myopia) remembered by friend;[44] she uses them to confirm what she

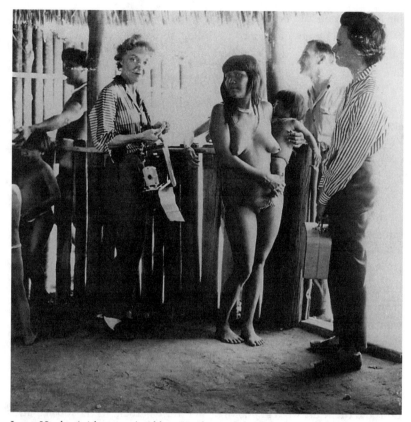

Laura Huxley (with camera), Aldous Huxley, and their interpreter, visiting Xingú Indians, August 1958. Photograph by Elizabeth Bishop. From Special Collections, Vassar College Libraries. Reprinted with permission.

can already see and knows after living there for fourteen years. Bishop then passes them to a Tasmanian passenger who in contrast sees nothing. "One's heart sinks," Bishop writes. "This was the first time the Tasmanian who had been twice around the world and was now half-away around for the third lap—and this was all he cared to know, apparently, of Brazil." Though syntactically fragmented, the piece promised to develop a criticism of tourism questioning the official line that it meant improvement to social conditions. In "Another American," undated and also unfinished, Bishop similarly connects tourism with optical instruments and their mediation. An American couple have "been all over . . . the world, almost! . . . five countries in six weeks," including "San Pollo," the woman tells the protagonist. The husband carries "a movie camera and under that arm a copy of TIME, a two-days-in advance copy." Since they're in the Amazon it's more likely he's an employee of *Time* than a subscriber. The narrative observes that "If one had been collecting Americans like butterflies" he especially is a species worth netting. The shift in perspective—who constitutes the wildlife in the Amazon?—is reversed as the short story removes even this ground. The woman watches the protagonist in the mirror, initially mistaking her for a Brazilian, looking for something foreign in her. But from cringing withdrawal the protagonist suddenly realizes her own "irrational self-pity of the self-exiled" and identifies with the Americans—and thereby identifies herself. "Then she/I told herself not to be a snob. After all, they were interested in seeing the world . . . and that was what was so wonderful about her race and her country, after all—their energy, the curiosity." The protagonist is of course herself "Another American." What's interesting about what we get to see of the drafting is that Bishop was considering point of view formally. Her handwritten annotations on her typescript include revision and juxtaposition of *I* for *she*, the first person for the third for her protagonist. Bishop was clearly wondering about where to render perspective from. It's quite possible that her inability to resolve point of view—the main edits to the draft—were what made her leave the piece unresolved.

The concern with mediation extends to newspaper translations, where we see Bishop's attachment to documenting reality but documenting oversights. Her promised account of the St. George's Day parade in Rio (dated 1963) begins with a newspaper quotation that segues into what the newspaper leaves out, details that strike the poet's eye. Other newspaper translations home in on her interest in relations between Brazil and America, the significance of U.S. financial aid, and occasionally but incrementally the effects of the military dictatorship, the restrictions on her friends' movement in contrast to her own freedom as an American. Translations from the Brazilian daily *O Globo* in 1967 through to the early 1970s concern the distribution by the U.S. Navy of cookies, tea, and chewing gum to *favelados;* a Janis Joplin concert in Rio thwarted because authorities fear the huge crowds of young people she would draw; and the identity papers or *carteiros* increasingly required. As she travels in perspectives she shifts between genres and forms. In "Suicide of a (Moderate) Dictator—A Report in Verse & Prose," Bishop treats to prose and poetic versions the facts of Vargas's suicide following the demand for his resignation after the scandal of the Lacerda assassination attempt. The poem, dedicated to Lacerda (surely ironically: "Perhaps truth is a shadow, Carlos," she has handwritten), heightens the contrasts with images of the ephemerality of media truths that will "rub off on our fingers / like the ink from unproof-read newspapers / crocking the way the unfocused photographs / of crooked faces that soil our coats," versus those of the scene of dogs being walked along the beach "as usual," a rainbow, and two boys flying kites. Another unfinished poem, "A Baby Found in the Garbage," catches in its incisive circularity the cold detachment of reporting, beginning with the still-breathing baby "Wrapped in the very newspaper / whose headlines she would make that day" when at the end of the poem she dies. At the same time Bishop's witnessing of social situations is mixed with the imaginary to convey empathy for events beyond the media's brief. The account promised of the "servant of mine from the northeast" might be among the 78 people who have been traveling for 8 days in the back of a truck to Rio. Already three people have died, and only one (a baby) could be buried when they stopped at night. Now a girl lies about to die, supported by her family, her body held by and uniting them all. The story's title is the truck's bumper sticker: "Farewell Teresa." Or from pathos to satire, it could come in the account of northeast immigrant to Rio who makes good and returns home to find it provincial, "Grand Opening." In prose, poetry, in memoir, fiction, in photography—in the incomplete processes of translation—Bishop reaches out to unearth Brazil. "A Trip to the Mines—Brasil" searches out for the graves of slaves now hidden in the obsolete gold mines they worked. Its several unresolved drafts don't unearth them.

Among Bishop's notes currently filed under *Brazil* is one page headed "Introductory Note." Like the newspaper translations and annotations that are also filed here, the introductory note is written too late to have been for inclusion in *Brazil*. Bishop states here that she stayed in Brazil for sixteen or seventeen years, so this would take us to a point at or after 1967 when she left Brazil for the United States. Bishop writes that her immersion in Brazil meant that she saw the country "from a double point of view—perhaps more than a traveler or tourist would see, or the Brazilians themselves." The note goes on that the work that follows is to be autobiographical as well as documentary. "This ~~collection~~ random collection of stories (true stories, mostly, travel sketches essays, poems, and a selection ~~of th~~ selections from the hundreds of newspaper clippings I saved over the years is partly a thank-you note for the hospitality I enjoyed, to the friends I made and lost and made." With her changes emphasizing that the work is non-narrative (*random* collection), Bishop's note echoes the generic multiplicity foreground in the Rockefeller application. We are reading the introduction to *Black Beans and Diamonds*. It also presents this work, like Lévi-Strauss in his prologue to *Saudades do Brasil*, as a valediction to Brazil interwoven with personal losses.

The explanation of those interwoven losses at the heart of *Black Beans and Diamonds* comes in a letter to the Rockefeller Foundation explaining why she hadn't finished the book. Dated October 16 with no year given but probably 1968 since her grant terminated that summer, Bishop writes what she calls a "very frank letter," totally unnecessarily given that all the foundation had asked for was her "informal evaluation of the assistance received." The letter flies in the face of professional correspondence, of all her professional correspondence. "Because of a series of unusual and unhappy occurrences in my personal life" she begins, "my answers to your questions will have to be very different from what they would have been if I had spent that time, as I had intended to, in working almost exclusively on my project: a book of prose pieces about Brazil. But I sustained a great loss, the prolonged illness and death of my closest friend & the breaking up of my Brazilian home of seventeen years, followed by three illnesses of my own." She is still planning on finishing the book, "trying hard to make up for the unavoidably lost time." But her losses meant her departure from Brazil and incompletion of this work. Her biographer, Brett Millier, says that Bishop was unable to complete her travel prose collection as opposed to her travel poems about Brazil because she was unable to generalize.[45] But there's more to it than that, or rather we see what's at stake in generalizing: the loss of the ability to express loss without mastery.

Bishop's incompletion of *Black Beans and Diamonds* traumatically repeats the events of late 1961 when she hadn't been able to complete properly and do the revision on *Brazil*. It hinges, as traumatic repetition does, on the same unresolved cause. Then Lota's involvement in the building of the park had meant Lota's immersion in her growing workload and Bishop's distraction from completion. Now Lota had a breakdown and Bishop found the project of completion impossible. While Bishop and Lota approved the military coup in 1964, like most people in Brazil they had no idea how it would turn out. After the coup in which Lacerda would be a principal actor knowing about it in '63, there was increasing tension between Lota and Lacerda. The new President Branco and his government grew uninterested in funding the park. Lacerda and Lota had different politics. Lacerda wanted to reclaim other public land around Rio for an international hotel, which would have provided him with a lucrative deal. Lota defended land for public use. The effect on Bishop's and Lota's relationship was immediate and inexorable. From 1964 on Bishop records in her letters Lota's worsening nervous exhaustion and says, in what may be a manner of speech but proves prophetic, that she doesn't want the park to "kill" Lota (*One Art* 427). By 1967 when she writes of wanting to escape "the violence" in Brazil (457), it is not clear whose violence she is referring to—of Lota or towards

Lota of politics—probably the enmeshed both. Struggling with her own work and illnesses, in July Bishop flew to New York, against her wishes but on the advice of Lota's doctors. Here Bishop was to bring together the *Black Beans and Diamonds* pieces—the second Brazil book. In September and this time against doctors' advice, Lota begged Bishop to be allowed to join her in New York. The night she arrived Lota took an overdose of valium. Though it looked at first as though she was going to survive she died five days later. In her account, fictional but based on research of documents and interviews, Brazilian novelist Carmen Oliviera has gotten at this traumatic chain of events, the ellipses and elisions from politics to the personal, from '61 to '64 to '67 as no one else has previously.[46] Bishop's photographs of Lota's park and the development along Rio's seafront somehow catch the same overshadowing and connection. In one photograph, so different from Kessel's which is taken at the most obvious angle, Bishop has photographed not from the customary east of the bay looking at the skyline but from the west looking out to the beach from the skyline. An evening photograph with the sun setting in the west, the skyscrapers themselves are not shown, but their long shadows on the white sands leave their ghostly mark.

After Lota's death Bishop decided she could no longer live in Brazil and in 1968 moved to San Francisco. (Her letter to the Rockefeller Foundation was written from here.) From '66 to '69 Rockefeller asked her to nominate other writers for the same award. One can imagine the guilt, the self-doubt and self-berating that Bishop must have gone through with each reminder of her own incompletion. But at least up to the mid '70s she was still planning to finish the book. In a letter to photographer Mariette Charlton written in 1970, Bishop seems to have given up the idea of her own photographs and now wants to commission others. Back in Ouro Prêto ("the worst mistake in my life" she realizes, the belief that she could return to Brazil) (*One Art* 510), trying to sell the house and move permanently to the United States, Bishop suggests to Charlton that "you might possibly, possibly like to come here and do some pictures for my 'book.'" She offers to pay fee plus expenses. "The book is away behind—three years or so!—but that wouldn't matter—because the pictures have nothing directly to do with the text. I just want GOOD ones, and not the usual ones at all—in fact I know what I want, exactly, but just can't take them myself, and I am sure you could. . . . Perhaps even saying 'exactly' is rude to a photographer, since you must know what would make better pictures than I do—and a lot must depend on luck, just as in poetry, but I'd give you my LIST."[47] And still in 1973 she was speaking, to Howard Moss, her longtime editor at the

New Yorker, of the "several hundred pages of my long-procrastinated book on Brazil on hand."[48] But *Black Beans and Diamonds* was never finished.

There's a way in which Bishop moves more fully into loss at the end of her life or rather awakens to it. In her final decade she was trying to finish several things. Among them was an elegy for Lota. Called "Aubade and Elegy"—like Schumann another dawn to an end, an awakening to death—Bishop left enough of its bones for us to see that she blamed politics for Lota's death. The notes in preparation for the poem remember

> the beautiful colored skin—the gestures (which yo[u] said you didn't
> have) / . . . the door slamming, plaster falling—the co[o]k and I laughing
> helplessly on the other side of the door / And oh the dream—t[h]e house,
> the desire . . . / and oh the co[u]ntry's ingratitude—misunderstanding—
> WASTE / . . . and courage courage to the last, or almost to the last— /
> Regret and guilt, the nighttime horro[r]s.

Bishop wrote several drafts of the poem, the best of which reads in part:

> Perhaps for the tenth time ~~today~~ already
> and still early morning I wake it's like waking
> wake and go under the black wave of ~~your death~~
>
> .   .   .   .
>
> the smell of the earth, the smell of the black-roasted coffee
> as fine as fine humus as black
>
> no coffee can wake you no coffee can wake you no coffee
> can wake you.

Another work that went unfinished, dating from the Brazil period, was entitled "Homesickness." Worked on for fifteen years, "Homesickness" was about Bishop's mother and *her* homesickness. David Kalstone was the first among critics to isolate as "the unspoken fact of Bishop's childhood: an absent mother."[49] This was a mother who went mad because, as Bishop renders it in "In the Village," she could not give up her mourning for her father; her scream hangs over Nova Scotia as the dressmaker tries to get her out of her mourning dress.[50] This was a mother who never recovered from loss. Bishop's mother was the first—though not the last—among Bishop's ghosts. (In an uncanny coincidence Bishop read *A Lover's Discourse* probably the year she herself died.)[51] While she was finishing "In the Village" and deciding to make her home in Brazil, she wrote in her letters: "It is funny to come to Brazil to experience total recall about Nova Scotia—geography must be more mysterious than we realize, even" (*One*

Art 249). Was Bishop at home enough in Brazil to become a child because of *saudades,* because of *its punctum?* For Bishop's was a childhood punctuated with loss and suffering. She herself suffered depression and twice took an overdose. It was in her childhood that she developed asthma, which she acknowledged could be connected to her depression and which her biographer believes was one of the forces behind her travelling: she went "in search of air she could breathe."[52] It was only with later losses that Bishop could realize *saudades*—look at the earlier losses. As Lloyd Schwartz writes in his reminiscence of Bishop in Brazil, "Having given up Brazil, she could finally become a Brazilian."[53]

Bishop's last finished book, her most abbreviated and formally exquisite as a butterfly wing, is predominated by poems about loss. A Crusoe now repatriated mourns his Friday but doesn't get over him (no *robinsonnades* here). A proto–dream house on a beach turns out to be boarded up. In the "Enormous morning" of "Five Flights Up" is discovered a "yesterday . . . almost impossible to lift." And of course there is initiation into loss, in the photographs of the *National Geographic,* in the first poem "In the Waiting Room." Bishop's seminal poem about loss, and one of the touchstones for telling loss, also appears here. "One Art" is an art, in how not to master loss. While critics have debated endlessly the source of the poem—who is the "you" addressed in this possible moment of "even losing you"?; it could be more Lota, or it could be the partner who stood by Bishop after Lota's death until Bishop's own[54]—the point is the catalogue of losses, as the adult now looks back on the child of "The Waiting Room," including that of her mother in "my mother's watch." Losses pile up ("two cities . . . / some realms I owned, two rivers, a continent"), counted but really incalculable. A villanelle, the poem's form is associated with mourning[55] and counting. The distinguishing feature of the villanelle is calculated repetition. Two one-line refrains must be repeated in each of the five triplet stanzas, before being brought together in the last two lines of the closing quatrain. Of poetic forms the villanelle requires most mastery.[56] Bishop's has been much admired by critics: "in the writing of such a disciplined, demanding poem lies the mastery of loss"; "One Art" is indicative of the way in which "writing is a way, not to overcome, but to come to terms with loss."[57] Yet while the poem's *studium* states that mastering loss is possible, even easy, that in the reiterated line-ends "the art of losing isn't hard to master" and "loss is no disaster," the poem's poignancy is to demonstrate the opposite. The *punctum* comes in a repetition, a return in the last line: "the art of losing's not too hard to master / though it may look like (*Write* it!) like disaster." The double *like* in the closing line is a giveaway of the failure to meet, masterfully, the intervening parenthetical injunction to *write* the loss. It is the point where, syntactically, the speaker loses it. Yet the repetition realizes loss better than anywhere in Bishop (in poetry?). Art of loss without mastery. For its own visions and for the perspective it would add to Bishop's canon, it's tempting to edit and publish *Black Beans and Diamonds*. But that would be to perform an art of mastering that she herself proved so fine in losing.

CHAPTER 5

MY SECOND SKIN

O R MY FIRST SKIN? I waver over what to call this return to my first book, which was called *Second Skins*. Especially since in saying "second skin" we cannot come any closer in language to embodying our corporeal skin. There is no idiom consisting of a first or original skin. "Under the skin" seems to me to be saying something different, something altogether more visceral, exposed: skin*less*. "Second skin" carries the greatest proximity to our literal skins. It is the metaphor closet to the skin we are in.

There's something like this equivocation in timing at work in the palinode. The palinode is a doubling back, a return to the ode. Yet in recovering what the ode left out the palinode makes its subject what should have been in the first. Indeed it goes back before the original. The palinode is take two but more authentic than take one. And as a return the palinode creates a new kind of text. The palinode is not among the customary modes for responding to one's errors. It is not a defensive turn against the reader in which the author accuses you of misreading and goes on to restate imperiously or painstakingly the argument (most common). Nor is it a full-scale retraction, an exercise in self-abnegation (I take it all back: for obvious reasons rarer). The palinode is rather a return that realizes that realization could only come with loss from the original. It may be a model of learning without deliberate self-advancement. As Hal Foster writes in the different context of his *Return of the Real,* a history of avant-garde art that may itself be read as a palinode since the author criticizes the linguistic turn in art theory for which he confesses he is in no small part responsible, the figure of return can disrupt a relentlessly evolutionary model of intellectual history in which one must abandon projects to take up new ones, always and fully break with the old.[1] The palinode creates something new in the repetition. It returns to expose the former surface, for there is in this exercise of turning in on oneself (although not turning on oneself) something gently self-excoriating: "scab-picking" as John Updike describes a tendency in much contemporary autobiographical writing.[2] The palinode picks at the first skin in order to lay open—but also to heal—the wounds remaining in the second.

Skin was very important to me in my book *Second Skins* (ode to my palinode here), as its title suggests. *Second Skins: The Body Narratives of Transsexuality* used transsexuality to bring back the materiality of sex that I argued theories of gender performativity current in gender studies left out.[3] Skin represented the most literal aspect of the body in transsexuality's "body narrative." As the largest and most visible bodily organ, yet also our interface between self and world and for many of us subject to psychic investment, skin literally incorporated identity. It is moreover the material through which transsexuals most substantially change sex, gender reassignment surgery consisting most visibly of a manipulation of the surface tissues of the body—and skin can run quite deep. Skin helped me move, so I thought, from *gender performativity* to transsexuality's *body narrative.* It contained the sexed referent that could anchor the free-floating gender signifier. And narrative (for my analysis consisted of reading the representation of sex in transsexual narratives) moved sex/gender on from the endless repetitions of gender performativity. In *really* changing sex I argued, transsexuals concluded a body narrative. With transsexual narratives I hoped to have wrapped up the plot of sex.

If I was aware then of the importance of skin as the literalization of the body of my body narratives, I was not aware to what extent photography carried the conclusion of but actually interrupted my narrative. It was in my epilogue that I finally turned to photographs. There I looked at how photographs of transsexuals evidenced the transitions of transsexual narratives, the intertwined transitions of sex and the story. The photographs presented visibly, really the evidence of sex as referent. The apparent referentiality of photography, its distinctive feature for showing its referent unmediated, seemed to me to correspond perfectly to the referentiality of sex at the end of transsexual narratives; it was a correspondence too perfect to forgo. So absolute was my faith in photography as presenting the referent of sex that I ended *Second Skins* with my own photograph. "I blow my cover," I wrote in my greatest moment of self-unveiling, "and embody my narrative with this photograph" (234). This sole autobiographical photograph in the book was supposed to literalize *my own* completion of a transsexual narrative as a female-to-male transsexual—now a man—and also simultaneously to complete my book. That was my last sentence. The photograph evidenced my point of no return. But the preceding, penultimate photograph was more important—the most important included in my book I now think—for literalizing the materiality of sex that I sought to recover through transsexuality (through photography). This photograph was an incredible close-up of a female-to-male's genitals before surgery but after hormone treatment. The photograph shows, I argued, my friend Zachary Nataf "as no longer female . . . but neither as a genetic male." Of a "clitoris-turning-penis," the photograph captured "this flesh as the referent of his narrative" (234). "Transcock," as it was retroactively named by photographer Del La Grace, seemed to encapsulate (literally: I was a real literalist) the substance of my work. Adamantine, huge, and irreducible, particularly when I projected it in slide shows at talks publicizing *Second Skins,* it had the effect, at least initially, of shocking my audience to see the referent I sought to make irrefutable. It was also the most cutaneous of my photographs.

My faith in photography as referential turned on a reading of Barthes's *Camera Lucida.*[4] In retrospect I realize this was a misreading: a failure to factor in what Barthes leaves out. Barthes of course crucially *doesn't* publish the most referential photograph for him, the Winter Garden Photograph of his mother. Amazingly I failed to mention this fact. Instead, seizing upon Barthes's initial setting up of the referentiality of photography, my reading remains confined to the first part of *Camera Lucida.* I didn't show (didn't see then) how *Camera Lucida* moves backward into the loss of the referent; I overlooked its palinode. *Camera Lucida* establishes reference only to show how photography loses it: *Ça-a-été;* the thing *was* there. The referent becomes irrevocable; the referent becomes real. Reading the referent back into the real, mistaking the latter for the former, I found presence in the lost past of the photograph. Thank goodness I managed at least to mention that *Camera Lucida* was Barthes's quest for his dead mother. Yet at the very moment I did so, I turned, through my etymological wordplay—through a performance of signifiers!—the absolute singularity of Barthes's relation to *his* photograph into gunshot for my cannons lined up against the linguistic turn and the rise of the signifier in gender theory. "Sifting through photographs of her, he looks for her flesh and blood *being,* a way to fill the absence of her body. From structuralism to poststructuralism to this

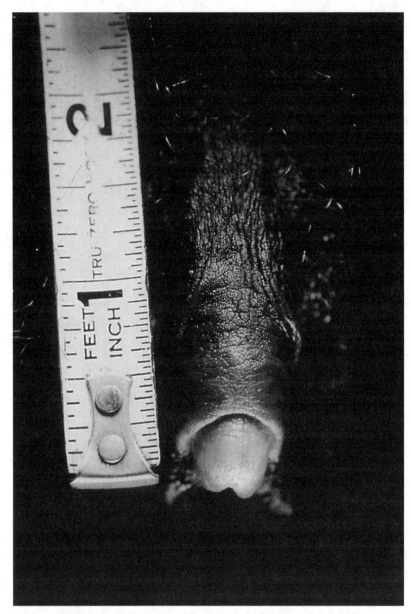

Del La Grace Volcano, "Transcock 1" (1996). Reprinted with permission.

signing off with the referent, the personal, and the search for his mother's presence (mater, matter): is there not something of an allegory in the final trajectory of Barthes's writings, a story for our specific theoretical time?" (211). I just couldn't get beyond that word "allegory," even though it took me away from the referential direction in which I sought to go, toward the figurative and further signification. I was even conscious at the time that Judith Butler, against whom I most directed my criticism of gender performativity, had used the base of this very word, in "allegorization," as a way to describe the performative relation of signifying drag to apparently natural heterosexual gender.[5] But, *faute de mieux,* I used the vocabulary and hurried on. In that sentence in which I sought to urge the importance of our doing so, I couldn't get *underneath* language.

In making Barthes allegory at the denouement of my narrative I didn't notice how Barthes's photograph stops narrative. In lieu of presence, the absence of Barthes's photograph interrupts his quest for his mother and sends him into palinodic decline—and silence: "nothing to say about the death of one whom I love most, nothing to say about her photograph" (93). I however, bustling onward and upward, had everything to say: about photography, about transsexuality. I read the linguistic-like codes in the photographs, the *studium* and never the *punctum,* responding to where the photographer, or the textual context, would have me look in my haste to close out anything accidental, anything that might stop my narrative. This is especially obvious when my reading was determined wholly by the captions of photographs; as it most often was. As Barthes had made quite clear in the earlier essay "The Photographic Message," captions along with layout and photographic composition are a crucial way in which photographs direct their reading or *studium:* the study of that which is most obvious about a photograph. These features constitute the "connotation procedures" through which the photograph connotes its message. They comprise photography's language and hence, Barthes writes of this medium that is really distinct as a message without a code, are "not strictly part of the photographic structure."[6] In response to a self-portrait of Loren Cameron for instance, I focused on the verbal frame of the image and read the photograph as "literally fram[ing] the viewer's gaze, reflecting back that look of fascination, objectification and desire s/he may cast" (230). In my opening image of a female-to-male transsexual at his desk with a pipe and pen, I dutifully noted the prominence of the props of pipe and pen, along with a beard, as evidence of the achievement of that body narrative. And it was the arrangement of four photographs of a male-to-female transsexual on a single page that enabled me to claim that they documented her sex transition. Even the putatively most referential photograph for me, "Transcock," relied on the code of the measuring tape for my reading, as many in my audiences tripped over each other in the eagerness to point out once they had recovered from the initial shock of the image.

To think now that I thought I could recover the referent even through *that* photograph! Without the brilliant enlarging techniques of La Grace's photography and the juxtaposition of the tape measure that encodes the image with size as a penis, the genitals would not, I must admit, be seen as a penis. In attempting to represent the referent, to symbolize it, I made it something else—part of the symbolic—and hence the referent *qua* referent escaped me.

But in mitigation Barthes *does* say that particularly with captions and text it's easy to fall prey to reading connotation in looking at photographs. Connotation uses the apparent referentiality of the photograph "in order to pass off as merely a denoted message which is in reality heavily connoted" (*Image* 21). You can see why I might have embraced the "passing off" of connotation procedures in transsexual photographs as the real (sexed) thing: read the clothing for the naked skin, the signifier for the referent. For if I read the *studium,* whose *studium* did I read and for whom? If I read the image according to how the photographer or the subject represented wanted me to see it, this had everything to do with where I was reading from. The return of the real that is a reaction against the postmodern "inflation of text and image" that Foster traces in his history of avant-garde art comes in two forms: first of all through the body, "through the violated body and/or the traumatic subject"; and second through autobiographical or ethnographic work in which the artist becomes representative of their community, "a turn to the referent as grounded in a given identity and/or a sited community" (xviii). My approach combined both of these turns against a postmodern inflation of text, for this is surely where I was writing from: as a transsexual; from and for a violated body; from that "as a" position Nancy K. Miller has called "representativity"—though she urges that we seek to avoid it in part by foregrounding our own bodies.[7] But how to avoid representativity when there is no (authentic) representation of oneself, in the combined imagistic and democratic senses of the word? Or more to the point, how to avoid reading oneself into the other when what one sees represented *is* oneself, when there is no real identity difference between who's represented and who's reading? In response to transsexual narratives but especially in relation to the photographs of transsexuals, I succumbed to a process of what I later discovered Susan Rubin Suleiman had just called "autobiographical reading": that is "the autobiographical imperative [that] applies not only to writing about one's life but to reading about it; reading *for* it; reading, perhaps *in order to* write about it."[8] Autobiographical reading, Suleiman writes of her own experience of reading memories of concentration camp survivors, "independently of any appreciation for the author's style or depth of vision, is shamelessly, unsophisticatedly, referential" (205). Crying not only on first but second reading of these memoirs, Suleiman realizes that what she's reading for her is herself: "What exactly am I looking for, and finding in these works? . . . I recognize the stories all too well. They could have been my own" (207). And although she doesn't theorize it as such, Suleiman seems to suggest that autobiographical reading, or at least the kind of autobiography that she reads and writes, is, like photography, caught up with the "shameless" and naïve desire for the "referential." One reads autobiographically because what one reads, what one wants to write autobiographically, is ultimately just out of reach of narrative's recovery: "the only kind of autobiography I find truly essential to read *or* write . . . is the kind that tries to recover, through writing, an irrevocable absence" (214). Reading and writing for transsexuality's absence, reading in the struggle to make it present, not surprisingly I got caught up in the connotation codes of transsexual photographs. Reading only with and for transsexuals, I read for my life.

Even so. How could I have missed Barthes's ultimate encounter with photography as wound? "I wanted to explore it not as a question (a theme) but as a wound," he writes undisguisedly in *Camera Lucida* (21). Buckling down to the *studium* in my ode, my first study, I covered over the *punctum,* "this wound, this prick" that for Barthes *is* the essence of photography (26), embodied in the Winter Garden Photograph and the reason he doesn't publish it: "(I cannot reproduce the Winter Garden Photograph. It exists only for me. For you, it would be nothing but an indifferent picture. . . . at most it would interest your *studium:* period, clothes, photogeny but in it, for you, no wound)" (73). But how to expose that wound, how to hold off the compulsion to re-dress it: a redressing that may cover but doesn't necessarily heal the wound? Barthes had actually left an explanation, and thereby made a prediction for his own future return, for how the connotation procedures are shattered off the real of the photograph, how the *punctum* or wound breaks through the *studium* that is strictly exterior to the structure of the photograph. At the end of "The Photographic Message" he had written that if "pure denotation, a *this-side-of language*" is possible, it is "at the level of absolutely traumatic images. The trauma is a suspension of language, a blocking of meaning" (30). This insight (which will become Barthes's second sight and his second skin) accords with Lacan's sense of how the real returns, how we make contact with "what resists symbolization absolutely": "The function of the *tuché,* of the real as encounter—the encounter in so far as it may be missed, in so far as it is essentially the missed encounter—first presented itself in the history of psychoanalysis in a form . . . of trauma."[9] Yet Lacan emphasizes that the real depends on an initial loss. Although the real is all presence ("there is no absence in the real"; "the real is absolutely without fissure"),[10] the return of the real requires our missed encounter: the first time around; originally. Barthes's description of the *punctum*—"it is what I add to the photograph and *what is nonetheless already there*" (55)—follows this same temporal deferral. The *punctum* is what we miss in our reading of the photograph, what is already there but which wounds us only on return (when we shut our eyes). It is what we see when someone brings "an oil-lamp into a dark place, so that those with eyes could see what was there."

In his *Return of the Real* Foster follows Lacan's theory to suggest that the splitting of the sign from the referent has left us with a notion of reality that can only be traumatic. After its loss the referent could only return as real. There has been a *"shift from reality as an effect of representation to the real as a thing of trauma"* (146). Foster's concept of *"traumatic realism"* (130–36) in our apprehension of the representation of reality both confuses what's representation and what's real, and mixes up what's created and new with what's reproduction and subsequent: first with second. Reading Warhol photosilkscreens of car crashes—where the reproduction with light-sensitive chemicals on a screen of the original photographs makes the wounded skin of the parties especially visible—Foster writes: "repetition in Warhol is not reproduction in the sense of representation (of a referent) or simulation (of a pure image, a detached signifier). Rather repetition serves to *screen* the real understood as traumatic. But this very need also *points* to the real, and at this point the real *ruptures* the screen of repetition" (132). The deferred trajectory of the real (like the palinode and photography it requires an original missing) may perhaps best be understood by that word "screen," which Foster uses in a carefully doubled sense. In the first sense Warhol's silkscreens actually veil the real. But the real then returns with unexpected force to break through or wound the screen of representation in that second sense that is on the contrary the visual display of the object. Slavoj Zizek, who has made this shift from reality to the real a key theme of his work, has also identified the same ambiguity of representation as screening out the real and simultaneously blowing up its screening: "Herein lies the fundamental ambiguity of the image in postmodernism: it is a kind of barrier enabling the subject to maintain distance from the real, protecting him or her against its irruption, yet its very obtrusive 'hyperrealism' evokes the nausea of the real."[11] Both Foster and Zizek moreover describe our confusion over the real as melancholic. Foster writes that "In recent intimations of postmodernism . . . the *melancholic* structure of feeling dominates"

(165). And in an image of cut skin that, like Foster's, corporealizes the idea of the readable surface of reality as a skin, Zizek suggests that "the inherently painful dimension of our contact with reality"—our desire to touch the real but our inability to hold it since every encounter, "even the most benevolent, *cuts into* the world"—renders our archetype Tim Burton's cinematic protagonist Edward Scissorhands. Edward Scissorhands, whose every attempt at contact results in unbearable wounding both to himself and others, "epitomizes the postmodern subject: a melancholic subject" (59). As Lynda Hart writes movingly of sadomasochistic scenes (I know: I'm piling up the texts when I should be getting real; layering skins when I should be peeling back my own skin)—but in a context that continues the image of our desire to touch the real as cutting through the other's and our own flesh—we have a "yearning for something that rips through the fabric of reality. We could think of it as a mourning for referentiality, the grief expressed for the loss of something one never had. . . . death is the referent, the moment when time stops—the present."[12]

What is this repeatedly invoked power of cut skin, particularly in a visual representation, to cut through the skin of representation and return the real? Perhaps transsexuality resonates for our moment, and I could equate it with the presence of the referent in *Second Skins,* because the process of surgical reassignment seems to offer a literalization of the traumatic loss of the referent and our attempt to regain it through trauma. Like Edward Scissorhands we cut *ourselves* up in the attempt to recover the referent of sex. Refusing to accept the loss of something we never had—a real sex; and this refusal brings transsexuality closer to melancholia than mourning—we turn in on our own skin. The hope is that surgery will provide us with immediate access to the referent—like photography. Indeed the two procedures of surgery and photography have been compared. For Walter Benjamin writing in an essay that sees in the photograph a demotic approximation to the referential, photography is like surgery because it "diminishes distance . . . and penetrat[es] into the patient's body."[13] For Barthes also, in *Camera Lucida* having one's photograph taken is like being subject to a surgery: "to become an object made one suffer as much as a surgical operation" (13). And with his history of TB Barthes would have had considerable experience of medical photography, of its ability to function like surgery in penetrating the body. X-rays cut through the body with sight, turning into an outside photographic skin a representation of what's going on inside (often traumatic) the otherwise opaque skin.

What's painful about photography and gender reassignment surgery both is that, in spite of how close they are to reproducing the referent, to making it present (and I emphasize they are our best means of approximation), they ultimately fail. Reading transsexuality and photography as referential (my photographic epilogue was entitled hopefully—but also tellingly—"Fielding the Referent": who, really, was out in left field?), I missed this loss. Now in an unbidden encounter I turn to see the lost referent return as real. Gender reassignment surgery fails most obviously in the case of female-to-male transsexual reassignment, which has found no way, half a century after its invention, of reproducing a functioning penis. It is almost impossible to develop a penis one can piss through without it developing disabling fistulas or complications. It *is* impossible to develop a penis with which one can have penetrative sex without first having to "pump it up" or insert a stiffening rod into the head (which may well shoot out during intercourse). And still one must chose between these "options," between *either* pissing *or* having sex—as if life could be decided between urinary or sexual function. And one makes this decision knowing (1) that *neither* will be fully successful and (2) that the end result will anyway leave severe scarring, the loss of flesh in the donor body part sometimes so shockingly large as to leave that part dysfunctioning. Literally, to have a penis one must give an arm and a leg. And then—sorry: but the trauma goes on—years after the surgery, the penis (often misshapen and ugly and looking nothing like a penis) can still fall off. Believe me, it happens. For male-to-female transsexuals, although by no means to the same degree, there is also some trace, some remnant, something that returns that can't be realigned or reassigned: a voice, height, hands, or, as was made traumatically evident in the recent experience of a dear friend of mine who was sure that at least in this way she passed perfectly, even postreassignment genitals. This failure to be real *is* the transsexual real.

This transsexual real is there in some of the photographs I showed in my book, although it's often not immediately or even completely apparent (the *punctum* is the partial detail that ruptures the *studium*). The *punctum* in the transsexual image is literally traumatic: the wounds of transsexuality, the scars from surgery or the physical traces that sustain this body as differently sexed. The scars or traces—for me it is an absence of parts—won't allow a prereassignment history to pass into, to pass as the apparent referentiality of a reassigned sex. In the Loren Cameron self-portrait the real is the scar that runs across the wall of the chest. One can barely make it out here (one of the reasons I chose this image), but in other photographs in *Body Alchemy* where Cameron is straightened up the scars are evident, unavoidable. What the scars make evident is the constructedness of transsexuality, the splitting of gendered sign from the sexed referent. For surely even if it does become possible to produce a perfectly reassigned sex in the future (tissue engineering is perhaps the way as I suggested—hoped—in my book, although what government health service or private insurance is going to fund this for transsexuals?), the irony will always remain that this referentiality was achieved only through the latest forms of technological construction. Here's the paradoxical deferral at work in the real: transsexuals can approach the referent of their sex only through reconstruction—a history that transsexual scars make evident. As reconstruction, transsexuality, too, like the palinode and photography, is an attempt to return, to get back the lost referent—the *ça-a-été* of sex, the body that should have been. And the scars on the skin are, like the photographs that don't hide them, that terrible thing: the return of the dead: they show the sex that was never really alive. In fact in many of his self-portraits Cameron leaves this trace of reconstruction in the form of the shutter-release bulb he holds quite visibly. The bulb, with its wire trailing outside of the frame of representation, points to the process of photographic construction. Emblematic of the brave facing up to the absence of the referent that *is* Cameron's photography, as it is *his* transsexuality (the *punctum* is subjective, stresses Barthes), the visibility of the technology means that the photograph does not try to pass itself off as referential, unmediated, but makes evident that it is a representation, a reconstruction. Cameron himself reads the shadow of the bulb as a metaphor for his path of self-construction as a transsexual: "People have asked me, however, why I don't try to conceal the bulb in my photographs. . . . I am creating my own image alone, an act that reflects the transsexual experience as well."[14]

The palinode like photography returns the real as ineffable. Flying to Brazil where I first presented this palinode as part of a seminar series that began my return to photography (my Brazilian colleagues, bless them, afterwards *congratulated* me on my transsexuality; they had a new and extraordinary response to loss, as I was to discover), I was reminded by a friend and my travelling companion of a footnote that had appeared in an early draft of my book but that had not made it through revisions into the final draft. This footnote, the existence of which I had completely forgotten, consisted of a discussion of a self-portrait by Cameron that appeared two years before publication of *Body Alchemy* in a female-to-male transsexual support journal.[15] Checking the journal to make sure I discuss the right image, I am startled to discover as true something I realize in retrospect I had already unconsciously known. This photograph did not make it into Cameron's final version of *Body Alchemy*. Like my footnote for me it proved unreproducible. Here's my footnote on Cameron's photograph,

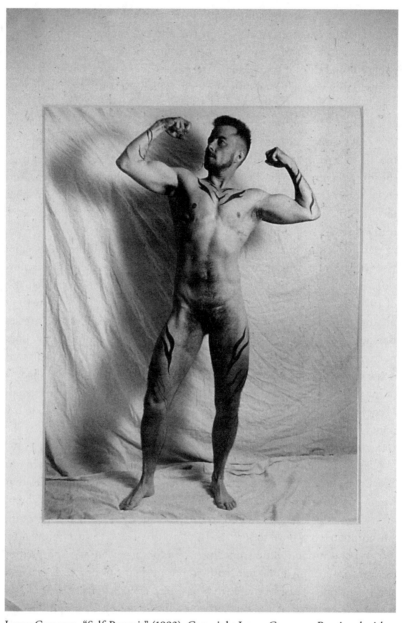

Loren Cameron, "Self-Portrait" (1993). Copyright Loren Cameron. Reprinted with permission.

finally found on a computer disk of discarded writings, written in 1994 at a crucial, decisive point in my transition. It appeared originally embedded in a discussion of German photographer Bettina Rheims's photographs of male-to-female transsexual Kim Harlow:[16]

FTM Loren Cameron's photographic self-portraits might be juxtaposed with Rheims's photographs of Harlow on this subject: the repetition of that splitting in self-representation. Although Cameron's photographs emblematically do not reverse or cover up the history of his transsexuality in the way that Rheims's portraits of Harlow do (quite the contrary), they strike me as being subject to something of that same splitting or doubling dynamic. Many of Cameron's shots are nudes. When the inscription of transsexuality on his body is occulted, that is, when he passes (i.e. as not transsexual), he appears as an integrally gendered subject. But when he represents his transsexuality, when he makes it visible, a splitting of the subject (and for me as viewer the split takes place in looking and looked at subject) seems to occur as a matter of course. The look/my look is drawn and fixed to what might be thought of as the transsexual markings on his body, as it tries to reconcile these markings with the remainder of the body. The splitting in viewed and viewer takes place precisely because of a (my?) failure at reconciliation of these parts/past. Cameron's stylized *(passing)* masculinity—his muscular chest and shoulders and the beautiful tattoos spread across them—only makes visible what is excessive or absent from the picture: what doesn't pass. My girlfriend's immediate reaction to these photographs voiced what I thought but couldn't say: "But he has no penis!" While Cameron's photographs are brave and brilliant testimony to the fact that transsexuality is certainly not unrepresentable, they do suggest that transsexuality exceeds the limits of (gendered) representation and, for me (at least for now), remains profoundly unreadable, irreconcilable within these limits.

One reason why I must have cut this footnote is that for a footnote it is ridiculously long. But there was an ample supply of long and abstruse footnotes in my book and the explanation doesn't seem sufficient. What really proved so necessary to cut, essential to overlook about this footnote for me, as perhaps Cameron's photograph was for him? Obvious to me now is that Cameron's photograph and my footnote are about the cutting and splitting in transsexuality, which were for me unspeakable. I couldn't name the nature of the splitting that took place both in the photograph and in the viewing subject; I am conspicuously vague here—"*that* splitting . . . *that same* splitting." The splitting that I was trying to describe was between what was representable (seeable, showable: the conjoining of the sign to the referent) and what was not (the real: the cut). This cutting in representation corresponded absolutely to the sexed splitting in the photograph. Simply, maleness, what can be shown in the image of Cameron's passing as a man, everything integral to that, proved speakable. What can't be reconciled with the apparently male subject in the photograph, what cut integrity, proved unspeakable. Or rather I should quickly particularize and say speakable/unspeakable *for me,* for my then girlfriend (at that point anyway) what *I* found unspeakable *she* spoke in her very first response to the photograph. I made this absolutely clear at the time: "My girlfriend's immediate reaction to these photographs *voiced what I thought but couldn't say: 'But he has no penis!'*" What she spoke and what I wrote and then cut was the unspeakability of transsexuality for me. Was this failure of Cameron's body to be genetically male-ly referential (and I emphasize this failure not just as his but as universally inevitable) speakable for my girlfriend because she was not transsexual? I was doubtful of this even at the time (evident from that questioning "my"? in parenthesis), that the lines of what could be seen and spoken of transsexuality were firmly pasted onto the division between nontranssexuals and transsexuals. And in retrospect as my girlfriend found *my* transsexuality increasingly unspeakable (literally: she couldn't speak about it for three years after we split, and is only starting to be able to discuss it and its role in our split now that she is with a genetic male, a man with a penis), I am certain that the division is not so correspondingly neat. As my final sentence in that note suggests, perhaps something about transsexuality remains not only unspeakable for me but for us all, irreconcilable—the referent unsuturable with the signifier, can I say?—within gendered representation.

What this unspeakability is I am trying to suggest (insane drive of the palinode: to speak the unspeakable; to recover the irrevocable) is the failure of us all, transsexuals and nontranssexuals alike, to achieve the real however much we desire to; indeed our failure to achieve it perhaps in proportion to our desire. Good old Lacanian conceit that I've only really understood for myself in return: it is loss in the real that engenders our desire for it, that engenders desire: photography, writing, transition. It's important, I think, that in this photograph Cameron does not show the shutter-release bulb. (Was this therefore taken by another photographer? Or, like Lévi-Strauss's self-portraits, on a self-timer? Probably the latter, since Cameron's career as a professional photographer has kept course with his transition as a transsexual, has apparently been determined by it.) This photograph is one of the few self-portraits of Cameron I've seen, and certainly the only full-length nude of him, that does not foreground, make visible as trace, the processes of technological (photographic/medical) construction. *For why the need to do so when the full frontal itself makes these processes of construction irrefutably evident?* What do we *not* see in this image except a genetic male? And my difficult placing of the "not" here is advised, because I think quite possibly we see everything in this photograph *but* a genetic male. We see a transsexual, a transsexual male, a self-constructed man, a body that is no longer woman but once was; we see the trace of a woman . . . The photograph itself—and surely this is where the eye is drawn: to what's not there, that absent male bodily referent—makes evident the missing penis. It can't be represented because indeed it's not achievable. I can hardly speak it.

But lose the referent and the real comes back. The return to what's missing impels a (self-) realization. Cut footnotes perhaps only serve to create the preconditions for a palinode: for what is the palinode if not an article-length footnote? In precedents of palinodes in theory what returns with startling consistency is an overlooked body part, often in a visual encounter—as frozen and clear as a photograph. For the writers of these palinodes the returning body part is typically a symbol of identity difference, the means to their realization of their own identity difference. But the body part is more than a symbol: in visual screenings—largely in photographs—it is literal too. And as literal *and* symbolic, not only moving between first and second texts but seeming to motivate them both (covered over in the first, remembered in the second), the body part somehow breaks free of the splitting between referent and signifier required of signification. These recurring body parts work a bit like Lacan's transcendental signifier: which is, of course, the phallus. In her palinodically titled "Afterthoughts on 'Visual Pleasure and Narrative Cinema' Inspired by *Duel in the Sun*," Laura Mulvey returns to her classic statement on Hollywood to consider, through film stills from *Duel in the Sun,* what she had left out of her previous account of cinematic narratives. In her concern with showing how Hollywood narrative is driven forward by a phallic gaze that castrates women in the film for a male audience ("subjected to her image as bearer of bleeding wound: she can exist only in relation to castration and cannot transcend it"), Mulvey realizes she had missed the female spectator's response.[17] She had thus missed her own pleasure in Hollywood narratives, cut her desire, which was symbolized in her earlier essay by the Lacanian phallus: "my own love of Hollywood melodrama . . . shelved as an issue in 'Visual Pleasure.'"[18] Recovering her pleasure now as she recovers herself, her own partiality to the phallus punctures, if it doesn't entirely reverse, Hollywood narrative. In an essay that makes clear its debt to Mulvey's first thesis on Hollywood's fetishization of women, Kobena Mercer criticized the photographs of Robert Mapplethorpe for similarly fetishizing—and feminizing—black men by fixating on their penises. Returning likewise out of doubt in the certainty and self-abstention characterizing his own first formulation ("I now wonder as I wander back into the text"), he recovers, too, his own pleasure: as a gay man he too loves penises. His desire makes him participant in the same "fantasy of power and mastery which I said was the projection of the white subject."[19] But perhaps the apparent coincidence of remembered or dis-membered body parts with deferred realizations in visual scenes is less arbitrary and more inevitable than may appear.

Perhaps the coincidence is classically uncanny. The model for deferred realization—Mulvey's and Mercer's and Lacan's and indeed from where the term comes to us—is Freud's case history on fetishism, that of the Wolf-Man.[20] A series of early sexual encounters had spurred the Wolf-Man's expected Oedipal conception of the female genitalia as a wound, in characteristic boyhood denial of women's sexed difference from his phallic own. Instead of pulling through the Oedipal plot and getting on with Freud's narrative, however, he had got stuck in and repeatedly returned to this moment. His adult life had been punctuated by a castration complex, channeled into a series of neuroses. Many were sexual: he alternated between sadism in which his penis was a weapon against women and masochism in which it was a target, on the point of becoming wound, mainly for other men. Some of them were not. Perhaps the most public way in which he acted out his horror in the uncertainty of sexual difference was by taking out a mirror to inspect repeatedly what he thought of as a wound in his nose: a hole—not visible to others—after he had picked a pimple on his skin. In analysis Freud goes back, goes back with the Wolf-Man to uncover the neuroses as the deferred realization or action of the castration complex: *nachträglichkeit* (189). Through a childhood dream along with other "screen memories" (163)—including the child Wolf-Man's account of being shown a picture book—the wound becomes readable on a screen. The crucial dream had consisted of a number of wolves sitting in a tree staring at the dreamer. Freud writes that three features continued to haunt the Wolf-Man about the dream: its immobility (the "perfect stillness and immobility of the wolves"); the power of the gaze (the "strained attention with which they looked at him"); and its enduring realness (the "lasting sense of reality") (177). The dream has a preternaturally photographic quality (stillness, gaze, reality); preternatural because it is a dream and unconscious, but also because it forms the projected surface for what is formative (pre-), primordial about the Wolf-Man's identity. At its exposed center is a primal scene, which Freud believes the Wolf-Man had encountered at eighteen months: possibly his first memory, but Freud here leaves undecided whether the scene was really witnessed by the child or whether it was solely fantasy. The dreamer associates the dream with a story he had been told just before he had the dream, of a maimed wolf: a wolf that had its tail docked. Suturing the dream with this story—and the Wolf's lost tail with the Wolf-Man's tale—Freud unlocks the castration complex screened in the dream but cloaked by repression into the neuroses.

After Freud had read his dream and his life the Wolf-Man never got back to a point before his trauma. He reentered analysis subsequently, with Freud and others. But he was considered sufficiently recovered, by himself and Freud, to lead a different life from that which had impelled him into analysis in the first place. Perhaps there is something that grows back around wounds and that's the skin. One of the remarkable properties of skin is its ability to regenerate: to produce second, even third layers when wounded. The palinode, though tied up with loss and belatedness—like transsexuality an attempt to *get it right this time*—is ultimately restorative in realizing loss. In his seminal palinode in autobiography theory, Philippe Lejeune captures this paradox. His expression of the palinode's recovery in loss borrows the Freudian fetishist's syntax of realizing wrongness: "I know but." "'I was wrong—but I was right to be wrong!' Undoubtedly self-criticism, like autobiography, is an impossible undertaking." "In spite of the fact that autobiography is impossible, this in no way prevents it from existing."[21] So: in spite of the fact that transsexuality is impossible this in no way prevents it from existing. Indeed, as with self-criticism, a similarly impossible undertaking, I would do it over again.

There is a recurring belief in photographs as a kind of skin. It is the most metaphysical and yet at the same time the most corporeal image of the photograph we have, and it goes back to a mystical conception of photography—to an ideal of photography that existed even before the chemical invention of photography. In it the photograph is the ghost of the photographed body, a revenant of the referent's lost skin. The image appears in the nineteenth century in the work of Oliver Wendell Holmes—a writer who was also a doctor—who embraced photography at its moment of birth for "its miraculous nature" which, even then, he claimed, "we forget . . . as we forget that of the sun itself, to which we owe the creations of our new art."[22] Holmes traces his cutaneous faith in photography back to an ancient assumption that our bodies are "continually throwing off certain images like themselves . . . subtle emanations" (72). He may have got it from Democritus, a 4 BCE traveling mystic who in his work on visual perception, *On eidola,* argued that we see objects only because they slough off membranes which then impinge on our eye; or more likely since this and all of Democritus's writings are lost, Holmes got it from Lucretius, who adopted the theory in his *De rerum natura* when he wrote

> there exist what we call images *(simulacra)* of things; which, like films drawn from the outermost surface of things, flit about hither and thither through the air; it is these same that, encountering us in wakeful hours, terrify our minds, as also in sleep, when we often seem to behold wonderful shapes and images of the dead . . . lest by chance we should think that spirits escape from Acheron or ghosts flit about amongst the living. . . . I say, therefore, that semblances and thin shapes of things are thrown off from the outer surface, which are to be called as it were their films or bark, because the image bears a look and shape like the body of that from which it is shed to go on its way.[23]

But with the power of technology to capture light, Holmes claims, for the first time photography had realized these "Forms, effigies, membranes or films"—fixed this lost *"cortex"* (72). In its unprecedented incarnation of the photographic instant, the photograph "has fixed the most fleeting of our illusions" (73), the "incidental glimpses of life and death" (79) that the artist typically leaves out but that the accidents of photography make their subject. These accidents themselves may be marked literally by vestiges of the skin. If we look at a photograph of a particular cottage in Stratford-upon-Avon, Holmes writes, "It is not impossible that scales from the epidermis of the trembling hand of Ann Hathaway's young suitor, Will Shakespeare, are still adherent about the old latch and door, and that they contribute to the stains we see in our picture" (80). Holmes embraces the epidermalization that carries over from the skin of the dead referent to the photograph, even though it means—as Benjamin will say a century later of photography's effect on the aura—loss of vitality from the original. Instead of going to a real place or making contact with a real object, with the invention of the new art, Holmes predicts, we will look at photographs and "call for its skin or form": "Every conceivable object of Nature and Art will soon scale off its surface for us. Men will hunt curious, beautiful, grand objects, as they hunt the cattle in South America, for their *skins,* and leave the carcasses as of little worth" (81).

This extraordinary notion of photograph-as-skin returns a few decades later, at the turn of the twentieth century, in Nadar's memoir, with the idea of the body shedding skins traced by a photographer this time back to Balzac.

According to Balzac's theory, all physical bodies are made up entirely of layers of ghostlike images, an infinite number of leaflike skins laid one on top of the other. Since Balzac believed man was incapable of making something material from an apparition—that is, creating something from nothing—he concluded that every time someone had his photograph taken, one of the spectral layers was removed from the body and transferred to the photograph. Repeated exposures entailed the unavoidable loss of subsequent ghostly layers, that is, the very essence of life.[24]

And with this description of the translation of bodily ghost to apparitional photograph, you won't be surprised to hear that Barthes's bibliography indicates that he read Nadar's memoir; for the photograph-skin recurs in *Camera Lucida*. And it is in *Camera Lucida* that we realize finally how much a faith in photography as *real* in spite of the loss of the referent was indebted to the *skin*. If for Barthes the "photograph is literally an emanation of the referent," a revenant of "a real body, which was there" (80), it is because the instant of photographic illumination produces a cutaneous connection between photograph and subject. This skin is protective, maternal; in Barthes's image the photograph is almost (not quite) womblike; it is the closest the child can get to the envelope that sustained him now he is outside his mother: "A sort of umbilical cord links the body of the photographed thing to my gaze: light, though impalpable, is a carnal medium, a skin I share with anyone who has been photographed" (81). In this medium whose *eidos* is death, suddenly, in the image of skin, there is birth after.

In one of the footnotes I *did* include in *Second Skins* (I wish I hadn't), I promised my next book would be about skin. Perhaps in writing this book on photography I've come close to that book on skin. What the image of the photograph as a skin brings to the surface and makes almost palpable is that the mystical realness of photography comes only with the loss of reality in the original. The photograph incarnates *because* it takes the body of the referent. Here's the trade. I may never recover my first skin. But the realization of that loss *is* my second skin.

THE REALIZATION OF LOSS

A THERAPIST ONCE TRIED TO PERSUADE ME to read old journal entries and bring in old photographs as a way to get over losses. I resisted. The exercise seemed far too literal for what I imagined of my psyche, and anyway as far as I could see I had no major losses.

Reading diary entries now of my first time in Brazil, I'm annoyed I didn't record what I remember as significant. After I'd presented some slides from my first book, I was approached by a member of the audience. He was in tears and embraced me. He embraced me for my sense of loss, he said. I hadn't known my talk was about loss.

Saudades is "endemic melancholy," two cultural commentators on Brazil recently suggest.[1] It is intrinsic to Brazilian self-conception. It is native, national, loss: the realization that we are born into loss; that it inheres in the human condition.

It was the first time I'd fallen in love with a notion or a nation. It was the first time I'd stayed with loss. I knew then I'd return.

I'm looking at Bishop's slides of Brazil at Vassar. I'm looking at Bishop's slides *with* Bishop at Vassar. At least, that's what it feels like. The curator of the Bishop Special Collection tells me that her photographs are rarely consulted, her slides even less so. I'm not surprised. To view them one must retrieve from the dark rooms of storage her slide projector. This is a cumbersome, antiquated piece of equipment from the 1960s. But it ran for me yesterday smooth as gliders.

Here is Bishop's Brazil unmediated. And yet . . .

> Is it right to be watching strangers in a play
> in this strangest of theatres?
> What childishness is it that while there's a breath of life
> in our bodies, we are determined to rush
> to see the sun the other way around?
> The tiniest green hummingbird in the world?
> To stare at some inexplicable old stonework,
> inexplicable and impenetrable
> at any view,
> instantly seen and always, always delightful?
> Oh, must we dream our dreams and have them, too?[2]

On July 4, I take a break from the library and visit Kykuit, Hudson home of the Rockefellers. The Rockefeller family was the first philanthropic dynasty, the prototype for making a family profession out of giving away the fortune. Yet their philanthropy was inextricable from, because made possible by, their also being the first multinational monopoly: the start of globalization. The source, John D. Sr., made his money from kerosene. He bought out—or shut out if they refused to join him—oil companies throughout the United States and from them formed his massive Standard Oil. Through this conglomerate he controlled much of the oil industry and, with the help of his sons, sought to influence international politics in the mid-twentieth century. His son Nelson helped steer the U.S. policy toward Latin America as a cold warrior in the '50s—and he visited Brazil for this purpose in the '50s and '60s. Nelson's more retiring brother, John D. Jr., turned giving into the family's raison d'être, in part as a way of making restitution midst the accusations of Rockefeller control and untrammeled incorporation.[3]

Taking the train alongside the Hudson from Tarrytown back up to Poughkeepsie, I'm put in mind of the Amazon. Immediately you know you're on the same continent. The breadth of the river. The hills on the opposite side, with their thick, huge-leafed foliage. Where else in the world such abundance: such wilderness? This, I say to myself with an Old World confidence, is America.

I'm reading Bishop's "A Cold Spring." At that exact moment, I look up and see that we're passing through Cold Spring station. Her poem is about the weather anyway, not the place. The weather now is positively Amazonian; a tropical rainstorm sheets it down. Nevertheless, it's the same uncanny feeling you get when the radio says the exact word you're saying or thinking, like "death." These coincidences often seem to hang on death. Ghosts coincide with the real.

I dream up a trip to Brazil that will take in all the sites and sights of my Brazilian photographers. Would the referent meet the real, I wonder? My trip will take me from the divided wealth of Parks's Rio; to the baroque, gold-mining towns and lunar landscapes of the state of Bishop's Minas Gerais. And back to Lévi-Strauss's Amazon.

In Rio, I decide against the "*favela* tour" that is now on offer, according to the tourist bumph they leave in your hotel room. Escorted by a local tour operator and with a stop-off so you can take photographs of the "spectacular views of Rio," you can see this other side to Brazil from the safety of your tour bus: the "real Brazil," they say. The bumph also urges that you not miss the Sugar Loaf, and advises on the most expensive restaurants in Rio.

Instead, I go with a Brazilian friend, who drives me round the developments of the wealthy Lagoa. On one side I recognize the Catacumba, the park where Flavio's *favela* once was. It's no longer the wilderness of Parks's visit. Yet *favelas* in Brazil do tend to be in wildernesses—to *be* wilderness. They perch like fabulous, mythic settlements atop their seemingly uninhabitable rocky outcrops. From planes, they look deceptively beautiful and ancient. In cities outside of Rio, they dot the wasteland between airports and the city's limits, shortening the space between: the space between the wealthy and poor; the urban and the rural. *Favelas* are one of the first and most frequent things you see in Brazil.

I've been warned by guidebooks and friends (even Brazilians) about the chasmic differences in wealth in Brazil and the provocative conspicuousness of affluent northern tourists. I'm fully prepared to be robbed in Rio. Instead I lose only my glasses in the Atlantic—my own fault (I'm trying to peer at something *under* the ocean, to see in the sea). The rest of my week is a blur—oddly reassuring though. This is my second time in Rio.

Ouro Prêto is very picturesque. It's all shapes and color, hills of tapestried landscapes forming the background to steep cobbled streets. The town is famous for its numerous churches, and these comprise a palette of yellows and whites and blues: all baroque. I take lots of photographs here in Minas. I photograph Aleijadinho's sculptures. His "lions" look more like monkeys, apparently because living in Brazil in the eighteenth century he hadn't seen a lion and didn't know what they looked like. A. had leprosy and progressively lost parts of his body. Working with more and more elaborate prosthetic extensions attached, he transferred his monstrosities from his beleaguered body to his lions.

Standing before Bishop's Casa Mariana I have a powerful sense of déjà vu, because of course I've already studied it in her photographs. As she recorded it with such painstaking precision while it was under construction though, and as her inscriptions on the back and front of her photographs offer detailed commentary on this process, Bishop's photographs seem more real than the scene before me. Redundantly, I take my own photographs anyway. Afterwards I'll have to peer at them and I'll still have trouble distinguishing which is Casa Mariana.

In the Amazon I'm not sure *what* to photograph because not sure quite what to focus on. What's surprising is that, in spite of all that green or maybe because of it, it feels like you're in black and white. I have no trouble at all identifying the Amazon from Lévi-Strauss's sixty-year-old photographs of his trips upriver here.

On the way to our base lodge, the space becomes less and less inhabited, and less and less touched. From a petrol station that is clearly recognizable as such, in the middle of the rivers when they're still oceanic sized. To churches and even a cemetery. Schools. "Farms"—of a sort—of zebu cattle, with their humps and their horns. Then of water buffalo which, better adapted to the flooding here, have since the '80s been gradually replacing the cattle. Farmers are given tax breaks to raise livestock. This has led to the so-called grass rush, the slash-and-burn techniques of forest clearance that are amongst the most destructive of recent impacts on the Amazon. Huts. And eventually just the walls of the green forest, closing in on either side of the narrowing river channels.

Then, suddenly, dolphins: freshwater dolphins. River dolphins are far less common than their marine cousins. (The only other places they can be found are the Yangtze in China and the Ganges in India: like the Amazon, their countries' holy rivers.) River dolphins are also much more humanoid in their shape than sea dolphins, with demarcated heads and *necks*.[4] And they're pink: positively, pleasurably pink.

The presence of the dolphin here suggests how the Amazon came to be formed. During the Pleistocene era (the Ice Age)—that is between 11,000 and 1.8 million years ago—ice sheets covered much of the Americas, as they did much of the world. In the interglacial periods of warmth, the ice covering the highlands (in South America, particularly the Andes) melted and the sea level rose, scouring the river channels and producing the Amazonian floodplain. The Amazon sediment resulting preserves a piece of this world from millennia ago. It is this, it is thought, that makes its ecology rich and life-giving.[5] The Amazonian tropical climate is also a leftover of a previous tropical climate that has not adapted to our drier climes.

No one's really sure how the dolphins got here but—since it's agreed they find their species origin in the sea—they, too, seem like vestiges of that previous world. The "*boto,*" as the Brazilians call the river dolphin, is the most mythicized inhabitant of the Amazon. Yet this river god (as Bishop's "Riverman" recognizes) is now threatened with extinction.

That evening as I arrive at our lodge, I'll trust the assurances about the generic passivity of piranhas and the nocturnality of caimans and swim with the pink dolphins.

One of the strangest things I see in the Amazon is the point where the black waters of the Rio Negro meet the white waters of the Rio Solimões, to form the River Amazon. What's weird is that the rivers meet but don't merge. You can still see the white in the black, the light in the dark. Or is it the other way round?

I take two photographs here. I have to admit later they're spectacular. When I have them framed and hung, people will mistake them for watercolors. But maybe it's the frames.

The first Brazilian opera tells the story of the myth that originated the waters' meeting. In Carlos Gomez's *O Guaraní,* an Amazonian Indian falls in love with a Portuguese girl. Their encounter is depicted in the opera house in Manaus. This is a spectacular and somehow very Brazilian affair, with its marble brought from Italy, its cast iron from Scotland—and the wood of *pau-brasil* from upriver.

Bishop, who also visited the joining of the waters of Solimões and Negro, left a draft of a poem "On the Amazon" that also speaks of encounters:

> crossing over
> the dark blue line
> and the river
> erases it all
> the world, all pink
> has dissolved at last
> and is going somewhere
> under a rainbow, too—

Rio Negro meeting the Solimões to form the Amazon. Photograph taken by the author, August 2000.

the rainbow has taken shape, but the world, all pink, strange to say
has dissolved at last
            and is going somewhere at last—
so *that* is the color of the world all together—

Another unfinished poem "Crossing the Equator" begins:

> We imagine an horizon, & it hardens
> into faultless definition: the horizon.
> It begins to illustrate imagination.
> Other things that are imagined
> are not often so obliging.[6]

Myths imagine an integral world before divisions. Before loss.

Crossings figure a lot in discussions of the Amazon:

1. As we enter the third millennium, it's being proposed, we stand at a cross-roads over the future of Amazonia.[7] The route choice we face is between continued corporate extractivism (the extraction of resources for corporate profit), leading to some kind of meltdown. And, in the other direction, careful, ecological, and sustainable management of the forest under local people. Chico Mendes, an Amazonian ecologist and rubber-tappers' union leader who was murdered in the late '80s for his activism, suggested—in support of environmentalists' plans against deforestation—"extractive reserves" as an economic alternative to forest exploitation.[8] In extractive reserves, workers live in the area they use and so are less likely to destroy it. They use it, but don't lose it.

Development in the Amazon began properly in the 1960s, though this continued the work of industrializing Brazil that was initiated under the Getúlio Vargas regime. After its successful coup in 1964, the military government undertook the project to colonize Brazil's massive interior. This was in part to deflect political unrest and to avoid making real social change elsewhere in the country. In the increasingly impoverished, drought-ridden northeast, the "landless" were causing problems. They were campaigning for the redistribution of land outside its concentration in *latifundia:* "large estates" held by landowners or companies. And at the same time, they were swelling the *favelas* in the newly prosperous, urbanized southeast. The military government also wanted to make Brazil a leading nation in the rapidly industrializing world. As containing the country's richest resources, the Amazon beckoned. The new general president promised the Amazon as "a land without people for a people without a land."⁹ The Amazon was to be paradise regained. Its development would run hand in hand with industrialization, militarization, and globalization. Paradise lost.

Current figures for rates of deforestation inevitably vary. From 11 million acres; to 2 million hectares—that is, 5 million acres; to 17,000 square kilometers per year. My head spins anyway at such numbers. But imagine something like Switzerland being lost every year. By 2020, in the worst scenario, 40 percent of the Amazon will be lost; in the best case, 25 percent will have gone. The three major causes of deforestation are, in order: industrial logging; land clearing for livestock; and extraction of raw materials in the form of minerals and ores for export to global markets.

Key to the colonization of the Amazon has been the construction of the Trans-Amazonian highways.¹⁰ The new road system opened the Amazon to trade routes leading to major urban centers in Brazil, and from there to the rest of the world. The road project was planned under the military government. But the actual building was made possible with the help of funds from the World Bank and Inter-American Development Bank. In return foreign companies investing in the area got concessions or investment deals at favored ("banana": falsely depreciated) prices. The loans that Brazil took to implement this project of industrialization have left it with the largest debt of any Third World country. Indeed, the largest debt of any country, after the United States.

The road building project continues to this day.¹¹ Aerial photographs reveal the extending, spaghetti-like tentacles of this arterial network and at the same time make possible new incursions into an otherwise seemingly unmappable and impenetrable forest.

The Amazon is now a literal crossroads.

2. An alternative crossroads, an alternative story. In the form of its cities such as Manaus, the rainforest is already a global frontier zone. Manaus was designated a free trade zone in the '60s (of course by the military government). Its visitor today will be struck by the numerousness of electronics stores selling the latest gadgets from Asia, Europe, and the United States at cut prices. They're higher here proportionally than in Hong Kong, Tokyo, or New York. Manaus is where Brazil comes to do its hi-tech shopping. The Nambikwara don't *have* to travel to North America anymore to buy cheap transistor radios.

Such rainforest cities are "technopoles" at the vanguard of globalization. They comprise another, more global, less material kind of crossroads—a crossroads for signs: "technological crossroads that link specific activities to global circuits of information and exchange."[12]

3. The crossroads of Amazonia is also for the rest of the world as well as Brazil. Why do we care about the Amazon's loss after all? Why should we care about the Amazon's loss?

Because the Amazon is our most precious preserve. It contains over half of the world's rainforest, and most of this is in Brazil; Brazil holds 40 percent of the remaining rainforest in the world. It is the world's largest and most diverse forest. It is home to one in five birds on all earth. Nowhere else do so many birds live—both in total number and in diversity of species. Its plants form the basis for many of the latest pharmaceuticals used to treat our current ills—leukemia treatments, antibiotics, antivirals, and anesthetics for example. And many of its plants, birds, and animals are as yet uncatalogued. Even unseen. There's so much bird life up in the forest canopies that, as one naturalist graphically puts it, "The observer can well break his neck trying to see up there and identify a bird whose voice he isn't familiar with."[13] And it contains one-fifth of the world's water supply, our most vital and increasingly scarcest resource.

For the Amazon is not simply a place of conservation, a vault for storing what's gone or soon to be gone. It sustains and gives life to the world's current ecological system. The destruction of the rainforest in South America has already been shown to have immediate and precise consequences on the North—to affect the rainfall in midwestern states, for example; to exacerbate, in the contribution of deforestation to climate change and global warming, the flooding and droughts that increasingly take place across our world today.[14] It's not an exaggeration to say that Brazil holds the determinants of our future.

And for the future of the Brazilian Amazon the latest research foresees not only continued but accelerating loss.[15] A conference of climatologists, environmentalists, and scientists just ending in London as I write this concluded that with the Amazon's deforestation we would see the collapse of the climate system.[16] Or rather we would not be here to see it.

The lung of the world. El Dorado. The Last Frontier. The Original State. The destruction of the Amazon would entail nothing less than the apocalypse of the world.

The Rio Negro is terrifying in its blackness. It really *is* black, the result of a vegetation that, because it is so rich, as it decomposes releases very high levels of tannin into the water. The tannin prevents light from penetrating the water, and this in turn produces an inordinate amount of oxygen in the river. The oxygen means less fish, therefore less birds—less life than in the "light" waters. The riverbanks of the Negro actually look more vital then, but the river is relatively impoverished compared to other Amazon tributaries.

The locals call it the "dead" or "silent" river.

Our jungle trek in the morning is an education. Our guide, G., shows us biodiversity in action. He points out *how* the relationship between plants and parasites is symbiotic. A termite nest balancing like a huge bulb on the top of a tree serves to sustain the life below it. The termites recycle the bacterial and vegetable matter, cleaning the plant and allowing it to reabsorb its sterilized decompositions in the form of nutrients. Parasites work like antibiotics work for us: to preserve the life of the biota.

In spite of its appearances, the Amazon's ecology is actually very fragile. Or rather it is strong only in its ecological complexity and exclusivity. It's a self-contained system. It is only biodiversity—the symbiosis on every level: between floodplains and terra firma, between plant and parasite; between the *living* and the *dying* here—that sustains the life system. The basis of the Amazon's ecology (of any ecosystem really) is, of course, light, but in a certain combination with darkness. Photosynthesis, which literally means a "making by light," is the process whereby plants synthesize organic matter from inorganic substances that are present in solar light. This process can only take place afterwards, in the dark. Insects, fish, and animals, which cannot use the sun's energy as a direct life-source, depend upon vegetation—these "autotrophers" or producers of energy—for our life-sources. Animals, birds, and fruit-eating fish in the Amazon have propagated and sustained the autotrophic forest by dispersing its seeds. The plants' seeds have in turn adapted and become resistant to the destructive elements present in these secondary trophers' gastric enzymes.

And what do humans do? Humans are far down in the trophic chain. We consume.

Life on earth depends on photosynthesis. It all comes down to this: plants' ability to transform light in the darkness.

You can't, after all, magic the recovery of the Amazon. Reafforestation, which *is* undertaken, has so far worked with nonnative species. Native species grow too slowly and are too diverse to be replicated. Nonnative species change the ecology anyway, and reafforestation with them takes between 100 and 150 years. Although, there are stories of the forest beginning to grow back, where the roads have been barely used, and reclaim the land of its own accord. But once the land is cleared, the forest never really recovers. The Sahara, too, was once a forest. Then there's more light than we can see, with no shade at all.

The story of the progress of the human species is the story of the destruction of forests.[17] The achievements of culture have been at the loss of nature. Monoculture—whether in the form of agriculture, industry, or national culture—spells the end of biodiversity. Farming in the Amazon produces floods, then, ironically, as the land loses its ability to absorb and hold water and erodes, drought.

The external, nonindigenous exploitation of the forest began, in a precursor of the dynamics of globalization, with research on some rubber trees conducted by an Englishman, via Kew. His efforts led to the transportation of the entire rubber industry to Malaya and, as a result, by the beginning of the First World War, the collapse of the Brazilian rubber market. In the period following the First World War, coinciding with the growth of the U.S. economy and *its* industrialization, the U.S. government sought to revive the Brazilian rubber industry in order to sustain its own cheap supply of rubber. The U.S. Rubber Company made deals under the Vargas regime to get concessions in return for investment. Henry Ford was among those who got exemption from taxes to cordon off large chunks of the Amazon into rubber plantations. In the lower Amazon he built Fordlândia, a city to complement his plantations and house their workers, and a narcissistic extension of himself. With its whitewashed wooden houses, its front gardens and fire hydrants, Fordlândia is a piece of small-town America: America *in* Brazil. At the start of the Second World War, when rubber was in its most critical short supply, the U.S. Department of Agriculture and Office for Inter-American affairs poured funds into Brazil to prop up its rubber industry. But then after the Second World War the logic of the "free market" of global capitalism took inexorable hold. Asia became the world's indomitable supplier and Brazil's rubber industry again collapsed—leaving just a few rubber-tappers in the Amazon to eke out a survival.[18]

But there's much hypocrisy, even imperialism, in the environmentalist arguments for conserving the Amazon. Up until the last decade, the U.S. and U.K. governments were still pressuring Brazil to exploit the forest. And multinational companies based in the United States and the United Kingdom continue to invest in development there. Now that we near exhaustion of resources in our own territories, have lost—or shrunk to parks—our own wildernesses, we place an imposition on Brazil to redeem us from our ills.

(National parks in the United States, by the way, originated under Theodore Roosevelt, who recorded how impressed he was with the Brazilian wilderness after his trip there in his book *Through the Brazilian Wilderness*.)[19] It is our desire for tropical hardwoods, for hamburgers and the extensive, unjustifiably expensive use of crops required to produce a single hamburger, that, after all, are ultimately behind the destruction of the Amazon. It is our gas emissions—harvest of our overconsumption—that lie behind the climate change for which we now demand the preservation of the Amazon as restitution. Of the carbon credits program, agreed in 1997 under the Kyoto Protocol to reduce greenhouse gases (which was vetoed by the United States), while there's much to be said in favor its intention, in practice it perpetuates economic exploitation of Southern Hemisphere countries that is globalization's form of colonialism. The program provides an escape route from our own excesses rather than demanding that we radically curb them. In exchange for their pristine environment, poorer nations can earn money by "absorbing" the pollution of wealthier nations. (But where exactly does that waste go? Not "to" the Amazon, literally.) In environmental protectionism resides imperial nostalgia.

The defensiveness of the Brazilian government is therefore not surprising. Their responses to the latest research, which is mainly undertaken by U.S. researchers and published in U.S. journals, see in it an undercurrent of ongoing imperialism. They argue that such research overlooks indigenous Brazilian projects that are underway. The Brazilians recognize in the above situation the economic colonialism that is typical of the global capitalism going under the name of "free trade." The latest loans from the International Monetary Fund ("essentially a covert arm of the U. S. Treasury") compelled Brazil into stalling a project to save the Amazon.[20] Brazil's "loans" (at extortionate rates of interest) and its "favored" designation as supplier of raw materials—in return for absorbing some of the surplus of consumer goods that swamp the developed world—compel it into undertaking rapid industrial development for economic reasons, simply to play catch-up with their neighbors in the North. The Brazilian government reminds northern conservationists that the Amazon is already inhabited and that it has a responsibility towards these people for improving their economic conditions. Environmentalists are hypocritical in demanding the "immobilization" of Brazilian economic development, from the affluence of their own developed countries. The Brazilian government's program for development, which includes the Amazon and entails its mass industrialization, is called "Avança Brasil": Go ahead Brazil; advance; don't hold back.[21]

Brazil's government contests the latest statistics about deforestation and claims that the losses are greatly exaggerated. The true extent of deforestation, it insists, is revealed by satellite photographs. Brazil has the largest and most advanced technological program in the world for monitoring forests from space, INPE, the National Institution of Space Research. Its Sino-Brazilian satellite beams images of the Amazon back to the world and to the World Wide Web.[22] It is upon photographs that the figures spin, and the future of the world turns.

Nevertheless, part of the "Avança Brasil" program consists of "The Project to Recover Altered Areas of the Amazon": a plan for reversing environmental degradation. But can you ever get back what's lost? Meanwhile, the hi-fis spill out onto the barely paved streets of Manaus as I catch my boat upriver.

Since Darwin's *Origin of Species*, the writing of the history of nature has served both to oppose and compound the creationist myths of religion, which are vestigial in the environmentalists' argument for preserving the original, the autochthonous. The latest natural histories of the Amazon argue that it's not virgin at all. The so-called virgin forest has actually been managed for millennia, and at the end of the Pleistocene riverine settlements were probably the most densely populated. What we experience as original is a crafted, human—produced—product.[23] It used to be held that the Amazon had been a more-or-less stable feature of our world over these past million years. But the rainforest's impenetrability—its apparent virginity—has deferred its archival exploration. Geologists are now even finding, beneath the riverine sediment, deposits of windblown sand. What is now rainforest may for a time have been—a desert. Maybe what was lost *does* grow back.

Posing a direct challenge to the former-held notion of indigenous cultures in the Amazon as inhabiting a "counterfeit paradise," the Amazon is now unearthing some of the first agriculture, culture, and technologies in the New World.[24] At Monte Alegre, a modern city positioned between Manaus and Belém, archaeologists are examining the ghostly traces of Paleo-Indian inhabitants. Alongside campsites and areas of apparent forest clearance and cultivation, they left painted caves—including one containing "an inverted figure with rayed head."[25] The cave paintings are evidence of a people who sought to represent their world and one of the markers of a sophisticated, artistic culture. They are proving key to the dating of these first settlements. And it's the new science of luminescence, which, by shining lights into their dark rooms, makes the history of the caves readable—and the culture of the Amazon thereby with them.

Monte Alegre, alongside the revelations/realizations of Monte Verde in Chile at the very tip of South America, suggests that South America may have been the birthplace of technology in the Americas. Archeological research at the turn of the millennium is revoking the theory long held that American occupation began with the crossing of the Bering Strait into *North* America. The dominance of this Clovis culture argument by U.S. archaeologists, and the consequent ignoring of research conducted by Latin Americanists until very recently, represents another kind of imperialism— an archaeological imperialism, as if the settling of the Americas was "the first great [U.S.] American invention—the Ice Age equivalent of the spread of Coca-Cola or baseball caps."[26] The North American Clovis settlement is typically dated to somewhere between 11,000 and 13,000 years ago. At possibly as much as 50,000 years old, the Monte Verde remains are beyond doubt pre-Clovis. And there's a chance that their inhabitants did not come here via land crossing into North America but direct from another conti- nent, by Paleolithic boat. Curiously, the supposition that the first Americans were from Asia, which would seem much rockier than the dating of the settlements, still generally stands. One of the first skeletons in Brazil has even been matched genetically to some found in a cave in China.

The debates about the hemispheric location and historical dating of settlement in the Americas entail a fight over origins. Who was first? Who belated?

How do you move in the world without losing it?

Where does America begin, where does it end?

When an asteroid hit the planet 65 million years ago and killed off 80 percent of existing species, it very nearly wiped the slate of the world clean. Six months of darkness followed the blast of light: a nuclear winter. It was an apocalypse. The first one. But this end was also a beginning. For nature loved the vacuum. And it came to create life as we know it. As we've come to live it.

Right before the asteroid made its impact—its "ground zero" was North America; actually the very furthest southern tip of North America, in Mexico to be precise—the continent of South America was gradually drifting toward North America. "Indeed, it probably made land contact just before Ground Zero. After this brief continental kiss South America began to waltz—at about eight millimeters per year—to the south-west, out into the Pacific. Whatever connection had earlier appeared between the two continents was now lost."[27] But then a dry land connection did open at some point later, the Isthmus of Panama, probably as long as 2.8 million years ago. This thin string of land still joins the continents, a kind of umbilical cord—though no one's dared which was first. Once rejoined, South America became the refuge for many species that were driven out of the north by the successive waves of immigrants—most dramatically by humans—over the last 13,000 or so years. Peccaries and tapirs traveled south. A range of cats. Camels and llama. Deer, skunk, and horses. All, originating in the north, made the trek south. Ironically, birds were one of the most widespread genera to make use of the land bridge. The one thing that these refugee birds have in common is that they're all now migratory land-birds. Flycatchers and warblers, for instance. But when they migrate each year they're not so much flying south in the winter as, when they fly north in the summer, going home. Some species went the other way, from south to north, most predictably perhaps the notoriously slow and evolutionarily backward sloth. Creosote bushes also crept north. Its toxins would prove very useful, millennia later, for northerner anthropologists travelling south again in preserving their notebooks from overly cooperative termites, and just a bit later, for bringing back their memories of Brazil.

What is the relation between two continents that have so much in common in evolutionary terms, where so many life forms are prodigious and peculiar to them? North America's latest and most extensive natural historian believes there may be an ecological principle that will come to explain their inextricable connection. Currently it is unrealized, so as he writes he "can only put it down to coincidence. Yet it is a coincidence as great and seemingly portentous as that which resulted in the sun and the moon appearing to be the same size in ou r skies."[28]

Bird-watching in the afternoon.

> Egrets. Tropical cormorant. Ducks *(irerê)*. Plenty of tern, wheeling.
> A kingfisher.
> A hummingbird I couldn't believe I was seeing, it was so tiny—
> green-throated, crimson breast, orange wings. The Crimson Topaz,
> rightly named: a jewel.
> Flocks of green parrot and blue macaw. And the golden parakeet,
> which with its yellow body and green flash on wings is dressed
> in the colors of Brazil.
> Toucans, comically heavy-billed, raucous and sociable.
> Kinds of cuckoos (apparently).

It was a show. Evening when the sun started to go down and the heat turned off was when the star performers took over.

Scissor-tailed nightjar, with its streamer kite-like tail: fly catching.
And a glorious, regal, fishing white hawk.

But around Vassar I see animals I've never seen before and that are extraordinary to think of running under lecture halls here and past north New York State's dilapidated factories. Still in America. Woodchucks, for example: flat-tailed and foolish, their fear at your approach fixes them in place. Lots of birds native to the continent. New World blackbirds, flashes of red wing startling on black body. Mockingbirds, which are much tamer and more common than I thought they'd be. They're arresting singers. They can now imitate car alarms. I look out for the confusion of car-owning residents.

The treasure, though, is a skunk I see in someone's front garden. Like Bishop's chain-mailed Brazilian armadillo scrambling to escape the bursting festival fire balloons of an encroaching city, it's an American atavism. Snuffling underneath the bird table, it was right at home but at the same time looked very, very strange. Black with a white wig running its entire length, like a body-sized toupee. Andy Warholish. The assistant curator said I was lucky I didn't scare it; otherwise its spray would have got me barred from the library.

This evening to G. and L.'s (G.'s French girlfriend) home for a slideshow of her photographs (she's a photographer) and G.'s talk on the history, ecology, and politics of Amazonia. The relationships of biodiversity and symbiosis are fascinating and far-reaching.

They argued that only ecotourism can save the forest. Ecotourism is the one industry apparently that can realistically sustain the local population while maintaining the environment largely unspoiled. We, who come from the most developed and wasteful societies in the world, to the best-preserved and most primitive, hold the solution. Here's the paradox at the heart of *saudades*. Our realization of loss provides the initiative—and the possibility of a revocation.

G.'s girlfriend came here originally as a tourist, to take photographs. Doubtless the camera will have a role to play whatever path we take.

This is the zero degree, the world at its origins: the real before the symbolic.

I sit in the dark room of G. and L.'s wooden house on the river and look at the slides.

This afternoon canoe trip with G. alone. The sounds surrounding us are more intense than the sights. Howler monkeys and capuchins. And birds, birds, birds. "We must listen to the wheat growing," urges Lévi-Strauss, in his plea for diversity.[29] You should hear the Amazon. It's total exposure to your senses—all of them open. And you become all receptacle. No self.

I put my camera aside. Right here in the canoe, I'm in the photograph. For once, or maybe longer, I'm all present.

NOTES

INTRODUCTION

1. Walter Benjamin, *Illuminations* (London: Fontana, 1992), 219.

2. Susan Sontag, *On Photography* (London: Penguin, 1977), 54, 154.

3. Roland Barthes, *Camera Lucida: Reflections on Photography* (London: Vintage, 1993), 77.

4. Simon During, *Modern Enchantments: The Cultural Power of Secular Magic* (Cambridge, MA: Harvard University Press, 2002).

5. Helmut Gernsheim, *A Concise History of Photography* (New York: Dover, 1986).

6. Robert Temple, *The Crystal Sun: Rediscovering a Lost Technology of the Ancient World* (London: Random House, 2000).

7. David Hockney, *Secret Knowledge: Rediscovering the Lost Techniques of the Old Masters* (London: Thames and Hudson, 2001). Philip Steadman makes a similar argument, about Vermeer, in *Vermeer's Camera: Uncovering the Truth behind the Masterpieces* (Oxford: Oxford University Press, 2001).

8. Hal Foster, *The Return of the Real* (Cambridge: MIT Press, 1996), 130, 165.

9. Dylan Evans, *An Introductory Dictionary of Lacanian Psychoanalysis* (London: Routledge, 1996).

10. Jacques Lacan, *The Four Fundamental Concepts of Psycho-analysis,* ed. Jacques-Alain Miller, trans. Alan Sheridan (New York: Norton, 1981), 53.

11. John North, *The Ambassadors' Secret: Holbein and the World of the Renaissance* (London: Hambledon and London, 2002).

12. Benjamin, 230.

13. Jacqueline Rose, *Sexuality in the Field of Vision* (London: Verso, 1986).

14. Sigmund Freud, *The Interpretation of Dreams,* trans. and ed. James Strachey (New York: Basic, 1965), 574.

15. Freud, *Moses and Monotheism: Three Essays,* in *The Origins of Religion,* trans. and ed. James Strachey (London: Penguin, 1990), 374.

16. Lacan, 47–48.

17. Hélène Cixous and Mireille Calle-Gruber, *Hélène Cixous: Rootprints; Memory and Life Writing,* trans. Eric Prenowitz (London: Routledge, 1997), 179, 189.

18. Michael Ondaatje, *Running in the Family* (London: Picador, 1984), 161, 162.

19. Gabriel Josipovici, *A Life* (London: European Jewish Publication Society, 2001), 7.

20. Tim Lott, *The Scent of Dried Roses* (London: Viking, 1996), 36.

21. Timothy Dow Adams, *Light Writing and Life Writing: Photography in Autobiography* (Chapel Hill: University of North Carolina Press, 2000).

22. Linda Haverty Rugg, *Picturing Ourselves: Photography and Autobiography* (Chicago: University of Chicago Press, 1997), 9, 238.

23. Paul de Man, *The Rhetoric of Romanticism* (New York: Columbia University Press, 1984), 69.

24. Nancy K. Miller, *Bequest and Betrayal: Memoirs of a Parent's Death* (New York: Oxford University Press, 1996). Marianne Hirsch, *Family Frames: Photography, Narrative and Postmemory* (Cambridge, MA: Harvard University Press, 1997). Annette Kuhn, *Family Secrets: Acts of Memory and Imagination* (London: Verso, 1995).

25. Philippe Lejeune, *On Autobiography,* ed. Paul John Eakin, trans. Katherine Leary (Minneapolis: University of Minnesota Press, 1989), 115.

26. Roland Barthes, *Roland Barthes by Roland Barthes,* trans. Richard Howard (New York: Farrar, 1977), 56.

27. J. Gratton, "*Roland Barthes par Roland Barthes:* Autobiography and the Notion of Expression," *Romance Studies* 8 (1986): 57–58.

28. Paul John Eakin, *Touching the World: Reference in Autobiography* (Princeton: Princeton University Press, 1992), 21, 4.

29. Patricia Berrahou Phillippy, *Love's Remedies: Recantation and Renaissance Lyric Poetry* (Lewisburg, PA: Bucknell University Press, 1995).

30. Plato, *Phaedrus,* trans. James H. Nicols (Ithaca, NY: Cornell University Press, 1998).

31. Saint Augustine, *The Retractions,* trans. Sister Mary Inez Bogan (Washington, DC: The Catholic University of America Press, 1999).

32. Geoffrey Chaucer, *The Complete Works,* ed. F. N. Robinson (Oxford: Oxford University Press, 1985), 265

33. Friedrich Nietzsche, *The Birth of Tragedy* (London: Penguin, 1993).

34. Søren Kierkegaard, *Concluding Unscientific Postscript to Philosophical Frag-*

ments, vol. 1, ed. and trans. Howard V. Hong and Edna H. Hong (Princeton: Princeton University Press, 1992), 621.

35. Kierkegaard, *Repetition: An Essay in Experimental Psychology*, trans. Walter Lowrie (London: Oxford University Press, 1942), 6.

1. Roland Barthes's Loss

1. Colin MacCabe, "Barthes and Bazin: The Ontology of the Image," in *Writing the Image after Roland Barthes*, ed. Jean-Michel Rabaté (Philadelphia: Pennsylvania University Press, 1997), 72. Daniel Ferrer, "Generic Criticism in the Wake of Barthes," in *Writing the Image*, 217.

2. Jacques Derrida, *The Work of Mourning*, ed. Pascale-Anne Brault and Michael Naas (Chicago: University of Chicago Press, 2001), 50. First published as "Les Morts de Roland Barthes," *Poétique* 47 (1981): 269–92.

3. Roland Barthes, *Camera Lucida: Reflections on Photography*, trans. Richard Howard (London: Vintage, 1993), 9.

4. Tzvetan Todorov, "The Last Barthes," trans. Richard Howard, *Critical Inquiry* 7 (1981): 449.

5. Jonathan Culler, *Barthes* (Glasgow: Fontana, 1983), 116, 122, 124.

6. Elaine Hoft-March, "Barthes's Real Mother: The Legacy of *La chambre claire*," *French Forum* 17 (1992): 62

7. J. Gerald Kennedy, "Roland Barthes, Autobiography, and the End of Writing," *Georgia Review* 35 (1981): 397.

8. Nancy Shawcross, *Roland Barthes on Photography: The Critical Tradition in Perspective* (Gainesville: University Press of Florida, 1997), 119.

9. Barthes, *La chambre claire: Note sur la photographie* (Paris: Gallimard, 1980).

10. For the former see Marianne Hirsch, *Family Frames: Photography, Narrative and Postmemory* (Cambridge, MA: Harvard University Press, 1997); for the latter see Kathleen Woodward, "Freud and Barthes: Theorizing Mourning, Sustaining Grief," *Discourse* 13 (1990–91): 93–110.

11. Sigmund Freud, "Mourning and Melancholia," trans. James Strachey, in *On Metapsychology*, vol. 11, *Penguin Freud Library*, ed. Angela Richards (London: Penguin, 1991), 262.

12. Paul John Eakin, *Touching the World: Reference in Autobiography* (Princeton: Princeton University Press, 1992), 20.

13. Ralph Sarkonak, "Roland Barthes and the Spectre of Photography," *L'Esprit Createur* 22 (1982): 48–68. Louis-Jean Calvet, *Roland Barthes: A Biography*, trans. Sarah Wykes (Oxford: Polity Press, 1994).

14. Chantal Thomas, "La Photo du jardin d'hiver," *Critique* 423–24 (1982): 799.

15. Barthes, "The Great Family of Man," in *Mythologies* (1957), trans. Annette Lavers (New York: Farrar, 1972) 100–102. Barthes, "The Rhetoric of the Image,"

in *Image Music Text*, ed. and trans. Stephen Heath (London: Fontana, 1977), 35. Barthes, *Roland Barthes by Roland Barthes*, trans. Richard Howard (New York: Farrar, 1977).

16. Barthes, "The Photographic Message," in *Image*, 16.

17. Barthes, *The Rustle of Language*, trans. Richard Howard (Oxford: Blackwell, 1986), 148.

18. Barthes, *S/Z: An Essay*, trans. Richard Miller (New York: Farrar, 1974).

19. Philippe Lejeune, *On Autobiography*, ed. Paul John Eakin, trans. Katherine Leary (Minneapolis: University of Minnesota Press, 1989), 22.

20. See respectively Mary Bittner Wiseman, *The Ecstasies of Roland Barthes* (London: Routledge, 1989); J. Gratton, *"Roland Barthes par Roland Barthes*: Autobiography and the Notion of Expression," *Romance Studies* 8 (1986): 57–65; and Patrizia Lombardo, *The Three Paradoxes of Roland Barthes* (Athens: University of Georgia Press, 1989).

21. Jane Gallop, *Around 1981: Academic Feminist Literary Theory* (London: Routledge, 1992).

22. Susan Sontag, "Writing Itself: On Roland Barthes," in *A Barthes Reader*, ed. Sontag (London: Cape, 1982), xviii.

23. Barthes, *The Grain of the Voice: Interviews, 1962–1980*, trans. Linda Coverdale (Berkeley and Los Angeles: University of California Press, 1985), 282–83.

24. Antoine Compagnon, "Who Is the Real One?" in *Writing the Image*, ed. Rabaté, 197.

25. Culler, 12.

26. Stephen Ungar, *Roland Barthes: The Professor of Desire* (Lincoln: University of Nebraska Press, 1983).

27. Lejeune, 134.

28. Barthes, *Writing Degree Zero*, trans. Annette Lavers and Colin Smith (London: Cape, 1967), 81.

29. James Beighton, "Le Texte Symptomal? Evidence of Depression in Barthes's Later Writings," unpublished essay, MA in English (University of Leicester, 1999). Lewis Wolpert, *Malignant Sadness: The Anatomy of Depression* (London: Faber, 1999) is one such study that Beighton uses.

30. Julia Kristeva, *Black Sun: Depression and Melancholia*, trans. Leon S. Roudiez (New York: Columbia University Press), 9, 40, 42.

31. Barthes, *Incidents* (Berkeley and Los Angeles: University of California Press, 1992), 73.

32. Maurice Blanchot, "Orpheus' Gaze," in *The Siren's Song: Selected Essays*, ed. Gabriel Josipovici, trans. Sacha Rabinovitch (London: Harvester, 1982), 179, 181.

33. Barthes, *Critical Essays*, trans. Richard Howard (Evanston, IL: Northwestern University Press, 1972), 268.

34. Barthes, *A Lover's Discourse: Fragments*, trans. Richard Howard (New York: Farrar, 1978), 98, 98.

35. Beryl Schlossman, "The Descent of Orpheus: On Reading Barthes and Proust," in *Writing the Image*, ed. Rabaté, 156.

36. Ovid, *The Metamorphoses*, trans. Mary M. Innes (London: Penguin, 1955), 225, 226.

37. W. K. C. Guthrie, *Orpheus and Greek Religion* (Princeton: Princeton University Press, 1993).

38. In chronological order: Roland L. Champagne, "Between Orpheus and Eurydice: Barthes and the Historicity of Reading," *Clio* 7 (1978–79): 229–38; Claude Reichler, "L'ombre," *Critique* 421–22 (1982): 767–74; Réda Bensmaïa, *The Barthes Effect: The Essay as Reflective Text*, trans. Pat Fedkiew (Minneapolis: Minnesota University Press, 1987); Lombardo (1989); Wiseman (1989); Schlossman (1997).

39. Reichler, 767.

40. Freud, *Civilization and Its Discontents*, trans. and ed. James Strachey (New York: Norton, 1961).

41. Wiseman, 181.

42. Schlossman, 150.

43. Daniel Grojnowski, "Le Mystère de *La chambre claire*," *Textuel* 34 (1984): 92.

44. Diana Knight, "Roland Barthes, or The Woman without a Shadow," in *Writing the Image*, ed. Rabaté, 138.

45. Calvet, 247. Essay translated in Barthes, *Rustle*, 296–305.

46. Barthes, *Barthes Reader*, 461, 465, 465.

47. Marcel Proust, *Swann's Way*, book 1 of *Remembrance of Things Past* (New York: Penguin, 1992), 217, 218.

48. Barthes, *Rustle*, 279, 280.

49. Kennedy, 395.

50. Gabriel Josipovici, *A Life* (London: European Jewish Publication Society, 2001), 281.

51. Barthes, *The Responsibility of Forms: Critical Essays on Music, Art, and Representation*, trans. Richard Howard (New York: Farrar, 1985), 293–94, 298, 298.

52. Eduardo Cadava, *Words of Light: Theses on the Photography of History* (Princeton: Princeton University Press, 1997).

53. Bensmaïa, *Barthes Effect*. Søren Kierkegaard, *Concluding Unscientific Postscript to Philosophical Fragments*, vol. 1, ed. and trans. Howard V. Hong and Edna H. Hong (Princeton: Princeton University Press, 1992).

54. Gary Shapiro, "To Philosophize Is to Learn to Die," in *Signs in Culture: Roland Barthes Today*, ed. Steven Ungar and Betty R. McGraw (Iowa City: University of Iowa Press, 1989), 3–31. Plato, *Phaedrus*, trans. James H. Nicols (Ithaca, NY: Cornell University Press, 1998).

55. Lejeune, "Le Roland Barthes sans peine," *Textuel* 34, no. 44 (1984): 18, 13.

56. Barthes, *Empire of Signs*, trans. Richard Howard (London: Cape, 1982), 82, 83, 83.

57. Alan W. Watts, *The Way of Zen* (1957) (London: Penguin, 1990), 63, 90, 97.

58. Guru Rinpoche according to Karma-Lingpa, *The Tibetan Book of the Dead: The Great Liberation through Hearing in the Bardo,* trans. Francesca Fremantle and Chögyam Trungpa (Boston: Shambhala, 1992), xxxxiii, xxvii.

59. Trungpa, *Cutting through Spiritual Materialism* (1973), ed. John Baker and Martin Casper (Boston: Shambhala, 1987), 49.

2. Claude Lévi-Strauss's Tristes Photographiques

1. Claude Lévi-Strauss, *Tristes Tropiques,* trans. John and Doreen Weightman (New York: Random House, 1997), 4, 5.

2. Lévi-Strauss, *Saudades do Brasil: A Photographic Memoir,* trans. Sylvia Modelski (Seattle: University of Washington Press, 1995).

3. Roland Barthes, "The Photographic Message," in *Image Music Text,* ed. and trans. Stephen Heath (London: Fontana, 1977), 15–31. Lévi-Strauss, *The Raw and the Cooked,* vol. 1 of *Introduction to a Science of Mythology* (London: Random House, 1994).

4. Louis-Jean Calvet, *Roland Barthes: A Biography,* trans. Sarah Wykes (Oxford: Polity Press, 1994). Barthes, *Mythologies,* trans. Annette Lavers (New York: Farrar, 1972). Lévi-Strauss, *Structural Anthropology,* vol. 1, trans. Claire Jacobson (London: Penguin, 1993).

5. Christopher Pinney, "The Parallel Histories of Anthropology and Photography," in *Anthropology and Photography, 1860–1920,* ed. Elizabeth Edwards (New Haven, CT: Yale University Press, 1992), 18–31.

6. Terence Wright, "Photography: Theories of Realism and Convention," in *Anthropology and Photography,* ed. Edwards, 20–21.

7. Lévi-Strauss, *The Savage Mind* (Oxford: Oxford University Press, 1996), 89.

8. Lévi-Strauss, *Structural Anthropology,* vol. 2, trans. Monique Layton (Chicago: University of Chicago Press, 1983), 132, 115.

9. Barthes, *Camera Lucida: Reflections on Photography,* trans. Richard Howard (London: Vintage, 1993), 76.

10. Lévi-Strauss, *The View from Afar,* trans. Joachim Neugroschel and Phoebe Hoss (Oxford: Blackwell, 1985), 249.

11. Lévi-Strauss, *Look, Listen, Read,* trans. Brian C. J. Singer (New York: Basic Books, 1997), 29–30.

12. Walter Benjamin, "A Short History of Photography," in *Classical Essays on Photography,* ed. Alan Trachtenberg (New Haven, CT: Leete's Island Books, 1980), 209.

13. Pinney, 74. Western mastery of vision is explored in Martin Jay, *Downcast Eyes: The Denigration of Vision in Twentieth-Century Thought* (Berkeley and Los Angeles: University of California Press, 1994).

14. G. Charbonnier, *Conversations with Claude Lévi-Strauss,* ed. and trans. John and Doreen Weightman (London: Cape, 1969), 125.

15. John Berger, *The White Bird* (London: Chatto and Windus, 1985), 176.

16. Lévi-Strauss, *The Way of Masks,* trans. Sylvia Modelski (Seattle: University of Washington Press, 1982).

17. Lévi-Strauss, *The Story of Lynx,* trans. Catherine Tihanyi (Chicago: University of Chicago Press, 1995).

18. Or, in the untranslated and single-printing first book, *La Vie familiale et sociale des indiens Nambikwara* (Paris: Musée de l'Homme, 1948)—which was an extracted journal article and later incorporated into work on the elementary structures of kinship—photographs of Indian family life.

19. Elizabeth Edwards, *Raw Histories: Photographs, Anthropology and Museums* (Oxford: Berg, 2001), 5. The argument about photography as revelation of the history of anthropology is also made in Edwards's collection, *Anthropology and Photography,* and in Anna Grimshaw, *Ways of Seeing in Modern Anthropology* (Cambridge: Cambridge University Press, 2001).

20. Pierre Bourdieu, *Outline of a Theory of Practice* (Cambridge: Cambridge University Press, 1977), 96.

21. George E. Marcus and Michael M. J. Fischer, *Anthropology as Cultural Critique: An Experimental Moment in the Human Sciences* (Chicago: University of Chicago Press, 1999), 29.

22. Marcel Hénaff, *Claude Lévi-Strauss and the Making of Structural Anthropology,* trans. Mary Baker (Minneapolis: University of Minnesota Press, 1998), 255.

23. Roslyn Poignant, "Surveying the Field of View: The Making of the RAI Photographic Collection," in *Anthropology and Photography,* ed. Edwards, 42.

24. Edwards, *Anthropology and Photography;* Grimshaw.

25. Bronislaw Malinowksi, *A Diary in the Strict Sense of the Term,* trans. Robert Gutterman (Stanford, CA: Stanford University Press, 1989), 140.

26. Lévi-Strauss, *The Naked Man,* vol. 4 of *Introduction to a Science of Mythology,* trans. John and Doreen Weightman (London: Cape, 1981), 268, "Translator's Note" 265, 630.

27. Susan Sontag, *Against Interpretation* (London: Vintage, 1994), 72. Jeffrey Mehlman, *A Structural Study of Autobiography: Proust, Leiris, Sartre, Lévi-Strauss* (Cornell, NY: Cornell University Press, 1974).

28. James Clifford, *The Predicament of Culture: Twentieth-Century Ethnography, Literature, and Art* (Cambridge, MA: Harvard University Press, 1988).

29. Edmund Leach, *Claude Lévi-Strauss* (Chicago: University of Chicago Press, 1989), 13.

30. Edwards, *Anthropology and Photography,* 7.

31. Barthes, *Image,* 26.

32. James C. Faris, "A Political Primer on Anthropology/Photography," in *Anthropology and Photography,* ed. Edwards, 255.

33. Lévi-Strauss, *The Elementary Structures of Kinship,* trans. James Harle Bell, John Richard von Sturmer, and Rodney Needham (Boston: Beacon Press, 1969), 84–107.

34. Johannes Fabian, *Time and the Other: How Anthropology Makes Its Object* (New York: Columbia University Press, 1983), 58–59.

35. Jacques Derrida, *The Work of Mourning,* ed. Pascale-Anne Brault and Michael Naas (Chicago: University of Chicago Press, 2001), 41–42.

36. Alan Watts takes apart cybernetic control in *The Way of Zen* (London: Penguin, 1990).

37. Lévi-Strauss, "Diogène Couché," *Les Temps Modernes* 110 (1955): 1217; my translation.

38. George Steiner, "Orpheus with His Myths," in *Claude Lévi-Strauss: The Anthropologist as Hero,* ed. E. Nelson Hayes and Tanya Hayes (Cambridge: MIT Press, 1970), 170–83.

39. Lévi-Strauss, *Saudades de São Paulo* (São Paulo: Companhia das Letras, 1996).

40. Cited in Eduardo Cadava, *Words of Light: Theses on the Photography of History* (Princeton: Princeton University Press, 1997), xxix.

41. Malek Alloula, *The Colonial Harem,* trans. Myrna Godzich and Wlad Godzich (Minneapolis: University of Minnesota Press, 1986), 7.

42. Paul Henley, "Fewer Words, More Pictures," *Times Literary Supplement,* February 2, 2001, 27.

43. John Collier, *Visual Anthropology: Photography as a Research Method* (New York: Holt, Rinehart and Winston, 1967), 4.

44. Jay Ruby, *Picturing Culture: Explorations of Film and Anthropology* (Chicago: University of Chicago Press, 2000), 4–5.

45. Nancy Scheper-Hughes, *Death without Weeping: The Violence of Everyday Life in Brazil* (Berkeley and Los Angeles: University of California Press, 1992). Marjorie Shostak, *Nisa: The Life and Words of a !Kung Woman* (1981; Cambridge, MA: Harvard University Press, 2000). Shostak, *Return to Nisa* (Cambridge, MA: Harvard University Press, 2000).

46. Philippe Lejeune, *On Autobiography,* ed. Paul John Eakin, trans. Katherine Leary (Minneapolis: University of Minnesota Press, 1989).

47. Barthes, *The Grain of the Voice: Interviews, 1962–1980,* trans. Linda Coverdale (Berkeley and Los Angeles: University of California Press, 1991), 357.

48. Annette Lavers, *Roland Barthes: Structuralism and After* (London: Methuen, 1982).

49. Derrida, *Writing and Difference,* trans. Alan Bass (Chicago: University of Chicago Press, 1978), 292. Renato Rosaldo, "Imperialist Nostalgia," *Representations* 26 (1989): 107.

50. Clifford, "On Ethnographic Allegory," in *Writing Culture: The Poetics and Politics of Ethnography,* ed. Clifford and George Marcus (Berkeley and Los Angeles: University of California Press, 1986), 113.

51. Quotations in French from Lévi-Strauss, *Tristes Tropiques* (Paris: Librarie Plon, 1955), 426, 31.

52. Marcel Proust, *Swann's Way*, book 1 of *Remembrance of Things Past* (New York: Penguin, 1992), 59.

53. Lévi-Strauss, *The Origin of Table Manners*, vol 3. of *Introduction to a Science of Mythology*, trans. John and Doreen Weightman (Chicago: Chicago University Press, 1990).

54. Clifford, "On Ethnographic Allegory," 112.

55. Sontag, *On Photography* (London: Penguin, 1977).

56. Bourdieu, *Photography: A Middle-brow Art*, trans. Shaun Whiteside (Oxford: Polity Press, 1998).

57. Sebastião Salgado, *Terra: Struggle of the Landless* (London: Phaidon, 1997); *Migrations: Humanity in Transition* (New York: Aperture, 2000).

58. Barthes, *Mythologies*, 94.

59. Darius Milhaud, *Saudades do Brasil*, Leonard Bernstein, cond. Orchestre National de France, EMI CDC-7 47845 2, 1978.

60. Sontag, *On Photography*, passim.

3. GORDON PARKS'S TAKING A LIFE

1. Roland Barthes, *Camera Lucida: Reflections on Photography*, trans. Richard Howard (London: Vintage, 1993), 34.

2. Graham Clarke, *The Photograph* (Oxford: Oxford University Press, 1997), 145.

3. John Collier Jr., *Visual Anthropology: Photography as a Research Method* (New York: Holt, Rinehart and Winston, 1967).

4. Roy Emerson Stryker, "The FSA Collection of Photographs," in *In This Proud Land: America, 1935–1943, as Seen in the FSA Photographs*, ed. Stryker and Nancy Wood (London: Secker and Warburg, 1974), 7.

5. F. Jack Hurley, *Portrait of a Decade: Roy Stryker and the Development of Documentary Photography in the Thirties* (New York: Da Capo Press, 1972), 56.

6. Stryker, cited in Alan Trachtenberg, "From Image to Story: Reading the File," in *Documenting America, 1935–1943*, ed. Carl Fleischauer and Beverly W. Brannan (Berkeley and Los Angeles: University of California Press, 1988), 61.

7. Lawrence W. Levine, "The Historian and the Icon: Photography and the History of the American People in the 1930s and 1940s," in *Documenting America, 1935–1943*, ed. Fleischauer and Brannan, 40, 56.

8. William Stott, *Documentary Expression and Thirties America* (London: Oxford University Press, 1973), 22

9. The following criticisms are Levine's and Clarke's respectively.

10. Clive Scott, *The Spoken Image: Photography and Language* (London: Reaktion Books, 1999), 31, 96.

11. Gordon Parks, *Moments without Proper Names* (London: Secker and Warburg, 1975).

12. Parks, *Midway: Portrait of a Daytona Beach Neighborhood* (Daytona Beach, FL: Southeast Museum of Photography, 1999).

13. Both reprinted in Parks, *Harlem: The Artist's Annotations on a City Revisited in Two Classic Photographic Essays,* ed. Michael Torosian (Toronto: Lumiere Press, 1997).

14. *Shaft,* MGM, 1971. *The Learning Tree,* Winger, 1969. Parks, *The Learning Tree* (New York: Ballantine, 1963).

15. Michael Torosian, introduction and interview, in Parks, *Harlem,* 13.

16. Richard Wright, *Twelve Million Black Voices: A Folk History of the Negro in the United States of America,* with photographs by Edwin Rosskam (London: Lindsay Drummond, 1947).

17. bell hooks, "In Our Glory: Photography and Black," in *Picturing Us: African American Identity in Photography,* ed. Deborah Willis (New York: New Press, 1994), 43–44, 48–49.

18. Parks, *A Choice of Weapons* (St. Paul: Minnesota Historical Society Press, 1986), 260.

19. Parks, *To Smile in Autumn: A Memoir* (New York: Norton, 1979), 210..

20. Nicholas Natanson, *The Black Image in the New Deal: The Politics of FSA Photography* (Knoxville: University of Tennessee Press, 1992), 183, 183, 186–87.

21. Parks, *Choice,* 231.

22. Susan Sontag, *On Photography* (London: Penguin, 1977), 42.

23. Susan Sontag, *Against Interpretation* (London: Vintage, 1994), 73.

24. Claude Lévi-Strauss, *Tristes Tropiques,* trans. John and Doreen Weightman (New York: Random House, 1997), 20.

25. Barthes, 92.

26. Parks, *Flavio* (New York: Norton, 1978), 14.

27. *Life,* June 16, 1961: "Freedom's Fearful Foe: Poverty," 94, 95; Parks, "Photographer's Diary of a Visit in Dark World," 96–98.

28. "A Great Urge to Help Flavio: Special Report," *Life,* July 7, 1961, 15–16.

29. "Flavio's Rescue: Americans Bring Him from Rio Slum to Be Cured," *Life,* July 21, 1961, 1+.

30. Marianne Hirsch, *Family Frames: Photography, Narrative and Postmemory* (Cambridge, MA: Harvard University Press, 1997), 7.

31. Wendy Kozol, *"Life's" America: Family and Nation in Postwar Photojournalism* (Philadelphia: Temple University Press, 1994), 78.

32. *The Crisis in Our Hemisphere: Crisis in Latin America,* part 1, spec. issue of *Life,* June 2, 1961, 1+. *Shocking Poverty Spawns Reds: Latin America,* part 2, spec. issue of *Life,* June 16, 1961, 1+. *Bolivia: U.S. Stake in a Revolution: Latin America,* part 3, spec. issue of *Life,* June 30, 1961, 1+. *Latin America's Story of Turbulence: Latin America,* part 4, spec. issue of *Life,* July 14, 1961, 1+. *Prisoners of Our Geography: Crisis in Latin America,* part 5, spec. issue of *Life,* July 28, 1961, 1+.

33. Lars Schoultz, *Beneath the United States: A History of U. S. Policy toward Latin America* (Cambridge, MA: Harvard University Press, 1998), 357.

34. Thomas E. Skidmore, *Politics in Brazil, 1930–1964: An Experiment in Democracy* (London: Oxford University Press, 1967), 195.

35. *Life,* June 2, 1961, 88.

36. Skidmore, 199.

37. E. Bradford Burns, *A History of Brazil* (New York: Columbia University Press, 1993), 444, 424.

38. Robert Coughlan, "The Staggering Problem," *Life,* July 28, 1961, 52A–58.

39. *Life,* July 7, 1961, 16.

40. John Tagg, *The Burden of Representation: Essays on Photographies and Histories* (Minneapolis: University of Minnesota Press, 1988), 157, 160.

41. A. J. Van Zuilen, *The Life Cycle of Magazines: A Historical Study of the Decline and Fall of the General Interest Magazine in the United States during the Period 1946–1972* (Uithorn, Netherlands: Graduate Press, 1977).

42. Coughlan, 57.

43. C. D. Jackson, "The Aim of *Life,*" *Life,* June 2, 1961, 1.

44. Richard M. Clurman, *To the End of "Time": The Seduction and Conquest of a Media Empire* (New York: Simon and Schuster, 1992), 19, 38.

45. Stott, 130.

46. Henry Luce, "The American Century," *Life,* February 17, 1941, 65.

47. Stott, 138.

48. Natanson, 64.

49. Barthes, 38.

50. Robert M. Levine, *The Brazilian Photographs of Genieve Naylor, 1940–1942* (Durham, NC: Duke University Press, 1998).

51. R. J. Doherty, *Social-Documentary Photography in the USA* (Garden City, NY: American Photographic Book Publishing, 1976), 86.

52. Julian Borger, "The Photo War," *The Guardian,* G2, April 26, 2000, 12–13.

53. John Tebbel and Mary Ellen Zuckerman, *The Magazine in America, 1741–1990* (New York: Oxford University Press, 1991), 227.

54. Jackson, 1.

55. Stott, 130.

56. Parks, *Choice,* 227.

57. *Life,* June 2, 1961, 81.

58. Burns, 432.

59. John Loengard, *"Life" Classic Photographs: A Personal Interpretation* (Boston: Little, Brown, 2000).

60. Alex Bellos, "Exposed to a Doubtful Dream," *The Guardian,* G2, June 4, 1998, 2.

61. http://www.pbs.org/newshour/bb/entertainment/jan-june98/gordon_1-6.html (accessed April 17, 2002).

62. Paula Rabinowitz, "Voyeurism and Class Consciousness: James Agee and Walker Evans, *Let Us Now Praise Famous Men,*" *Cultural Critique* 21 (1992): 166.

63. Parks, *Born Black* (Philadelphia: Lippincott, 1971).

64. http://www.pdngallery.com/legends/parks/mainframeset2.shtml (accessed April 17, 2002).

65. Parks, *Born,* 68; *Harlem,* 10.

66. *Flavio,* NBC, 1966

67. *Life,* June 16, 1961, 96, 98.

68. David J. Hellwig, ed., *African-American Reflections on Brazil's Racial Paradise* (Philadelphia: Temple University Press, 1992).

69. The census just before Parks's intervention cites blacks and *"pardos"* ("mulattoes") as constituting 68.6 percent of Rio's *favela* population compared with 29 percent of the total city population. Julio César Pino, *Family and Favela: The Reproduction of Poverty in Rio de Janeiro* (Westport, CT: Greenwood Press, 1997), 48.

70. Parks, *Born Black,* 28.

71. Parks, *Moments,* 101.

72. *Half Past Autumn, NewsHour* transcript January 6, 1998, http://www.pbs.org/newshour/bb/entertainment/jan-june98/gordon_1-6.html (accessed April 17, 2002).

73. Parks, *Arias in Silence* (Boston and London: Little, Brown, 1994).

74. Pino, 138.

75. Toni Morrison, *Sula* (London: Chatto and Windus, 1973).

4. ELIZABETH BISHOP'S ART OF LOSING

1. Quotations of published poems from Elizabeth Bishop, *The Complete Poems: 1927–1979* (New York: Farrar, 1999).

2. Bishop, *One Art: Letters,* ed. Robert Giroux (New York: Noonday Press, 1995), 329.

3. Bishop makes the later claim in conversation with George Starbuck, in *Elizabeth Bishop and Her Art,* ed. Lloyd Schwartz and Sybil P. Estess (Ann Arbor: University of Michigan Press, 1983), 318. Lee Edelman discusses the misreferencing in "The Geography of Gender: Elizabeth Bishop's 'In the Waiting Room,'" *Contemporary Literature* 26 (1985): 175–96.

4. Paul Fussell, *Poetic Meter and Poetic Form* (New York: McGraw Hill, 1978), 175.

5. Bonnie Costello, *Elizabeth Bishop: Questions of Mastery* (Cambridge, MA: Harvard University Press, 1991), 6. Harold Bloom, "Foreword," in *Elizabeth Bishop and Her Art,* ed. Schwartz and Estess, x. Adrienne Rich, "The Eye of the Outsider: Elizabeth Bishop's *Complete Poems, 1927–1979,*" in *Blood, Bread and Poetry: Selected Prose, 1979–1985* (London: Virago, 1987), 124–35.

6. Anne Stevenson, *Five Looks at Elizabeth Bishop* (London: Bellew, 1998). The description comes in Gary Fountain and Peter Brazeau, *Remembering Elizabeth Bishop: An Oral Biography* (Amherst: University of Massachusetts Press, 1994), 274.

7. George Monteiro, ed., *Conversations with Elizabeth Bishop* (Jackson: University Press of Mississippi, 1996), 24.

8. Bishop, *Exchanging Hats: Paintings,* ed. William Benton (Manchester, England: Carcanet Press, 1997).

9. Bishop, "Gregorio Valdes," in *The Collected Prose,* ed. Robert Giroux (New York: Noonday Press, 1984), 51–60.

10. Quotations of all unpublished material unless otherwise indicated from the Special Collections, Vassar College Library, with permission. I have proofed obvious spelling or typographical errors and omitted Bishop's drafts before her corrections unless making a point about changes. All ellipses my own; any exceptions will be noted.

11. Robert Dale Parker, *The Unbeliever: The Poetry of Elizabeth Bishop* (Urbana: University of Illinois Press, 1988).

12. Fountain and Brazeau, 182.

13. John Tebbel and Mary Ellen Zuckerman, *The Magazine in America, 1741–1990* (New York: Oxford University Press, 1991), 229.

14. Ashley Brown, "Elizabeth Bishop in Brazil," in *Elizabeth Bishop and Her Art,* ed. Schwartz and Estess, 223.

15. Bishop, trans. and ed., *The Diary of Helena Morley* (London: Bloomsbury, 1997), xxvi.

16. Schwartz and Estess, 194.

17. Schwartz and Estess, 305.

18. Maria Lúcia Milléo Martins, "Elizabeth Bishop and Carlos Drummond de Andrade: Verse/Universe in Four Acts" (Ph.D. diss., University of Massachusetts, Amherst, 1999), 170.

19. Bishop, *Collected Prose,* 229, 233, 233.

20. Cited in Brett C. Millier, *Elizabeth Bishop: Life and the Memory of It* (Berkeley and Los Angeles: University of California Press, 1993), 517.

21. Bishop and the Editors of *Life, Brazil* (New York: Time, 1962).

22. Schwartz and Estess, 312.

23. Howard Abramson, *"National Geographic": Behind America's Lens on the World* (New York: Crown, 1987). Catherine A. Lutz and Jane L. Collins, eds., *Reading "National Geographic"* (Chicago: University of Chicago Press, 1993).

24. Siegfried Kracauer, quoted in Eduardo Cadava, *Words of Light: Theses on the Photography of History* (Princeton: Princeton University Press, 1997), xxvi.

25. Originally published in *Life,* June 2, 1961, 82–83, 88.

26. C. R. Boxer, introduction to Bishop, *Brazil* (London: Sunday Times World Library, 1962).

27. Monteiro, 80

28. Bishop, "On the Railroad Named Delight," *New York Times Magazine,* March 7, 1965, 30–31, 84–86. The Brazilian criticism—and Bishop's response—is discussed in Victoria Harrison, *Elizabeth Bishop's Poetics of Intimacy* (Cambridge: Cambridge University Press, 1993), 167.

29. Thomas E. Skidmore, *Politics in Brazil, 1930–1964: An Experiment in Democracy* (London: Oxford University Press, 1967). Skidmore, *The Politics of Military Rule in Brazil, 1964–85* (New York: Oxford University Press, 1988).

30. Camille Roman, *Elizabeth Bishop's World War II–Cold War View* (New

York: Palgrave, 2001). Sandra Barry, *Elizabeth Bishop: An Archival Guide to Her Life in Nova Scotia* (Nova Scotia: Elizabeth Bishop Society of Nova Scotia, 1996). Bettsy Erkkila considers the leftist possibilities of Bishop's poetics in "Elizabeth Bishop, Modernism, and the Left," *American Literary History* 8 (1996): 284–310. Renée R. Curry charges Bishop with racism in *White Women Writing White: H. D., Elizabeth Bishop, Sylvia Plath, and Whiteness* (Westport, CT: Greenwood Press, 2000).

31. Lorrie Goldensohn, *Elizabeth Bishop: The Biography of a Poetry* (New York: Columbia University Press, 1992), 228.

32. Monteiro, 75.

33. Millier, 87.

34. Fountain and Brazeau, 98, 111–12.

35. Monteiro, 44.

36. Quoted in Schwartz, "Elizabeth Bishop and Brazil," *New Yorker,* September 30, 1991, 93.

37. Fountain and Brazeau, 173.

38. Bishop, letter to Robert Lowell, July 6, 1965. Reprinted by permission of the Houghton Library, Harvard University; shelfmark *bMS Am 1905 (226).* The first ellipsis is Bishop's own. Thanks to Maria Lúcia Milléo Martins for bringing this letter to my attention.

39. Alex Bellos, *Futebol: The Brazilian Way of Life* (London: Bloomsbury, 2002).

40. Monteiro, 29.

41. Harrison, 172.

42. Aldous Huxley, *The Art of Seeing* (London: Chatto and Windus, 1943).

43. Quoted in Costello, 63.

44. By Ashley Brown in Schwartz and Estess, 223.

45. Millier, 287.

46. Carmen L. Oliveira, *Rare and Commonplace Flowers: The Story of Elizabeth Bishop and Lota de Macedo Soares,* trans. Neil K. Besner (New Brunswick, NJ: Rutgers University Press, 2002).

47. Bishop, letter to Mariette Charlton, June 15, 1970. Reprinted by permission of the Houghton Library, Harvard University; shelfmark *bMS Am 2001 (12).* I am once again indebted to Maria Lúcia Milléo Martins. Bishop's ellipses.

48. Cited in Harrison, 172.

49. David Kalstone, *Becoming a Poet: Elizabeth Bishop with Marianne Moore and Robert Lowell,* ed. Robert Hemenway (London: Hogarth, 1989), 5.

50. Bishop, "In the Village," in *Collected Prose,* 251–76.

51. Susan McCabe, *Elizabeth Bishop: Her Poetics of Loss* (University Park, Pa.: Penn State University Press, 1994), 104.

52. Millier, 75.

53. Schwartz, "Elizabeth Bishop and Brazil," 97.

54. For the former see Goldensohn, and Thomas J. Travisano, *Elizabeth Bishop:*

Her Artistic Development (Charlottesville: University Press of Virginia, 1988). For the latter see Millier and Harrison.

55. Stephen Matterson and Darryl Jones, *Studying Poetry* (London: Hodder Headline, 2000), 87.

56. James Fenton, *An Introduction to English Poetry* (London: Penguin, 2002), 20.

57. Millier, 513. McCabe, 1.

5. My Second Skin

1. Hal Foster, *The Return of the Real: Avant-Garde Art at the End of the Century* (Cambridge: MIT Press, 1996).

2. John Updike, *Self-Consciousness: Memoirs* (London: Penguin, 1990), 44.

3. Jay Prosser, *Second Skins: The Body Narratives of Transsexuality* (New York: Columbia University Press, 1998).

4. Roland Barthes, *Camera Lucida: Reflections on Photography*, trans. Richard Howard (London: Vintage, 1993).

5. Judith Butler, *Bodies That Matter: On the Discursive Limits of "Sex"* (New York: Routledge, 1993), 237.

6. Barthes, "The Photographic Message," in *Image Music Text*, ed. and trans. Stephen Heath (London: Fontana, 1977), 20.

7. Nancy K. Miller, *Getting Personal: Feminist Occasions and Other Autobiographical Acts* (New York: Routledge, 1991), xiii.

8. Susan Rubin Suleiman, *Risking Who One Is: Encounters with Contemporary Art and Literature* (Cambridge, MA: Harvard University Press, 1994), 200.

9. Jacques Lacan, *Freud's Papers on Technique, 1953–1954,* ed. Jacques-Alain Miller, trans. John Forrester, book 1 of *The Seminar of Jacques Lacan* (New York: Norton, 1991), 66. Lacan, *The Four Fundamental Concepts of Psycho-analysis,* ed. Jacques-Alain Miller, trans. Alan Sheridan (New York: Norton, 1981), 55.

10. Lacan, *The Ego in Freud's Theory and Technique of Psychoanalysis, 1954–55,* trans. Sylvana Tomaselli, book 2 of *The Seminar of Jacques Lacan* (New York: Norton, 1991), 313, 97.

11. Slavoj Zizek, "Grimaces of the Real, or When the Phallus Appears," *October* 58 (1991): 59.

12. Lynda Hart, *Between the Body and the Flesh* (New York: Columbia University Press, 1998), 163.

13. Walter Benjamin, "The Work of Art in the Age of Mechanical Reproduction," in *Illuminations,* ed. Hannah Arendt, trans. Harry Zohn (London: Fontana, 1992), 217.

14. Loren Cameron, *Body Alchemy: Transsexual Portraits* (Pittsburgh, PA: Cleis, 1996), 11.

15. *FTM Newsletter* 27 (April 1994).

16. Kim Harlow and Bettina Rheims, *Kim,* trans. Paul Gould (Munich: Keyahoff Verlag, 1994).

17. Laura Mulvey, "Visual Pleasure and Narrative Cinema," *Screen* 16 (1975): 6.

18. Laura Mulvey, "Afterthoughts on 'Visual Pleasure and Narrative Cinema'' Inspired by *Duel in the Sun*," in *Feminism and Film Theory*, ed. Constance Penley (New York: Routledge, 1988), 69.

19. Kobena Mercer, "Reading Racial Fetishism: The Photographs of Robert Mapplethorpe," in *Fetishism and Cultural Discourse*, ed. Emily Apter and William Pietz (Ithaca, NY: Cornell University Press 1993), 320. The first essay, reprinted here, was published in *Photography/Politics: Two* (London: Comedia/Methuen, 1986), 61–69.

20. The Wolf-Man, *The Wolf-Man by the Wolf-Man, with the Case of the Wolf-Man by Sigmund Freud and a Supplement by Ruth Mack Brunswick*, ed. Muriel Gardiner (New York: Noonday Press, 1991).

21. Philippe Lejeune, "The Autobiographical Pact (bis)," in *On Autobiography*, ed. Paul John Eakin, trans. Katherine Leary (Minneapolis: University of Minnesota Press, 1989), 134, 131–32.

22. Oliver Wendell Holmes, "The Stereoscope and the Stereograph," in *Classic Essays on Photography*, ed. Alan Trachtenberg (New Haven, CT: Leete's Island Books, 1980), 73.

23. Lucretius, *De rerum natura*, cited in Robert Temple, *The Crystal Sun: Rediscovering a Lost Technology of the Ancient World* (London: Random House, 2000), 259.

24. Nadar, "My Life as a Photographer," trans. Thomas Repensek, *October* 5 (1978): 9.

EPILOGUE

1. Robert M. Levine and John J. Crocitti, eds., *The Brazil Reader: History, Culture, Politics* (Durham, NC: Duke University Press, 1999), 469.

2. Elizabeth Bishop, "Questions of Travel," in *The Complete Poems, 1927–1979* (New York: Farrar, Straus and Giroux, 1999), 93. Further references to Bishop's published poems are to this book.

3. *The Rockefellers, American Experience* transcript, PBS 2000, http://www.pbs .org/wgbh/amex/rockefellers (accessed November 1, 2002).

4. F. N. and Susan Johnson, *The Dolphin Story: An Introduction to the Biology of Dolphins* (Carnforth, England: Castlerigg Publications, 1976).

5. Nigel J. H. Smith, *The Amazon River Forest: A Natural History of Plants, Animals, and People* (New York: Oxford University Press, 1999).

6. Quotations of unpublished Bishop material from the Special Collections, Vassar College Library, reprinted with permission.

7. Anthony Hall, ed., *Amazonia at the Crossroads* (London: Institution for Latin American Studies, 2000).

8. Chico Mendes, *Fight for the Forest: Chico Mendes in his Own Words,* trans. Chris Whitehouse (Birmingham, England: Third World Publications, 1989).

9. Neil MacDonald, *Brazil: A Mask Called Progress* (Oxford: Oxfam, 1991), 32.

10. R. J. A. Goodland and H. S. Irwin, *Amazon Jungle: Green Hill to Red Desert? An Ecological Discussion of the Environmental Impact of the Highway Construction Program in the Amazon Basin* (Amsterdam: Elsevier Scientific Publishing, 1975).

11. John Vidal, "Road to Oblivion," *The Guardian*, June 13, 2001, G2 6–7.

12. John Browder and Brian Godfrey, *Rainforest Cities: Urbanization, Development and Globalization of the Brazilian Amazon* (New York: Columbia University Press, 1997), 13, 14.

13. Helmut Sick, *Birds in Brazil: A Natural History*, trans. William Belton (Princeton: Princeton University Press, 1993), 7.

14. David Werth and Roni Avissar, "The Local and Global Effects of Amazonian Deforestation," LBA [Large-Scale Biosphere-Atmosphere Experiment in Amazonia, a special section of the journal], *Journal of Geophysical Research: Atmosphere*, series D, 107, no. 55 (2002): 1–8.

15. William F. Laurance et al., "The Future of the Brazilian Amazon," *Science* 291 (2001): 438.

16. Bianca Jagger, "Threat to the Trees of Life," *The Guardian*, G2, November 6, 2002: http://society.guardian.co.uk/societyguardian/story/0,7843,833969,00.html.

17. Warren Dean, *With Broadax and Firebrand: The Destruction of the Brazilian Atlantic Forest* (Berkeley and Los Angeles: University of California Press, 1995).

18. Dean, *Brazil and the Struggle for Rubber: A Study in Environmental History* (Cambridge: Cambridge University Press, 1987).

19. Theodore Roosevelt, *Through the Brazilian Wilderness* (London: John Murray, 1914).

20. Chalmers Johnson, *Blowback: The Costs and Consequences of American Empire* (New York: Henry Holt, 2000), 210, 213.

21. "Plans for the Sustainable Development of the Amazon," February 2001, Brazilian Embassy in London, http://www.brazil.co.uk (accessed November 1, 2002). "Avança Brasil" has a Web site at http://www.abrasil.gov.br.

22. Tony Reichhardt, "Brazil's Space Programme Comes of Age," *Nature* 398 (April 1, 1999): 10. The satellite photographs are relayed from São José dos Campos's Global Resource Information Database Web site at http://www.grid.inpe.br.

23. Colin McEwan, Cristiana Barreto, and Eduardo Neves, *Unknown Amazon* (London: British Museum Press, 2001).

24. Anna Roosevelt, ed., *Amazonian Indians from Prehistory to the Present: Anthropological Perspectives* (Tuscon: University of Arizona Press, 1994), 4.

25. Roosevelt et al., "Paleoindian Cave Dwellers in the Amazon: The Peopling of the Americas," *Science* 272 (1996): 374.

26. Thomas D. Dillehay, *The Settlement of the Americas: A New Prehistory* (New York: Basic, 2000), xvi.

27. Tim Flannery, *The Eternal Frontier: An Ecological History of North America and Its Peoples* (London: Heinemann, 2001), 34–35.

28. Flannery, 139.

29. Claude Lévi-Strauss, *Structural Anthropology,* vol. 2, trans. Monique Layton (Chicago: University of Chicago Press, 1983), 362.

INDEX

Jay Prosser is lecturer in the School of English at the University of Leeds. He is the author of *Second Skins: The Body Narratives of Transsexuality* and coeditor of *Palatable Poison: Critical Perspectives on "The Well of Loneliness."*